Hospitality Human Resource Management

HOSPITALITY HUMAN RESOURCE MANAGEMENT

Dr. Ramesh Chand

CENTRUM PRESS
NEW DELHI-110002 (INDIA)

CENTRUM PRESS
H.O.: 4360/4, Ansari Road, Daryaganj,
New Delhi-110002 (India)
Tel: 23278000, 23261597, 23255577, 23286875

B.O.: No. 1015, Ist Main Road, BSK IIIrd Stage,
IIIrd Phase, IIIrd Block, Bengaluru-560085 (INDIA)
Tel: 080-41723429

Email: centrumpress@gmail.com
Visit us at: www.centrumpress.com

Hospitality Human Resource Management

First Edition, 2013

ISBN 978-93-81460-00-9

PRINTED IN INDIA

Printed at Balaji Offset, Delhi.

Contents

Preface

The rapidly changing hospitality industry and the sophistication of travellers require more nimble, opportunistic, and tightly executed strategies. Hospitality leaders who are effective at strategy formulation, implementation and evaluation are able to create value in a highly competitive marketplace. One of the most important departments of any hotel staff is human resources management. Proper human resources management can be the difference between a really well run hotel and a poorly one hotel. The human resources manager can control almost the whole feeling and presence of the entire hotel. This makes the importance of human resources management for hotels very evident. There are several different areas in which human resources management is very important. One of these areas is for newly hired employees. The employees that are hired in a hotel can really alter the quality of service and the whole atmosphere of the hotel. This means that it is very important to pick upbeat, dedicated workers for each position. It is the job of the human resources manager to make sure that good people are chosen to work in the hotel.

In many cases many hotel workers are only participating in hotel work because they can find nothing else to do. Not very many people have a dream of running or serving in a hotel environment. However, there are some people who do want to work in that capacity, and it is the job of the human resources manager to find those people. Retention of employees is another large problem in the hotel service business. Since so many of the employees do not have hotel work as their ending career goals, many of them only work in a hotel for a short amount of time. Other employees may have to be let go because of poor work ethics or other issues. However, there are ways that a hotel human resources manager can curb some of the desire and likelihood that employees will move to other jobs quickly. The importance of human resources management for hotels is very large in this area.

Atkinson (1984) introduced the concept of the 'flexible firm', and suggested there were three kinds of flexibility:

- Functional flexibility, so that employees have multiple skills and can be moved between a range of jobs.
- Numerical flexibility, by the use of part time and temporary contracts so that the numbers of employees can be easily increased or decreased in line with the demand for labour.
- Financial flexibility, which provides for pay levels to reflect the state of supply and demand in the external labour market.

The concept of the flexible firm involves employing a core of permanent, full time, relatively well paid and well trained staff, supported by peripheral workers who move in and out of the labour force in line with demand. The peripheral workers can have a range of different types of contract; for example, Lunn Poly employ part timers who can be asked to work anywhere between 4 and 37 hours a week, although the average is around 18.

There is, then, an evident need for organisations to carry out human resource planning. However, it has been observed that there are so many problems to overcome, and so many uncertainties in the local, national and international environment, that it is pointless spending a lot of time and effort on an activity which so frequently produces the wrong answers. In particular, the travel and tourism industry has a number of features which can make predicating staffing needs very difficult. For example, the demand for holidays can be affected by a range of factors, from weather conditions to the strength of sterling, while industrial action by air traffic controllers and political unrest generally have an impact somewhere in the world each year. This may make the task more problematic, but does not mean it should not be attempted at all!

Stages of Human Resource Planning

It is possibly to identify a number of stages in human resources planning:

- Assessing demand—this involves looking at the objectives the organisation is trying to achieve overall, and then assessing the number of people it will require.
- Assessing supply—this involves taking an inventory of the number and type of people employed today, and then

making a projection of how the position is likely to change in future years.

- Balancing supply and demand—there is likely to be a disparity between the number of people available and the number of people needed.
- Human resource planning—this involves determining the necessary actions so that the supply of labour matches the demand for labour.

An organisation must satisfy three conditions if the above stages are to be carried out effectively:

Human Resource Planning must be Fully Integrated with Corporate Planning

It is impossible to make decisions about staffing requirements unless decisions have also been made about the products and services the organisation will offer in the future. Decisions must also be made about the human resource policies of the organisation, for example, in terms of the levels of training to be offered and the salary levels to be paid.

Comprehensive Human Resource Records and Statistics must be Available

It is impossible to forecast the level of staffing available unless there are accurate and up-to-date records and statistics available. Human resource planning requires both information on individual employees, and also statistical information on trends in the labour force, such as the number of people leaving over a year.

The Organisation must Define its Objectives

The organisation must decide the period over which the forecast should be attempted, and also the degree of accuracy and detail which it requires. There will be certain areas which are critical to the success of the organisation, and on which the human resource planner should concentrate attention.

For example, a travel agency chain may set itself the target of increasing the number of travel shops by 5 per cent in the next 12 months, or a tour operator may decide to enter the cruise market, or a theme park may decide to build a number of new rides and a hotel. All of these decisions require resources to make them happen, whether capital, material or human, and planning to ensure that things happen at the right time.

However, staffing requirements are expressed not only in terms of quantity, but also in terms of type and quality. Thus, it is insufficient to say we need 10 people to fill 10 posts; they must have the knowledge and experience to be able to do the 10 jobs. This implies a need to conduct a 'skills audit' to discover the skills and abilities of the existing staff and an analysis of the job descriptions of the vacant posts to ensure that the people are recruited.

Human Resource Forecasting

An organisation has to predict the number of people it will need in the future. These people are only available from two sources: those people who are currently working within the organisation, and those people currently outside the organisation. Whilst seemingly obvious, this indicates clearly the two which the human resource planner must investigate.

Within the Organisation

This requires an analysis of the skills and experience of current employees, their length of service, training potential, and also their personal preferences. Some assessment of the likelihood of them leaving the organisation must also be made.

Outside the Organisation

This requires an analysis of the availability of people with specific skills outside the organisation. Even in times of high unemployment, certain occupational groups will still be in great demand. Some assessment must also be made of the likelihood of the organisation being able to attract the people it will require.

Assessing Staffing Supply

The purpose of human resource planning is to estimate the size of any future shortages or surpluses in particular skill groups so that action can be taken if necessary. In order to succeed at human resource planning, it is essential to have an accurate picture of the organisation's existing labour resources and then to assess the extent by which this stock will have been reduced by labour turnover by the end of the forecast period. At the same time, an assessment must be made of the extent to which the future requirements for labour will be available.

Internal Supply

Human resource records should record the number of staff in different categories, their age, sex and length of service. Records must be kept of the absence levels of staff in specific occupations and also on the turnover of staff. It may be helpful to conduct exit interviews to establish the reasons why staff are leaving the organisation. The information gained will allow predictions to be made about the numbers of days likely to be lost through absence, and also how many staff are likely to leave the organisation. The age and length of service of employees may also affect future wastage rates. Younger employees are more likely to leave the organisation than older employees, and people who have a longer length of service are less likely to leave than those who have only been with the organisation for a shorter period of time.

External Supply

An estimate must be made of the supply of labour outside the organisation. This is based on the total population figures, but also on the numbers in particular age groups, for example schools leavers or university graduates. The educational system will also determine the numbers available with particular qualifications at a range of levels; for example, over the last ten years there has been a tremendous increase in the number of travel and tourism graduates in the labour market. There are also social factors which influence the number of people available, such as the availability of child care provision.

Effect of New Technology

It has been said that Britain is undergoing a second Industrial Revolution, brought about by the increased availability and sophistication of computers. New technology has an impact both on the demand for different products and the methods used to provide different goods and services. For example, within the travel industry there has been a move towards 'ticketless' travel which has reduced the commission available to travel agents. The availability of new machinery can either be used to increase the output from the same number of staff or to maintain the output level with a smaller number of staff. However, increased automation may also call for different skills from employees and may also change the way in which work is organised. This is already happening in travel agencies, where some employees are mainly booking clerks, entering details in a computer, while others are able to make full use of the available technology to provide high quality advice on a range of destinations.

The Human Resource Plan

The next step is to draw up a plan to ensure that the demand for labour will be met by the appropriate level of supply. More specifically, it will specify future recruitment requirements, training and development to be undertaken, and any necessary redundancies. The process of forecasting future labour requirements may also indicate areas in which improvements in productivity could be made.

Perhaps the most important point to remember about human resource planning is that even detailed human resource plans are useless in themselves. Their only value lies in providing the manager with information to make decisions. If the figures show that absence or labour turnover is rising in a particular department, then action must be taken to find out the reasons why so that further action can be taken to reduce it. Monitoring is vital so that any change in the actual position compared to the fore cast position will be noticed and then action can be taken either to change the trend or to change the forecast. The result of this may be to modify long term plans, policies or objectives.

Recruitment and Selection

The previous sections on the role of human resource management and on human resource planning have stressed the need to select the 'right people', and this is achieved by using recruitment and selection techniques. The CIPD publish a Code of Practice (1995) on Recruitment which 'aims' to promote and maintain high standards of professional practice by encouraging recruiters to adhere to best practice'. The Code contains advice and guidance on a range of aspects, including ensuring equality of opportunity.

It is helpful to divide the process into four distinct stages and examine each one in turn:

Recruitment:

1. Assessing the job,
2. Attracting a field of candidates.

Selection:

1. Assessing the candidates,
2. Placement and follow up.

Assessing the Job

The first question to be asked is 'Do we need to fill this vacancy?' In the current climate, where many organisations are attempting to reduce their numbers by natural wastage, the answer to this question may well be 'no'. However, if the question is not asked at all then there is no opportunity to examine the work done by the post-holder in an attempt to see whether it could be reorganised in a more efficient manner. One technique which may be helpful in examining the work done is job analysis which is an analytical study of a job to determine the essential component factors.

The job analyst will ask four basic questions to determine what a job involves:

- what the job holder does,
- how the job holder does it,
- why the job holder does it,
- what does the job involve.

Job Description

The information about a job will normally be presented in the form of a job Description. This will detail the organisational position of the job in terms of department, location, who the post-holder reports to, and which posts they are responsible for. The job description will also outline the resources available to the post-holder and any specific constraints. The main part of the job description comprises a list of the duties and responsibilities involved in the job, together perhaps with some indication of the amount of time spent on individual activities. There has been a move away from detailed job descriptions in some organisations as it is felt they can inhibit flexibility. However, there is still a need for some indication of the personal competencies which are necessary to perform a particular job. Armstrong (1999: 280) draws a distinction between work-based or occupational competencies, which refer to what people should be capable of doing and the standards that people are expected to attain, and behavioural or personal competencies, which are the personal characteristics of individuals which they bring to their work roles.

Person Specification

When all the above information has been collected, it will be possible to determine the knowledge and skills required to perform the job successfully. A popular classification of human attributes which can be useful in compiling a person specification is Rodger's Seven Point Plan. The purpose of the Plan is to set a standard under a range of headings against which individual candidates may be measured. The Seven Point Plan covers:

- Physical make up (e.g., clear speaking voice)
- Attainment (e.g., academic and other achievements)
- General intelligence (e.g., other evidence of mental ability)
- Special aptitudes (e.g., foreign languages)
- Interests (e.g., physical, mental or social)
- Disposition (e.g., preference for working in a team)
- Circumstances (e.g., where they live and how far they have to travel to work).

When preparing the person specification, requirements should be stated under each heading. The temptation will often be to draw up an over-idealised specification, perhaps requiring GCSE Maths when really an understanding of how to calculate percentages would be sufficient. It may be helpful to consider those attributes which are essential, those which are desirable and those which are undesirable and would automatically disqualify any individual who possessed it. An example of the latter may be an applicant for a position of regional sales manager who has a conviction for driving while under the influence of alcohol.

Attracting a Field of Candidates

There are three main sources of recruitment: internal sources; external agencies; and advertisements.

Internal Sources

There may well be somebody already employed in the organisation who could perform the job competently. Indeed, some organisations have an agreement with their staff that all vacancies should be advertised internally to give existing staff a chance of promotion. However, there should be a balance between bringing in people with new ideas from outside the organisation and offering promotion prospects to existing employees. An advantage of promoting existing staff is that their abilities are well known whilst their knowledge of the organisation should allow them to make a more immediate contribution in their new job than an outsider.

External Agencies

There are a range of different agencies, some of which are Government-funded and others which are operated privately. Job Centres are located in most suburban shopping centres and provide a basically free service to both employers and job seekers. They tend to concentrate mostly on manual and clerical jobs, although they provide specialised services for particular groups, such as disabled workers and the long term unemployed. Careers Services are particularly useful for school and college leavers as they have close links with educational institutions. Private agencies frequently specialise in certain fields, such as travel and tourism, or in particular areas of the market, such as secretarial staff, IT staff, drivers or temporary workers. These agencies charge the employer for their services.

Advertisements

Most organisations will use advertisements at one time or another, and they can form a substantial part of recruitment costs. They must be written very carefully and be placed in the appropriate place at the right time if they are to prove cost-effective. The aim of recruitment advertising is to produce a compact and well-qualified field of candidates who are motivated to accept the job. This implies that sufficient candidates must apply to offer a reasonable selection, but not so many that they present an administrative burden. The candidates should meet the requirements of the person specification, and they should have obtained a favourable impression of the organisation.

It may be helpful to state in the advertisement that a copy of the job description will be sent with the application form. This will give potential candidates a much better idea of what the job entails and enable them to decide at an early stage if they feel that the job is not what they are looking for. This will save the employer administrative time and expense in dealing with applications which will not lead to an appointment. It also recognises that recruitment is a two-way process and that the candidate needs to have the information to select a suitable employer in the same way the employer selects a suitable candidate.

Application Forms

A well designed application form will request the information which is required in a systematic manner. A specific item of information will be in the same position for each candidate which should allow speedier comparisons. There should be sufficient space in which to write the required information. Many application forms for more senior positions require the candidate to state at some length why they feel their experience and qualifications make them a suitable contender for the job.

Assessing the Candidate

The first two stages should have produced a shortlist of qualified candidates. The subsequent selection stage, using a range of selection methods, then involves deciding on the most suitable. The most common selection method is the interview which may be supplemented by selection tests, group methods, and references.

Selection Tests

A range of tests are available which are designed to assess various attributes. These include tests of practical skills, such as filing or typing, and verbal and numerical abilities. There are also psychometric tests designed to provide information on personality characteristics. Many of these must be administrated by a trained psychological to facilitate interpretation of the results.

Group Selection Methods

These involve bringing a group of candidates together and giving them tasks to do. This is often used to recruit tour operators' overseas representatives, where their ability to get on well with other people and be able to present material clearly and concisely can be assessed. They may be given a topic to discuss, be asked to deliver a 'welcome talk', or sell excursions. Trained observers watch each individual's contribution and make an assessment of their personal skills and their ability to work with a group of people. These exercises may be time-consuming, but properly used can obtain information which would be very difficult to obtain using other methods.

References

The purpose of a reference is twofold. Firstly, it is designed to obtain, in confidence, factual information about a prospective employee and, secondly, it may ask for opinions about their character and their likely suitability for the post in question. Some people argue that references rarely supply any useful information, while others argue that they provide a valuable safety net. They are probably most useful when they ask for specific information on starting and leaving dates, salary history, and sickness record.

Selection Interview

The interview is trying to find an answer to two simple questions: can they do the job, and will they do the job? At the same time, however as well as trying to select the best candidate for the job, the interview is also trying to persuade the candidate to accept the job. The majority of candidates will be unsuccessful but it is, nevertheless, important that they too receive a favourable impression of the organisation.

That is, there may be a temptation in times of high unemployment to feel that it is less important to try to sell the job because it is a buyer's market. However, if the organisation is trying to recruit the best people for the job, those people are likely to receive offers from other organisations as well.

Thus, it is equally important to convince the candidate that the job is right for their as to assess whether they are right for the job. Research has shown that interviews can produce very poor selection decisions-most people only have to look around their own organisations to see evidence of this. Better results can be obtained if the interview has been trained, and if they carry out adequate preparation prior to the interview. The interview room itself should be free from interruptions and arranged for either a formal or an informal interview as appropriate. A one-to-one interview may be conducted fairly informally around a coffee table but a panel interview involving three or more interviewers may dictate a more formal seating plan.

One-to-one Interviews

A single trained and experienced interviewer may well produce the best results. The candidate is likely to be more relaxed in this situation and the conversation will, therefore, flow more easily. The main problem, however, is that the organisation then relies on the judgement of one individual who may be biased in certain directions. This type of interview is more common in the private sector.

Panel Interviews

These can vary in the number of interviewers, although they have been known to enter double figures. The smaller the numbers, the more likely they are to be effective as large numbers are very difficult to control. The panel members should agree beforehand on their respective roles and they should be carefully controlled by a chairperson. The advantages of a panel interview are that the people involved can share the responsibility for making the decision and that experts in particular areas can ask questions on their own specialism.

During the Interview

At the start of the interview, the interviewer should try to create a rapport so that the candidate begins to relax and settle down. Typically, the interviewer may ask about the candidate's travelling arrangements, how well they know the area or some other non-threatening topic of conversation. Inexperienced interviewers tend to ask. "Did you find us easily?" and then launch straight into the interview. It is well worth taking more time to relax the candidate, particularly if they are young or obviously nervous. The interviewer will often tell the candidate a little about the organisation and the specific job applied for. Care must be taken not to talk for too long as the candidate will probably be nervous and unable to easily absorb the information.

The actual questions should then be put to the candidate and the interviewer should carefully listen to the answers. This can be quite difficult in practice, as the inexperienced interviewer will tend to be thinking about how to ask the next question rather than listening to the answer from the last one. Thus, a useful technique is to follow up each question with at least one supplementary question designed to probe what the candidate has just said.

Different techniques are useful in different situations. Leading questions will usually provide little information as to the candidate's true feelings, whilst multiple questions can lead to confusion. Generally speaking, open questions are more useful than closed questions as they encourage the candidate to talk. One technique which can produce reasonably consistent and reliable results is the 'behaviourally situated' interview. This technique is based on the belief that the past performance is the best predictor of future performance. The candidates are asked pre-prepared questions such as:

- describe a situation where you used your influencing skills to achieve a successful result, or
- describe a situation where you had to overcome difficulties to complete a task.

The questions are chosen to reflect the type of situations which are likely to be crucial to effective job performance. It is important that the interviewer should really probe to discover exactly what the candidate did to achieve the outcome.

It has been suggested that the interviewer should talk for no than 30 per cent of the time because while they are talking are not learning anything. It may be helpful to take notes as a reminder of the answers, particularly if a number of candidates are to be seen at the same time. The candidate should also be given the opportunity to ask any questions they might have and then the interview should be brought to a close. The interview should be told when they can expect to receive any information and also how to claim their expenses if appropriate. Each candidate should feel that they have had a fair hearing and have been given sufficient information so that they can make their own decisions as to whether they would like to do if were offered. It is much better that a candidate refuses a job offer because they feel the job is unsuitable rather than accepting, only to leave the organisation after a short period of time.

After the Interview

Any notes which have been made during the interview should be written up immediately afterwards, before the next candidate is seen. The selection decision is then made by comparing all the available information on a candidate with the requirements of the job. It may be helpful to use some form of rating scale based either on the Seven Point Plan or on the specified criteria for the job as a systematic means of recording information on each candidate. If a number of interviewers have seen the same candidate there may be some fairly lengthy discussions before a measure of agreements can be reached. Candidates who are unsuccessful should be informed promptly and courteously.

No matter how carefully the recruitment and selection procedures have been carried out the new employee will still need assistance if they are to become fully effective as quickly as possible. The administrative details must be handled competently and the new employee must receive appropriate induction training. Even an experienced operative will require training in the particular procedures to be adopted in their new organisation, as well as needing information on the organisation itself and such practical matters as stationery supplies and when they will be paid.

Training and Development

Training is of vital importance if the organisation is to ensure that it has the right people available at the right time. It should be considered as an investment in the organisation's most valuable resource, the people it employs However, in times of financial difficulty it is often one of the first activities to be curtailed. In the past, a lot of training has undoubtedly been carried out for its own sake rather than helping the organisation to meet specific objectives. The aim then should be to ensure that training is designed to meet specific needs.

Potential Benefits of Training

Training is provided to:

- Provided specific skills—it can be easier to train your own staff in essential skills rather than relying upon the labour market to provide them.
- Improve performance and productivity—teaching the best methods of working can increase the quantity and quality of the output.
- Reduce wastage—employees who make mistakes are wasting both time and perhaps materials.
- Reduce accidents—the correct method will also be a safe method.

- Reduce labour turnover—employees who are unsure about what they are supposed to be doing and who receive complaints because they make mistakes are more likely to be absent or to leave the organisation.
- Individual advancement—employees will improve their personal position by acquiring new skills.

Many employees have a probation period during which their performance is closely monitored and they receive training and feedback on how well they are adapting.

It is sometimes said that training is designed to effect a change in three main areas, namely, knowledge, skills and attitudes. Knowledge-based training is sometimes called education as it involves the assimilation of a number of facts, for example, the codes used for different airports. Skills-based training will enable the trainee to do something at the end of the training, for example, type at 40 words per minute. Training designed to change attitudes can be the most difficult, such as encouraging a calm and patient response when faced with an irate and demanding customer.

Although all training will be directed towards bringing a change in knowledge, skill or attitudes, or a combination of them, it is possible to identify particular types of training:

Induction Training

This can fall into two categories. Firstly comes the introduction to the organization which every new employee will need. The second part involves initial training related to the specific job they will be required to do.

Skills Training

This is an extension of the induction training and is designed to enable employees to perform all parts of their job competently.

Management Training

This may be carried out within the organization, or by attendance on external courses, and is designed to encourage the skills required to manage other people.

There will be wide range of training needs of any organization and only a limited amount of money available in the budget. In these circumstances, decisions must be made as to which activities take priority so that the training provided will be both relevant and cost-effective. The best way of achieving this is by drawing up a training policy which has the support of the highest level of decision makes within the organization.

Decisions have to be made about the staff and resources which are to be devoted to training, as these in turn determine the actual the staff and resources which are to be devoted to training, as these in turn determine the actual training carried out. Training cannot be carried out in isolation; it must be integrated with the other activities of the organization.

Thus, if the policy is to recruit school leavers and then train them, the resources must be available to do this. If the organization is installing new machinery or expanding into new markets then the staff must be trained in the necessary skills. Training is simply one more method of helping the organization to achieve its overall objectives.

The Training Cycle

If training is to be carried out in the most efficient manner, it is important that it is approached in a systematic fashion. There is a Four Step Approach, the Training Cycle, which can be applied to all types of training at all levels.

Identify Training Needs

It seems obvious to say that it is necessary to find out what training people need before giving them any training yet, in many organizations, this does not happen. People are sent on training courses because their colleagues have been sent on the same training course, rather than because the course is actually right for them. In order to determine an individual's training needs, it is necessary to carry out a training needs analysis. Examine their job description to see what they are required to do and then interview the individual and their supervisor to see what they can do already.

The difference between the two is called the Training Gap and it is here that training should be directed. There are also other ways of deciding what training needs to be done and these are more suitable for deciding what training requires to be done on an occupational or departmental level and on the organizational level. Training may be related to.

Set the Objectives for Training

Training may be related to:

- Changes in legislation: this can involve changes in policies, practices or procedures.
- Changes in equipment: people must be trained to operate and maintain the new equipment.
- Changes in product: there may well be new techniques involved.
- Productivity figures: these may indicate where improvements can be made.
- Accident figures: high numbers of accidents may indicate training should be given in safe working practices.
- Wastages figures: large amounts of spoiled materials may indicate a need for training.
- Customer complaints: those may indicate where things are going wrong.

Labour turnover: people who are finding it difficult to do their jobs are more likely to leave the organization.

A word of caution is necessary, as there may be an assumption that training can solve all problems. It is true that training may be able to help in all of the above examples, but it will be only of limited assistance if the problems basically stem from obsolete equipment and poorly-designed procedures.

Plan the Training

Once decisions have been made about who needs what training, then further decisions must be made about how this is to be achieved. In particular the following questions must be answered:

- WHO: who will carry out the training?
- WHERE: where will the training take place?
- WHAT: what specific knowledge, skills and attitudes will be included?
- WHEN: when will be the date, time and duration of the sessions?

Having answered these questions, then arrangements must be made for the people, equipment and rooms to be made available as required.

On-the-job and off-the-job Training

There is sometimes an assumption that training only takes place in a classroom away from the job. In reality, people learn most about their job by actually doing it. Effective learning takes place when people are given an opportunity to practice particular skills and are then given feedback on their performance. It may well be that a short period of off-the job training can best be followed by guided practice on-the-job, by somebody who has been trained in instructional techniques.

Evaluate Training

Most organizations will have carried out the previous three steps, to a greater or lesser extent, when arranging a training programme. However, in many cases little or no attempt is made to systematically evaluate the training with the attention of feeding back these results to future training programmes. It is so wonder that training is one of the first areas to be cut back if there is no data available on the extent to which it is helping the organization to achieve its overall objectives.

Evaluation can be carried out at different levels and thus provide answers to different questions:

- Did the training achieve what it set out to do?
- Were the original objectives appropriate?

The success of a training programme can also be measured at different points in time:

- Reaction evaluation: this involves asking the trainees to assess how much they learned and whether they 'enjoyed' the training. This is the most common form of evaluation, but is of limited usefulness.
- Learning evaluation: this involves testing the employees at the end of the course to see if they have achieved the objectives. To be fully effective, a test should also be given prior to the course to ensure that the learning is a result of the course.

- Performance evaluation: this involves making an assessment of the performance of the trainee when they have returned to their job to see if they are implementing their training in practice.
- Organisational evaluation: this is the ultimate test which is designed to show whether the organization as a whole is performing better as a result of the training.

It will be clear that the most valuable information relating to the impact on the organization is the most difficult to obtain and is most affected by external variables. Thus, although British rail invested a great deal of money in their 'Charm Schools' which were designed to improve the social skills of their staff, it is impossible to say whether this alone contributed to increased passenger revenues. However, it undoubtedly led to a reduced number of complaints about the attitudes of certain members of staff, which could in itself be considered to be sufficient justification for the training.

The cost involved in training must be carefully controlled to ensure both that the most cost-effective methods are being used and that benefits to the organization outweigh the money spent on training.

It is only by monitoring the situation closely that the organization will be able to maximize the benefits of an investment in training. At the end of the day, training must be seen to be producing the desired results in terms of contributing to the overall organizational objectives.

Performance Appraisal

In every organisation, there is a need regularly and systematically to take stock of current manpower. The aim is to assess people's performance in existing jobs and their potential for future jobs. The technique used to achieve this is performance or staff appraisal. Properly conducted, performance appraisal can achieve the following:

- It gives line managers the opportunity to assess the employees' strengths and weaknesses.
- It gives employees the opportunity to assess their current

position within the organisation, and to review their personal future.

- It provides the opportunity for action to be taken to provide training and development which will enable the individual to more closely match the requirements of the job.

The importance of the word 'action' must be noted. Undoubtedly the most frequent criticism of appraisal scheme is that much talking is done and many forms are filled in, but nothing actually happens as a result. In essence appraisal entails one individual sitting in judgement on another. Many managers dislike the idea of 'Playing God' and employees may be reluctant to receive criticism, particularly if they feel the organisation itself is making it difficult for them to achieve their goals.

Some organisations try to shift the focus of appraisal so that the manager helps the employee to identify their own strengths and weaknesses and from there pinpoint their own training and development needs. The success of this sort of approach will depend on the relationship which exist between the manager and the employee.

Staff appraisal ranges from intermittent, informal and often ill-informed discussion between managers and individual members of staff, to highly formal appraisal procedures, based on extensive sets of forms and laid down times, rules, and frequency of assessments.

Generally, an important point is that any decisions made as a result of the appraisal process should be based on sufficient, relevent and objective information.

Value of Performance Appraisal

Appraisals are not an end in themselves, but a means to an end. Research has shown that appraisal schemes aim to achieve one or more of the following purposes:

- to improve current performance;
- to identify future potential; and
- to link pay realistically with performance.

It is, of course, very difficult for any one scheme to successfully achieve all of the above. For example, if one is attempting to improve current performance, this assumes a fairly frank discussion about strengths and weakness. However, if the employee is aware that a future pay increase rests upon their performance during an appraisal interview, they are likely to be less forthcoming about their weakness and concentrate on their strengths.

A similar distinction can be drawn between schemes which aim to improve current performance, and those which aim to identify future potential. The former will require detailed discussions with the employee in order to review past performance, set performance targets, and motivate the employee to achieve these. However, the latter objective requires less discussion with the employee as the information required to identify 'high flyers' can perhaps be more readily obtained from other sources.

Designing a Scheme

When designing the scheme, early consideration must be given to the categories of staff which it is appropriate to include and whether it will be necessary to incorporate different aims and procedures as a result. Some organisations only include white-collar staff in their scheme, or white-collar staff between certain levels.

Acceptability of Scheme

The scheme must be designed to suit the needs of the organisation and must have the full support of senior management. It must also be acceptable to line managers, employees and the trade unions, if appropriate. Trade unions have a traditional mistrust of appraisal schemes as they feel it allows scope for management to show favouritism. To achieve acceptability the scheme must be fully explained to all parties, training must be given to the managers involved, and the system should be designed to involve a minimum of bureaucracy.

Performance and Reward

If a decisions has been taken that pay increases will in some way be linked with an assessment of performance rather than using an incremental payment scheme, then this process should be separate from the process used to help the individual improve their current performance. The reasons for this are set out below:

- A full and frank exchange of views becomes less likely.
- It may be better to link pay with some objective measures rather than a manager's subjective judgement.

- Managers may avoid differentiating between their staff and give everyone the same increase.
- Those disadvantages may at least be minimised by separating the two processes in time and also preferably in paperwork and procedures.

The Appraisal Interview

This forms the basis of the scheme and is conducted at regular, usually annual, intervals. It is not intended as a substitute for day-to-day management, so feedback, both positive and negative, should be given as appropriate as near as possible to the specific events. Its purpose is to take an overview of the last year's performance and from there plan and appropriate course of action for the future. This is done by taking into account both the needs of the organisation and the personal preferences of the individual.

The interview can be seen as rather threatening by the employee, so care must be taken to ensure a genuine two-way flow of information. If handled well, the employee can leave the interview feeling that there has been an opportunity to discuss in detail their hopes and problems, and feeling that action will be taken to sort out specific issues. On the other hand, if handled badly, the employee may feel resentful because the manager did not listen to the comments and opinions expressed and used the interview as an opportunity to criticise.

Objective Setting

The most effective interviews usually involve the evaluation of performance against preset targets which had been jointly set by the manager and employee. There may be the disadvantages that the interview concentrates on only a limited part of the job as a result. The main advantage is that results-oriented appraisal is likely to be more impartial and therefore may be more acceptable to the parties involved.

Paperwork

It has already been said that appraisal is a means to an end but, if an organisation produces elaborate documentation, then the completion of the forms themselves is seen as being increasingly significant. If managers are unconvinced about the usefulness of the exercise, or feel uncomfortable about the process, they may conduct the interview at a superficial level in order to complete the form. Certain basic information will be required, such as the job description for the post, any statements of objectives agreed previously, plus basic human resource information on the employee. In addition, the following types of forms may prove helpful:

- Self-appraisal form: used by the employee prior to the interview to assist them in thinking about their own performance.
- Free written report: either a blank sheet of paper, or including a number of headings, which encourage the managers to comment as they see fit without being over-constrained.
- Comparative rating form: the manager is asked to rate the employee on a number of scales covering different aspects of job performance.
- Combination report: this combines rating scales with an opportunity for more descriptive comment.

Whichever forms are used, simplicity in design and ease of use are vital factors to be considered.

Employee Rewards

The notion of 'reward' includes both financial and non financial benefits which are given to the employee. The financial rewards include basic pay, commission, overtime, and bonuses. However, some organisations also provide other benefits, sometimes known as indirect pay, in the form of pensions, life assurance, health assurance, and subsidised loans.

Annual holidays are not strictly remuneration but are also regarded as a benefit Non-financial benefits may include recognition as an 'employee of the month', or the opportunity to attend training courses.

An employee reward system 'consists of an organisation's integrated policies, processes and practices for rewarding its employees in accordance with their contribution, skill and competence and their market worth'.

The purpose of a reward system is to attract, retain and motivate staff, and its success can be measured by how well it achieves these things. Both the employer and the employee have different requirements from a reward system and sometimes these may in conflict with each other. The employer will, in general, want to minimise the expenditure on wages, whilst the employee will want to maximise their earnings.

The employer will want as much work as possible, at the appropriate quality, while the employee will want stable earnings. The employee will want to feel they receive a 'fair' reward for their efforts compared with other people in the organisation and with similar jobs outside.

The level of pay in any organisation is determined by a combination of a number of factors. These include the external value of the job as determined by market forces, the comparative value of jobs within the organisation, sometimes determined by job evaluation, the value of the person as measured by performance appraisal or other measures and , in some cases, the influence which can be exerted by trade unions.

There is generally believed to be a certain balance between supply and demand so that people who have skills which are in short supply will be able to command more than those who have skills which are easily obtained elsewhere. This is one of the reasons why pay is low in the travel in and tourism industry, as many of the jobs require relatively low skills levels and therefore replacement staff can be found easily.

A number of people in the industry receive a form of bonus or commission dependent upon the sales which they receive. This can take a number of forms, such as $X per booking or passenger, or the opportunity for top sales people to 'win' a holiday. It can also take the form of a bonus paid to everyday depending on the sales or profit made by the whole organisation. The idea is to relate the efforts of the worker or the team of workers to a reward. The major variable is the ratio of effort to earnings: in some schemes this is set so very little effort can produce proportionately high earnings whereas in others a lot of effort can produce a small increase in pay.

The human resource management approach would look at the extent to which the payment system matches other parts of the overall human resource strategy and the extent to which it contributes to the overall corporate strategy. For example, an organisation which was trying to provide a high quality service should not have a payment system which only rewarded the quantity of output. Alternatively, an organisation should not only reward individual achievement if the employees need to work together as a team in order to perform the job effectively.

The reward system is a very powerful expression of what the organisation values and is prepared to pay for and it plays a significant part in the communication of the organisation's values, performance, standards and expectations.

2

Human Resources Development in Hospitality

Overview and Objectives

Tourism sector industries generate a large number of highly diversified jobs in different branches of activities such as hotels, restaurants, travel agencies, tour operators, leisure activities and passenger transport. Human resources are a key element in ensuring the quality and content of tourism products. There is a growing need for skilled manpower able to meet the needs of a changing environment and to maintain the competitiveness of tourism enterprises. In a competitive labour market, the tourism sector suffers from a relatively poor image and finds it difficult to retain employees on a long-term basis. In the light of these changes and challenges, strategies for managing and promoting human resources have a central role to play in a sustainable development approach to tourism. The understanding of labour markets in the tourism sector remains inadequate.

The effects of the new practices introduced by certain governments and the industry to improve skills and enhance the competitiveness of the sector in the labour market have not been widely shared and assessed. The pursuit of strategies to promote the skills needed in a globalising tourism industry must be continued. Lastly, in a context of liberalisation and globalisation of tourism services, the possibility of harmonising the differing regulatory approaches to the labour market in the tourism sector should be discussed in depth with all actors on national and international labour markets.

The conference on "Partnership in Vietnam's tourism human resources development" was the second annual conference held by the Vietnam Human Resources Development in Tourism Project at the Furama Resort, Danang.

The conference on "Partnership in Vietnam's tourism human resources development" was the second annual conference held by the Vietnam Human Resources Development in Tourism Project at the Furama Resort, Danang. It took place on 30th November 2006 and followed the conference on "Vietnam tourism human resources development and regional integration", held in Hanoi during December 2005. Among the 150 participants (international and local) were representatives from Vietnam National Administration of Tourism, the National Steering Committee for Tourism, representatives from ministries, the Delegation of the European Commission to Vietnam, the Secretariat and National Tourism Organisations of ASEAN, provincial tourism departments, representatives from hotel and travel enterprises, tourism training institutions, etc. By attending the conference, regional tourism representatives viewed the activities of Vietnam's tourism human resources development at first hand, and Vietnam's tourism administrators and experts gained further insights into regional practice.

After the introduction by Mr. Jozef W.M. van Doorn, the Co-Director of the Project, presenting the Project's outputs to date, Mr. Jaap Funnekotter, Chairman of the conference, reviewed outcomes from last year's conference. Conference 2006 followed the same format as last year's edition in order to create continuity, so speakers from both public and private sectors presented their experience of partnership in tourism human resources development. After the presentations, there was a panel discussion on the topic: "Has any synergy between the educational institutes and the hotel and tourism enterprises taken place in the last year?" along with some further discussion of best practices.

Attending the Gala Dinner, participants were introduced to a training DVD on housekeeping according to the Vietnam Tourism Occupational Skill standards (VTOS). This is one of 14 videos that will be developed by the Project as support for training. It is designed to be used in conjunction with the Project's Trainer Development Programme training manuals, or for entry-level staff training within enterprises.

The second day of the conference was spent on a field trip to My Son and Hoi An, two of the World Cultural Heritage sites.

UNWTO Summit Discusses New Reforms for Human Resources in Tourism

According to the January 2009 issue of the UNWTO World Tourism Barometer, in 2008, international tourist arrivals worldwide increased by 2%. The Middle East registered the best performance among all world regions with 11% growth in international tourist arri.als in 2008 over the previous year. Based on passenger traffic data from worldwide airports for the first two months of 2009, it appears that of all the world regions, the Middle East is the least affected y the global crisis thus far. It was the only region with a positive traffic growth of 3.1%.

The Summit has demonstrated the complexity of labour markets in the region and constantly returned to the fact that the rapid growth of tourism in the region brings with it issues of labour supply gaps and skills shortage. The Qatar Summit identified a range of human resource challenges for tourism.

Tourism employment comes in the shape of a broad spectrum of roles and varied tasks, across all sectors benefiting in particular women, the young and the unemployed. Tourism is well known as a generator of employment, so a well-trained tourism labour force will both anticipate and remedy such economic crisis.

Longer-term challenges include the poor image and lack of understanding of tourism jobs, and the fact that availability of labour and skills is highly variable across the region.

The Summit addressed these issues into four key pillars of reform:

The first one is the need to change the mindset of both governments and communities towards employment in tourism, as well as the need for the industry to change its view of human resources to one that values peoples, their skills and knowledge, develops them and treats them as valued resources.

The second pillar means the necessary understanding of labour markets. With the Tourism Satellite Account (TSA) methodology, it is now easier to understand and measure labour markets, diagnose the problems and act. Governments will be able to plan for future labour and traning needs.

Re-engineering education and training, the third pillar of reform, will demand national standard setting in partnership with industry and the development of articulated and legible pathways to allow students to gain qualifications, and ensuring that programmes are creatively packaged, innovative and utilize edge technology for lifelong learning.

The final pillar of reform relates to the work and leadership of both the UNWTO and Qatar in addressing these challenges and engaging stakeholders to craft new strategies. The solutions demand the forging of effective partnerships and working together to implement the recommendations of the Summit, as well as the findings of the Bali conference and the ILO's Decent Work Agenda.

Professor Chris Cooper, summit moderator, commented:

"The message of this summit is clear-tourism is a people-centred industry, the sector must invest in the education, training and development of the labour force to secure the future." Alongside the Qatar Summit, the 32nd meeting of the United Nations World Tourism Organisation commission for the Middle East took place on April 22nd and 23rd.

Dr. Taleb Rifai, Secretary General of the UNWTO, presented to the members of the Commission a snapshot analysis of the current economic downturn's impact on tourism in the Middle East and North Africa. Country briefs and response measures were also discussed in a regional perspective.

The Secretary General presented the research programme: "Tourism towards 2030", as well as regional training programmes and possible adjustments in the light of the global economic downturn.

This meeting of the UNWTO commission for the Middle East reviewed the preparations for the eighteenth session of the General Assembly of UNWTO, that will take place in October 2009.

On the occasion of the conclusive press conference, Mr. Ahmed Al Nuaimi, Chairman of Qatar Tourism and Exhibitions Authority, declared, "I am really pleased Qatar Tourism and Exhibitions Authority hosted this UNWTO conference. With 250 participants, we shared different experiences and had very fruitful discussions that enabled us to create a roadmap with four pillars of reform. Tourism is a key economic pillar and we need to ensure the future of the region."

Tourism Human Resources in Shortage, Weak

Weakness in Foreign Languages

According to statistics of the Vietnam National Administration of Tourism (VNAT), the total number of workers in the tourism sector is around 850,000 at present, including 250,000 workers who directly serve tourists. However, only around 50% of them are trained.

The tourism sector needs an additional around 35,000 trained workers each year but training centres can provide only about one-third of the volume. Besides weakness in terms of professional knowledge and skills, the largest disadvantage of Vietnamese tourism workers is foreign languages. Besides English, the major foreign language, Vietnamese tourism workers are also weak in other languages like Japanese, Chinese and Korean.

Specifically, the number of Korean travellers coming to Vietnam is increasing fast (ranking second after Chinese) but Vietnam currently has only 50 tour guides who can speak Korean. For the Japanese market, the third potential market of Vietnam, just 8% of tour guides speaking Japanese can fluently speak this language.

English: Below Standards

As part of a programme to raise the quality of the tourism human resources of Vietnam, the Test of English for International Communication (TOEIC) Vietnam has currently made a survey to test the English ability of some occupations in the tourism sector.

Based on the need of using English in each position, TOEIC Vietnam performed nearly 400 surveys of the need for English skills of nearly 200 hotels of three- to five-star standard and travel agents throughout the country. The major subjects of those surveys are directors, human resource managers and direct managers like team leaders who clearly understand the need for English of their staffs.

Random surveys of 1,000 workers at tourism companies reveal that the English skills of most of them are low and below the standards required by their employers.

The survey also points out that hotels of higher standard have high percentages of staffs that don't meet standards in English. According to Doan Hong Nam, director of the TOEIC Vietnam, the standards that we apply to evaluate the English skills of tourism workers is to ensure the minimum quality of service so the survey results show that the English skills of surveyed tourism workers is even lower than the low standards.

This is not only a hindrance for the development of the tourism sector but others as more and more foreign tourists are coming to Vietnam to seek business opportunities. Mr. Nam said that Vietnam needed to quickly improve the quality of the current tourism services by issuing common standards for foreign languages for each position in the tourism sector. This is a necessary foundation for the training tasks of training centres and tourism firms.

Philippines: DoT holds 1st Tourism Human Resources Congress Today

In line with the Department of Tourism's (DoT) "Gandang Pilipinas, Galingng Pilipino" GP2 campaign which aims to further develop tourism services, DoT Secretary Roberto "Obet" M. Pagdanganan will lead the launch of the 1st Tourism Human Resources Congress today at The Peninsula Manila Hotel.

Pagdanganan said the activity, which will be held until tomorrow (June 18), will further enhance the industry's manpower resources enabling them to meet the international standard of tourism service.

"In order to cope with the global challenges in the tourism industry, we must arm ourselves with the changes in the international market. Quality services and products are fast becoming a norm in the new global economy. We must make precedence by introducing speed, innovation and customization," he added. The Tourism Industry Board Foundation, Inc. (TIBFI) organizer of the event, is a non-stock, non-profit institution composed of representatives from the government (which include the DoT as founding member), private and labour sectors.

The foundation aims to provide manpower development, ensuring an adequate supply of trained workers who will match the skills of the labour force with the manpower requirements of the tourism industry. TIBFI invited distinguished guest speakers including World Tourism Organization (WTO) representative Professor Chris Cooper to talk about the TedQual Programs, which focuses on quality service assurance and the WTO products and services standard.

Human resources directors and heads of various tourism sub-sectors, associations, industries and government agencies (TESDA, CHED, Government Training Institutions), tour guides and the academe including state colleges and universities are invited to participate in the two-day assembly. Registration fee is R1,500.

The Tourism Industry

* Tourism is the largest earner of foreign exchange in Antigua & Barbuda.
* It is estimated to be the largest employer when all enterprises providing direct and indirect services to the sector are combined.

Tourism and The Labour Force

* Though there are no definitive statistics on the labour force involved in tourism in Antigua & Barbuda, a recently produced Antigua & Barbuda Tourism Strategic Plan (2005-2009) stated that surveys suggest that approximately 8,000 workers or 26% of the total labour force could be employed in the accommodation sector: hotels, guests houses, apts., villas, with other sectors of the industry creating a further 3,000 jobs.
* Therefore, the total number of workers employed in the tourism sector is 11,000 representing 40% of the total labour force.
* When compared to statistics which indicate that globally tourism accounts for 8.3% of the total work force, Antigua & Barbuda can clearly be considered one of the, if not the most tourism dependent countries in the world.

Tourism Human Resource Audit

* A tourism human resource audit should be conducted to give true and reliable data relating to the tourism work force.

* Such data must of necessity address the issues of:
* male/female ratio
* age-group
* percentages employed in various sectors, for e.g. accommodation, F&B, yachting, adventure, etc.
* education
* It is important to note that the paucity of reliable data is a regional problem and unfortunately the experience of many economic sector areas, the tourist industry being no exception.
* As recently as February 2006, CTO in recognition of this situation include the improvement of data collection as one of its Key Focus Areas.

Assessing Training and Education Needs

* In a 1998 study conducted by the CTO within its member countries, the focus was on assessing training and education needs for the tourist industry in the new millennium.
* The study was designed to provide data about the nature and level of skills deficiencies in the industry so as to inform Caribbean Governments and regional training agencies where their training priorities should lie and how their training $$ should be spent.
* It was intended that the study would provide a launching pad for tourism training in this millennium as well as to represent a benchmark for future studies.
* The information provided on HRD in the Caribbean region as a whole (through this study), is quite applicable to the Antigua & Barbuda situation.

Highlights of the Study

* Industry Profile:
* Majority of the responding organizations were from the Accommodation sector, with F&B and Transportation sectors running a far second and third behind, respectively.

* Events and Conferences and Attractions provided least number of respondents. Reflection of the level of development of these two sectors in the Region.
* ¼ less than 5 yrs. Old/ ¼ over 20 yrs. Old
* Majority of the work force permanent full-time staff with more males than females (56% to 44%). Over 70% under 40 yrs.
* Recruitment and Retention of Staff
* Local and regional tourism training institutions are not a preferred source of employees.
* Most organizations recruit their staff from secondary/ primary schools and from university, depending on the level of staff.
* Many also hire from their competitors or from among relatives and friends.
* Recruitment and Retention of Staff (cont'd)
* Generally, managerial and professional vacancies are difficult to fill.
* Also difficult to recruit skilled/semi-skilled persons in the accommodation, F&B and adventure sectors.
* Unskilled positions generally easier to fill.
* Industry Training and Development
* Only 1/3 of the establishments in the survey had a full-time trainer on staff.
* Training done primarily in customer relations and technical skills.
* Of 1/3 of the respondents providing information on training budget, 2/3 spent less than US$5,000 for a year.
* Industry Training and Development (cont'd)
* On the job-training is the preferred training strategy for all levels of staff.
* External trainers and local tourism training institutions used but to a much lesser extent.

* Local and regional tourism training institutions are not perceived by the industry as important or effective in satisfying its training needs.

Training Needs Identified

* General and technical training deficiencies identified at different staff levels.
* General training needs:
* Interpersonal skills deficiencies found at all staff level
* Marketing and management deficiencies at managerial level
* Computer literacy and foreign language deficiencies (also found)
* Technical training needs: these were linked to deficiencies within the various tourism sectors; accommodation, food & beverage, transportation, travel trade, adventure and tourism services.

Accommodation

Technical Skills:

* Culinary
* Maintenance
* Housekeeping
* F & B Service e.g. Bartending, Waiting
* Front Desk
* Tour Guiding
* Customer Service
* Other, e.g. Safety & Security, Tourism Awareness, Computer

Food & Beverage

Technical Skills:

* Culinary
* Food & Beverage Services e.g. Bartending, Waiting
* Customer Service
* Other e.g. Inventory Control, Maintenance, Cashing, Sanitation

Transportation

Technical Skills:

* Ticketing
* Customer Service
* Tour Guiding
* Maintenance
* Other e.g. Customer Procedures

Travel Trade

Technical Skills

* Ticketing
* Tour Guiding
* Other e.g. Customer Service, Maintenance, Computer, Marketing

Adventure

Technical Skills

* Tour Guiding
* Watersports e.g. Boating, Sailing, Scuba Diving, Fishing
* Maintenance
* Culinary
* Other e.g. Customer Service, Golf, Housekeeping, First Aid, Piloting, Food & Beverage Service

Tourism Services

Technical Skills:

* Statistical Analysis
* Property Management
* Environmental Protection and Conservation
* Public Relations

Attractions

Technical Skills:

* Tour Guiding
* Customer Service

* Other e.g. Ticketing, Heritage Conservation/Preservation, Museum Management, wildlife Management, Environmental Protection, Marine Biology, Heritage Studies

Meeting Technical Training Needs

The Antigua and Barbuda Hospitality Training Institute.

Antigua & Barbuda Hospitality Training Institute.

* Mission To provide training and education with a commitment to excellence; to equip persons to work in the Tourism and Hospitality Industry with a high degree of professionalism

One Year Certificate Programme

* Food and Beverage Service
* Training at Skills level
* Basic Cookery
* Knowledge & Skill in basic Cookery techniques
* Housekeeping
* Training at skills level

2 Year Diploma Programme

* Culinary Arts
* In depth practical and supervisory level training
* Reception and Sales
* Broad base training in Front Office Operations
* Hospitality Management
* Knowledge and skill to embark on supervisory or junior management level

Accreditation

* 2 Year Diploma Programmes
* Hospitality Management
* Culinary Arts
* University of the West Indies
* Monroe College

In-House Training Courses

* Butchery Techniques
* Caribbean Cuisine
* Art and Science of Service

Collaboration with Tourist Operators

* Federation of Tour Operators
* Food Hygiene & Safety Seminar
* Antigua Hotels and Tourist Association
* Internship for students
* Membership on Board & Sub committees
* Partnership with Trans Caribbean Marketing & US meat Export Federation

Regional Collaboration through Caribbean Tourism Organization

* Core Curriculum
* Certified Hospitality Educator
* Dynamic Supervisory Management Programme
* Quality Assurance and Articulation
* Human Resources Conference
* Promotional material on careers in Tourism

Sources of Funding

* Consolidated funds of Antigua & Barbuda Government
* European Commission
* Organization of American States
* First Caribbean International Bank

Annual Government Funding Allocation

* ABHTI Estimates 2006 $1.8 Mil 21%
* ASC(Antigua State College) $5.7 Mil 65%
* ABICE $1.2 Mil 14%
* ABIIT unknown-

* Total $8.7 Mil 100% Revenue (2005) ABHTI $122,000 ASC $60,000

Conclusion

* Tourism is a high-touch, high-tech, high-involvement industry where it is the people who make the difference.
* The ability for the industry to succeed and the future performance of the industry and related activities will depend largely on the skills, qualities and knowledge of its employees. Indeed the challenges facing the industry can only be met successfully by a welleducated, well-trained, bright, energetic, multi-lingual and entrepreneurial work force.
* A high-quality tourism work force can only be achieved through high standards of tourism education and training which in turn will impact our destination's ability (the ability of our twin-island state) to compete successfully in this global competitive industry.

Special Symposium on APU's Tourism Human Resource Development Project

A Special Symposium on APU's Tourism Human Resource Development Project titled, "Creating the Future of Regional Tourism-Fostering Talent for the Next Generation" was held at Beppu B-con Plaza on Friday, March 10. The Special Symposium was held for people who will have major roles in the future of the tourism and service industry including the accommodation sector.

APU's "Tourism Human Resource Development Project" was commissioned by the Ministry of Economy, Trade and Industry as part of its "AY2005 Power Supply Regional Service Human Resource Development Business."

Mr. TOYODA Masakazu, Director-General of the Commerce and Information Policy Bureau of the Ministry of Economy, Trade and Industry Mr. TOYOTA Masakazu commenced the first-half of the Symposium with a keynote address on "Promoting the Hospitality Industry." Afterwards, the President of the All Japan Ryokan Association, Mr. Kohara Kenji gave a presentation on "Creating a Tourism-Orientation Nation." A panel discussion on the theme of "Creating the Future of Tourism in Kyushu-Regions and Business/ Developing Human Resources" took place in the second-half of the Symposium. The participants listened attentively to the animated exchange of ideas.

Human Resources in Tourism: Still Waiting for Change

People, we are frequently told, are a critical dimension within the successful delivery of tourism services. ''The story of successful tourism enterprises is one that is largely about people—how they are recruited, how they are managed, how they are trained and educated, how they are valued and rewarded, and how they are supported through a process of continuous learning and career development'' points to recognition of this philosophy in the mission statements of hotel companies within which a far higher proportion of respondents include reference to human resources than is the case within manufacturing companies.

This contemporary manta or reflection of the '''soft' rhetoric of people as an organisations's greatest asset'' (Bolton & Houlihan, 2007, p. 1) may have had equal veracity at various points during the development of tourism over the past century, but the practical implications of the claim, in terms of the role that people play, will have been interpreted in different ways at varying points over this timeframe. In particular, there is an apparent paradox in the dramatic evolution of the global tourism sector over the past half century and, within it, the manner and conditions in which people deliver tourism services which have remained timeless in many respects but also subject to significant change.

During this time, debate about labour intensity, the number and cost of people required to work in many areas of tourism, has sat alongside discussion of the skills necessary to deliver quality tourism services, remuneration and working conditions and the role that technology plays in both supporting and changing this delivery.

Inevitably, the nature of such analysis has shifted over time. In particular, the profile of many workers, but by no means all of those in tourism's work force, and the role that they play in the labour markets of developed countries, has been subject to change.

At the same time, tourism work must be set alongside major economic and labour market restructuring in post-industrial societies so that direct comparison between tourism and traditional heavy manufacturing work in shipyards, mines and steel works, which formed an important element of the early industrial sociology in the emerging service sectors, is less relevant. Rather, tourism work now sits alongside and is compared to other activities within the dominant service economy of developed countries, and the analytical paradigm for such comparison should consider employment opportunities in the sector in a rather different light. Whether such comparison leads to a positive assessment of work in tourism is a matter that we shall consider in this paper.

In the light of external change, in developed countries, certain aspects of human resource management in tourism demonstrate evolution over time, by responding across the breadth of the contextual environment within which tourism is located, notably in socio-cultural, marketrelated and technological terms. Such change is clearly evident within some of the large tourism companies in transport, entertainment and accommodation.

At the same time, the headlines of change do not reflect reality across the totality of the tourism sector. There is a real contrast between major multinational tourism companies and smaller operators within some sub-sectors of tourism (particularly accommodation and restaurants) which contain areas of work where many things have not changed over the past 20 years—productivity remains stubbornly low, working conditions are poor and remuneration levels are well below national averages in many countries. In some areas of tourism, businesses have been unable to cope with the pressures of external change-induced competition so that, for example, work opportunities in traditional travel agents have declined in many countries.

By contrast to the developed world, in poorer countries, the picture is rather more homogeneous whereby much work in low labour cost economies, including that of the tourism sector, has an appearance of timelessness so that change, if any, has been at the margins of the overall employment experience. This paper seeks to make a partial assessment of the impact of external change on the human resource environment within tourism over the past 20 years, with particular focus on work and employment themes within the sector. In addressing a topic as broad as this, there is a real danger of uncritical generalisation within a highly heterogeneous sector such as tourism.

There is real and on-going debate with regard to definitional issues in the tourism sector and this has presented some challenges in the context of this paper. Discussion here seeks to embrace an inclusive interpretation of tourism with illustrations of human resource practices across various sub-sectors. This challenge is illustrated by highlighting features such as the diversity within tourism with its various sub-sectors (accommodation, food service, transport, facilitation, heritage); the size of operations; the location of these operations; business arrangements that are in place to deliver services within tourism; and the economic context within which operations do their business.

Published empirical and conceptual analysis of human resource issues in tourism has focused disproportionately on the hospitality sub-sector and, inevitably, evidence here is substantially drawn from hotels and restaurants to the possible neglect of major areas of employment such as transport. This is a challenge faced by others in considering human resource themes in tourism in this way.

Our assessment is further complicated as a result of ambiguity in understandings of what the term, human resources and its management, encompasses. This ambiguity includes the consequences of changes that have taken place at a functional level as the traditionally accepted concept of personnel management has given way to a broader functional application in human resource management, operating as part of a company's wider business and strategic environment. Human resource themes are also applicable at both the levels of the firm and in a macronational or regional context. This paper adopts conscious selectivity in focusing on human resources in the specific context of the work place and considers whether and how the employment environment has altered over the past 20 years.

Attempting a retrospect, with regards to a theme such as human resources in tourism, presents a challenge in determining an appropriate benchmark against which to measure possible change. Notionally, a 20-year yardstick is used, taking us back to the mid-1980s. At the same time, it is important not to ignore the insights from earlier times and to consider these in a contemporary context. Conceptually, the most useful and comprehensive framework against which to judge change is that provided by

Wood's (1992, 1997) consideration of work in the hotels and catering sub-sector of tourism.

While Wood's discussion purposefully does not address the breadth of what is taken to be tourism here, it provides a valuable insight into research and analysis across the largest of tourism's subsectors, but one that is both the best studied and most problematic. Wood's assessment of the evidence discussed in his book, much of it drawn from the 1970s, 1980s and early 1990s, is that Hospitality work is largely exploitative, degrading, poorly paid, unpleasant, insecure and taken as a last resort or because it can be tolerated in the light of wider social and economic commitments and constraints. Our concern here is to consider whether the context of and practice in contemporary tourism is such as to allow work in the sector to have moved significantly beyond the bleakness of this assessment and, if it has, to consider the extent to which wider contextual change has imposed itself on the management of human resource within tourism.

Therefore, this paper is concerned with assessing the nature and extent of contextual change on the management of human resources across the international tourism sector. This is a very broad aspiration, given the scope and scale of tourism as an economic activity, consisting of widely differing sub-sectors and located across virtually all communities, countries and cultures. The themes and contexts addressed here, therefore, must necessarily be selective, and include dimensions that appear to have broad salience across major tourism destinations, both established and more recently emerging. The paper commences with a brief look back to the nature of work in tourism as depicted in early research into the sector, substantially the sources which led Wood to his bleak assessment.

The paper then focuses on a number of themes which allow us to evaluate the extent of change and its impact—undertaking an assessment of the practice of the management of human resources in contemporary tourism; followed by consideration of the consequences of global and social forces on perceptions of work and careers; the impact of ICT on work and employment in tourism; changing interpretations of skills within tourism; and, finally, the increasingly diverse nature of the tourism work force in developed countries. The paper concludes with an assessment of whether change, within these selected areas, outweighs the dead hand of the status quo that may appear to pervade tourism employment in other respects.

Where we have Come From

Recorded and formal accounts of what was and is involved with work in tourism, beyond passing fragmentary evidence, are relatively recent. One of the first in-depth pictures of aspects of tourism work comes from the 1930s and the writing of George Orwell (1933). His description of the work of the plongeur within the working hierarchy of Paris hotels is as perceptive as it is moving and, in many ways, provides a benchmark against which much subsequent sociological discussion of working conditions in the tourism and, particularly, the hospitality industry can be assessed.

Orwell's approach is to describe his own experiences of working in Paris hotels and his relationship with colleagues and superiors from the perspective of the foreigner and the 'down and out'. Orwell's objective is to expose the extremes of social deprivation during the depression of the 1930s and, as such, is one of extreme pessimism. He considers the work of the plongeur in its social context.

When one comes to think of it, is strange that thousands of people in a great, modern city should spend their waking hours swabbing dishes in hot dens underground. The question I am raising is why this life goes on—what purpose it serves, and who wants it to continue, and why I am not taking a more rebellious attitude. I am trying to consider the social significance of the plongeur's life. I think I should start by saying that the plongeur is one of the slaves of the modern worldy he is no freer than if he were bought and sold. His work is servile and without art; he is paid just enough to keep him alive; his only holiday is the sack.

Orwell was looking at society through eyes that would have sat comfortably alongside that of other social commentators of the time, such as Seebohm Rowntree, a major contributor to understanding of poverty in Britain during the first half of the twentieth century. Rowntree prepared three assessments of social conditions in York and these progressively analysed the causes of poverty at the respective times, gathering increasing optimism as greater levels of state engagement with work, health and related social matters impacted upon British society and the work place. Rowntree and Orwell shared a faith in the capacity of the state to improve the lives of the poor and were part of a movement that spawned detailed analysis of social conditions through initiatives such as the Mass Observation project. This included the domain of work.

Political change since the early 1980s has, perhaps, weakened the basis of such faith, notably through the impact of "Thatcherism" in the UK and elsewhere. Therefore, contemporary commentators question the basis for optimism in assessing the conditions of work to which may service workers, including those in tourism, are exposed. For example, Orwell's disenfranchised and marginalised world of the plongeur has resonance in more contemporary studies. Toynbee (2003), walking in the footsteps of Orwell, describes life in low-wage Britain, including her experiences in sectors of hospitality, and this world is not dramatically different from that of 1930s Paris within which Orwell talks about work as a "sort of delirium" within which "we were going as though we had only five minutes to live"y It was now that the tempo of the shift moved from hard and fast work to a controlled frenzy of washing up. Conversation came to an end. We were, I suppose, cheaper than industrial dishwashing machines but we imitated them quite well.

The tough reality that is presented in early descriptions, building from the influence of Orwell's analysis and, subsequently, reflected in Toynbee, can also be seen in other more recent studies of the industry (primarily but not exclusively, hospitality), many of which focus on problematic aspects of tourism work in a comparative social context. There is, therefore, little evidence, notwithstanding exceptional best practice examples by some organisations from across the industry, that working conditions in tourism have improved significantly from the time of Wood's pessimistic assessment.

Returning to Orwell, however, also brings us to his depiction of the craft and professionalism of hospitality work, set so starkly alongside the grim "below stairs" experience out of which the waiter seamlessly moves.

It is an instructive sight to see a waiter going into a hotel dining-roomy. As he passes through the door a sudden change comes over him. The set of his shoulders alters; all the dirt and hurry and irritation have dropped in an instant. He glides across the carpet with a solemn priestlike air.. And you cannot help thinking, as you see him bow and smile, with the benign smile of the trained waiter, that the customer (is) put to shame by having such an aristocrat serve him.

There is another side of the coin which perhaps depicts tourism work in a rather more positive light and one which highlights what Riley et al. describe as "the obvious contrast of glamour on the one hand and low menial status on the other". One example of the glamour, that is equally precise and from the same period as Orwell, is represented by the accounts written, between 1937 and 1942, in five books by Ludwig Bemelmans.

However, in contrast to Orwell, Bemelmans is the supreme optimist and describes hotel work from the point of view of someone climbing to a senior position in a luxury New York hotel. In a similar vein, Le Sueur's (1998) account of managing a hotel in Tibet presents an upbeat and very positive perspective on work at this level within the industry. The airline sector was also, historically, held up as the glamorous side of work in tourism, particularly in the 1950s and 1960s, and was widely depicted as one of the "blue ribbon" sectors for employment within personal services. During the 30-year period up to airline deregulation in the United States (1979) and Europe (early 1990s), it is fair to say that employment in the airline sector, especially with major national flag carriers, had many of the security of tenure attributes of public sector work and its attendant benefits combined with high levels of trade union participation while, at the same time, offering perceived glamour and a "fun" image. Calder describes this in terms of "A job in aviation—glamorous, secure, well-paid employment".

This perspective of airline work has been critically assessed by, among others, Bolton and Boyd (2003), Tyler and Taylor (1998) and Williams (2003) and further debunked as a result of high profile disclosures relating to work in some new model low-cost airlines as well as post-2001 changes within the aviation industry. However, vestiges of status and glamour remain current in the airlines of many developing countries. Other areas of tourism work, while not well covered in the research literature, also point to clear ambiguities with respect to the working environment of tour guides and tour operator representatives.

Riley's application of internal labour market models to tourism provides a useful analytical framework in seeking to understand and explain the lack of significant change with respect to working conditions and remuneration in many areas of tourism work. Riley and Szivas describe tourism as a sector "where easily acquired, transferable skills co-exist and engender weak internal labour markets in organisations that economically are bound to a rate of throughput." Riley (1996) points to the features of employment in these conditions in terms of recruitment, training and professional status and, unsurprisingly, notes that many areas of tourism work typify weak internal labour market characteristics.

Alongside this assessment sits trends within most developed countries and within economic regions such as the European Union which point to erosion of elements of labour market strength and a general weakening of work place conditions. This has been driven by both economic and labour relations changes, notably in countries such as Spain and the United Kingdom but also, to a lesser extent, in bastions of strong labour markets such as France and Germany. As we shall see, access to low cost sources of migrant labour in many European countries has further acted to weaken labour market conditions within businesses in the tourism sector, despite the introduction of national minimum wage levels in countries such as Ireland and the UK.

An assessment of progress or otherwise, with respect to the overall working conditions and remuneration levels of tourism employees, does not provide clearcut answers. There has been progress in some countries and within many, particularly, larger, organisations where case examples of high quality working lives and opportunity can be found to match that within most other sectors of the economy. However, much tourism work remains menial and under-valued and the plethora of smaller organisations also point to working environments where practices remain Dickensian and show little change from Wood's let alone Orwell's depiction.

Reflections on the Role of Human Resources in Tourism

The underlying premise of Failte Ireland's ground breaking strategic plan for human resource development in Irish tourism is predicated upon the argument that "good HRM practices will be adopted because they deliver bottom line profitability". This primarily economic justification for investment in HRD has underpinned much of the history of this field, whether in the guise of personnel management, strategic human resource management, high commitment management or the management of human capital, among other iterations.

This, in turn, is manifested in a range of good practices, adopted by companies recognised for their leadership in the management of people within the tourism sector. Failte Ireland (2005a, 2005b) identify a number of good practice themes, based on a study of excellence in the tourism sector in Ireland and other countries.

Bolton and Houlihan (2007), in their powerful plea to reintroduce a human dimension to our consideration of HRM, note that these dimensions are uni-dimensional in their focus on employer benefits so that they ignore any notion of reciprocity. They effectively encapsulate this oneway street in their assessment of the HRM contract in terms of its humanity.

Bolton and Houlihan's case is, on the face of it, simple. Arguments in favour of work place flexibility among other forms of accommodation and change in the work place are generally, business and employer driven. Notwithstanding blandishments that advocate recognition of employee lifestyle requirements and work-life balance, some of which is enshrined in legislation addressing matters such as paternity leave, the overwhelming evidence is that reciprocity with regard to flexibility and accommodation in the work place is relatively rare, both for remunerated employees and among volunteer workers in tourism and heritage organisations.

Bolton and Houlihan point to imbalance in the expectations of contemporary industrial relations within tourism. As a weak labour market sector, tourism in most developed countries has never been highly unionised and what strength trade unions may have offered in seeking greater reciprocity in the human resource contract has been eroded further in recent years. High profile disputes in international tourism companies have taken place in recent years, primarily in larger organisations located in transport related sub-sectors. Examples of these include disputes in Irish Ferries, Gate Gourmet.

Unions have succeeded in achieving partial amelioration of employer plans, but in no sense can these be taken as indicative of change in a general labour market process which is designed to weaken the position of employees within the sector. Indeed, in the wider context of services, especially in smaller businesses, Korczynski argues that if trade unions "are to have meaning for frontline workers, their strategies must be informed by the daily work experiences of these workers" and that strategies that are derived from such experiences are likely to appear contrary to traditional union practice. He notes the failure of trade unions to adapt to the needs of the contemporary service economy but, in the context of most businesses in tourism, this does not really represent change from past experience within which trade unions were of but marginal relevance within the sector. There are specific contexts within which trade unions can operate effectively in tourism. "Traditional" airlines are one example as are hotels in Dublin, Ireland where Piso (2003) reports structural factors in the local labour market as being supportive of union participation. Perhaps the main barrier to unionisation in tourism's private sector is the attitude of management. Royle (2000), in considering work in the McDonalds fast food chain across a number of European countries, identifies the strategies employed by the company to ensure that unions cannot operate effectively.

Within tourism businesses, a process of organisational delayering and the reduction in specialist human resource staff means that many human resource responsibilities have substantially been devolved to front line managers. Brewster and Larsen (1992) suggest that there are a number of reasons why many human resource activities have been devolved to line managers, and these are cost reduction, to provide a more comprehensive approach to HR Management, and to place the responsibility with the people who are most responsible for it.

Renwick's (2003) study established that line managers are now responsible for a larger number of employees than ever before, which in turn means that there are more issues in this area for them to manage. Storey (1992, 1995, 2001) suggests that if the work force is so critical to organisational success, the responsibility for human resource activities rests with all line managers and should not be left to HR specialists. While larger organisations have undoubtedly invested in providing front-line managers with the new HR skills necessary for the responsibilities identified, there is little evidence that the majority of smaller tourism businesses have done much to meet this need. As a result, it is arguable that the quality of human resource management has deteriorated.

Approaches to human resource management that are suitable for a complex sector such as tourism remain contentious. The evidence is that larger organisations have become more professional in their application of key HR principles within the work place, but that such professionalism frequently remains absent in smaller businesses. The notion of reciprocity, which we introduced with regard to work place flexibility, can also be largely absent when organisations implement wider HR policies and practices. People management may be recognised as a concern for all those in positions of responsibility in organisations, but there is little evidence that those charged with this responsibility have a full comprehension of what this strategic role means in practice.

This failure or neglect is not just one that is of concern at the level of the tourism firm but reflects a charge that can equally be directed at tourism development policies and practices at a community, regional or national level. Liu and Wall are rightly critical of this neglect when they state that "tourism's human resource issues are poorly conceptualised and the many studies of tourism development approaches, both theoretical and practical, provide no consolidation of useful recommendations to situate the human dimension as an integral part of a comprehensive planning framework for tourism". There is little evidence that this recent criticism has any less validity today than it might have done in the mid-1980s, and this is a real indictment of the large number of master plans and similar documents for tourism that have been funded by international agencies during this time.

A Global Industry, A Global Work Force

The tourism sector offers many and varied opportunities for working lives across its diverse sub-sectors and at different levels throughout the world. The industry's heterogeneity, geographical spread and stochastic demand cycle provides both opportunity and challenge in terms of mapping these against the aspirations and expectations of those attracted into the tourism industry, either as new entrants to the labour force or in the context of change opportunities within their working lives.

In most developed countries, traditional models of one sector working lives, built on the notion of a logical and progressive career "ladder" represents a reality which will face fewer and fewer entrants to the jobs market in the future. For some people, this is not a concern or a fear but provides the basis for challenge and opportunity, the ability to take control of aspects of their lives and to respond to changes within the external environment in a positive manner. Unlike their grandparents, today's school leavers and college graduates are more likely to think of their working lives in terms of finite segments rather than sustained and permanent careers, viewing the future in terms of what have been called "boundaryless careers" or "fragmented futures". Sennett, in recognising this phenomenon from a somewhat different perspective, notes that "flexible capitalism has blocked the straight roadway of career, inverting employees suddenly from one kind of work into another".

The trend data in many countries also point clearly to people being more mobile in their working lives and spending less time in the same job. For example, with respect to the UK, Macauley highlights evidence that "in 1996, half of all employees had been working for the same firm for 5 years or less. This had fallen to 4 years by 2001". The same source, points to the decreasing proportion of both full- and part-time employees who had been in their current job for at least 12 months during the same timeframe.

Similarly, the same UK labour market has seen a significant increase in the proportion of people in nonpermanent jobs. McOrmond (2004) reports on changes between 1993 and 2003 which point to increasing temporary engagement by, in particular, those aged below 24 years and those aged over 50 years. Notably, the intermediate group, both male and female, saw a decrease in temporary employment over the same time period. Given the importance of younger workers to the tourism sector, this trend is evidence of this process of fragmentation and its likely impact within the industry and has stimulated response through, for example, recruitment from new labour markets. Notwithstanding the trend indicated here, temporary employment in the UK, by wider European standards, remains quite low at about 7% of the total work force compared to a figure of 32% in Spain, 20% in Portugal and almost 18% in Finland. The temporary employment of female workers is consistently higher than then of males throughout the European Union. The structure of tourism is particularly conducive to supporting vocational mobility, particularly because of stochastic demand within the sector. However, the working environment in many sectors of tourism is such that labour turnover is higher than in other sectors of the economy.

Weir (2003) reports labour turnover in the UK and notes that the hotel and restaurant industries display the highest job separation rates of major sectors. High labour turnover is a reflection of the work environment within tourism and also of economic prosperity and opportunity combined with changing demographic structures and increased educational opportunity in developed countries. In the Irish Republic, for example, a centralised recruitment service for craft-level courses in tourism has seen demand move from a situation of very significant under-supply of training places in the late 1980s to one today where many courses are significantly under subscribed and some have been withdrawn.

Bauman's (2005, 2006) concept of liquidity is equally effective in explaining movement from one dimension of life to another and between relationships, whether in personal or working terms. Liquidity also points to blurring in the distinctions between working and nonworking lives, or as Hochschild puts it "family life had become like 'work' and work had become more like 'home'". Adler (2004) reinforces this notion in his discussion of how the initiation of new work place practices, based on interdependence, can spread over into the home and change domestic behaviour in terms of a weakening of traditional gender roles. Fluid movement between working life segments allow individuals frequent mobility between different sectors of the economy, periods of study within models of lifelong learning and episodes that consist of travel or volunteering sabbaticals. Vocational mobility is greatly facilitated by recognition of the underpinning "generic" skills set which much education and working experience provides today and which permits ease of both formal (qualifications driven) and informal (experience driven) transition, particularly within the tourism sector's weak labour market conditions.

Fragmentation or fluidity may be a relatively new phenomenon in the context of many sectors of the economy, but the reality of such employment models, generally employer rather than employee driven, is well established in many areas of tourism. Writing more than a decade ago, Riley infers that, in moving towards a future of "rising insecurity of job tenure, more unsocial hours working, more uneven workflow, a greater sense of immediacy in tasks", production industries are, essentially, playing what might be called "catch down" with a range of low skills service industries, including tourism.

Fragmentation or fluidity have long been features of work in these sectors, as noted by Orwell (1933) and are driven by, among other things, employer management of stochastic demand and growing responsiveness to customer demand or whims. What is new, however, is that work place mobility and job change are increasingly employee driven, with workers unwilling to make long-term commitments to one organization or work place. Unlike the disapproval that fragmentation or liquidity in working lives may have attracted in the past, today such mobility is less likely to be seen in terms of a lack of commitment or disloyalty to an employer nor does it necessarily create a sense of fear and insecurity for those moving between various working phases. Perceptions of working lives held by younger people today are focused more on short-term wealth accumulation or debt reduction and much less on job status, security or permanence of employment than was the case with previous generations. Therefore, within the timescale allotted to work in a particular company or sector, commitment may be strong despite the transitory nature of the employment relationship.

Alongside the flexibility which characterises working relationships within the contemporary global work force, vestiges of the past remain within the labour market. Major cities undergoing post-industrial transformation can face the paradox of high residual, long-term unemployment, mainly within the former work force of heavy industries such as automobile manufacturing alongside a large number of unfilled vacancies in contemporary tourism businesses, most of which can only be filled from student or migrant worker labour pools. Sennett (2006) talks about the "spectre of uselessness" which haunts post-industrial society, in his terms the result of automation and technology substitution in the industrial work place but equally relevant where communities have witnessed growth in service, notably tourism, work and parts of the work force have not been enabled to buy into this new model of employment. At the heart of the causes of this uselessness is Bauman's notion that "the impetuous growth of new knowledge and no less rapid ageing of the old combine to produce human ignorance on a massive scale, and continuously replenish, perhaps even beef up, its supplies".

At its simplest, leading businesses have already recognised the changing nature of the employment relationship and have responded by a reconfiguration of operations and service delivery at certain levels within the traditional quality spectrum. As a leader within this process, McDonalds early on accepted that they would offer, at best, transitory job opportunities for many school and college students as well as others in the work force.

Therefore, they ensured that processes can be learnt very quickly by able people who are productive within a short period of time. Both parties know very well that there will not be a long-term commitment to the working relationship but that, while it lasts, both sides seek to maximise respective benefits.

For McDonalds and similar operators, this involves streamlining and simplifying processes and relying on the energy and enthusiasm of their workers for the delivery of their services. McDonalds have recently taken acknowledgement of the transitory nature of employer–worker relationships a step further with their announcement of the McPassport, providing opportunity for their employees working anywhere within the European Union to transfer to positions in McDonalds' shops across boundaries elsewhere in the EU, for short or longer periods of time, thus facilitating lifestyle and educational opportunity.

Other tourism businesses have recognised the value of this approach. In major cities in the UK and elsewhere perhaps half of all tourism workers are notionally full-time students. As a result, the tourism industry is configured to depend upon this source of labour and education providers have also had to adjust their delivery models accordingly. For businesses, there has been some modification of both product and technical skills demands with a greater focus on "generic skills" of communication, personality (aesthetic and emotional labour) as well as greater use of technology. Traditional training, as offered through tourism colleges in the form of formal courses and qualifications, plays a lesser role in meeting industry needs within this new model of tourism employment. The decline in relevance of and demand for technical courses in tourism also increases the marginalisation of those with low qualifications in contemporary society (the traditional recruitment pool for such courses) who, as a result, may be further economically and socially excluded. In their place, the flexible student labour market offers employers many perceived advantages which traditional training routes do not.

Likewise, many tourism businesses in rural areas have turned to short-term labour pools of students and others from abroad, in Ireland/UK to learn English (from countries such as Spain or Germany) or for their year out (from New Zealand or Australia) as ready made, articulate and, in some cases, lower cost alternatives to local labour. "Lifestyle"—attractive employment in Donegal, West Cork or Kerry in Ireland can be offered seasonally to workers from elsewhere in Europe at lower cost and difficulty than would be involved in drawing on local labour markets. Training required and offered is minimal and there is hassle-free disengagement at the end of the tourist season.

An extension of this employment culture is reflected in the increasing use of other flexible labour strategies within tourism. Shackleton (1998) points to the contribution of targeted part-time labour in the development of 'superservice' in food retailing. Likewise, agency staff, in some areas of tourism employment, are of increasing importance, particularly in urban locations. Hotel housekeeping and banqueting are the main work areas where agencies provide a "just in time" model for businesses which allows for rapid response to variable demand and eliminates surplus staffing on an employer's books. This also creates an environment where longer-term employment relationships and structured longitudinal training models have little relevance.

These expedient models of employment are most prevalent within the systematised, middle quality rankings and "fast" delivery sectors of the tourism sector. The concept of a career within this sector for all but a minority in positions of managerial responsibility is of limited and decreasing value. The role of education and training in the context of transitory working lives, both within the external college environment and in industry itself, is to support mobility, mid-life entry and re-entry to the sector and development in relation to new technologies and products.

This represents a fast-moving, ever-changing and challenging model of life-long learning which, in the future, will play an important role in support of the "popular" sector of the tourism industry. "Fragmented" and transitory employment relationships and practices may still leave problems for those "high end" businesses which remain locked within traditional skills paradigms and which employ craft personnel in the conventional mode. For them, the concept of the traditional, longitudinal career within a chosen craft area has relevance and career management in this sense requires active participation by employees themselves, their employers but also by those responsible for maintaining, managing and enhancing quality within tourism. At the same time, paying for and marketing the outcomes of such skills necessitates premium pricing and careful management of the price–value relationship.

The working lives projected for today's young people bear little relationship to the linear career models aspired by their grandparents and will be characterised by change, short-term goals and on-going renewal. Those planning for human resource development in tourism may need to more responsive to the challenges and opportunities presented by fragmented learning and working lives and recognise, as Adler and Adler (2004) do, the diversity of motivations and interests that workers typically bring into their employment relationships with tourism sector employers. Change, with regard to this theme, has moved employee aspirations for reciprocity in the utilisation of flexibility up the agenda so that notions of work place flexibility, as introduced by Atkinson (1984) and others, can no longer be seen solely in terms of approaches that are designed to benefit organisational needs.

The response to global trends in tourism, by educational and training providers, has been mixed. Baum (2000) points to the institutional and cultural barriers to change within most educational systems, factors that mitigate against the adoption of common tourism programmes and qualifications across national boundaries, notwithstanding the intentions of initiatives such as the Bologna agreement in Europe. The range of national case studies that address educational and training themes in tourism and the wider economy also points to the intransigence of diversity.

At the same time, there has been a growth in programmes in tourism education offered to a worldwide audience on-line and demand for education in this field through overseas study in Australia, Hong Kong, the UK, the USA and elsewhere remains high. However, such provision is largely structured upon demand from students from developing countries seeking to acquire skills and knowledge as imparted by academic and professional experts in the developed world. This is a questionable model of knowledge transfer and one that Botterill and Baum (2006) describe as neo-colonial in impact. It is similar to the underpinning assumptions behind the growth of tourism education in many developing countries over the past 20 years, assumptions that see European and North American models delivery put uncritically in place in the colleges and universities of recipient countries.

The Impact of ICT on Work and Employment in Tourism

There is little questioning of the impact of technological development on all aspects of working and living in developed countries and, to an increasing extent, within the developing world as well. The impact of such change on the work place and beyond is well documented. These assessments highlight the importance of changes in the work place linked to a wide range of issues, including perceptions of time and work intensity within the work place; organisational fragmentation; flexibility and enabling the recognition of work-life balance issues in the work place; the polarisation of skills and the decline in demand for less skilled workers; disparities in remuneration linked to use/non-use of ICT in the work place; outsourced working; home and teleworking; social inclusion, ICT and the work place; ICT and knowledge management; and technology substitution among a much wider range of concerns. These changes in the work place mirror wider adoption and use of technology within society and, in many respects, feed off familiarity with and expectations of technology that stem from everyday life. A comprehensive assessment of the impact of ICT and wider technology on the work place and working lives in tourism and beyond has the potential to be a subject for separate analysis in its own right. Here, we touch on a number of key themes and issues drawn from this discussion.

What is true, with regard to ICT in a general sense, is equally valid as an assessment of change within services and tourism and, in particular, within the context of work and employment and the changing role that people play as a result of such change. It is not an understatement to argue that ICT and wider technological change have revolutionised aspects of tourism operations (particularly distribution) while leaving others virtually untouched (food preparation and service in many smaller operations).

In terms of employment in tourism and the past 20 years, technology has had a direct effect on both the elimination of work areas and on the creation of others. Some destinations, dependent on airline and other transport stop-overs for their tourism business, have been by-passed by advances in transport technology so that the work associated with this industry may no longer exist. For example, Gander in Newfoundland, Canada, a major refuelling stop for trans-Atlantic flights until the early 1980s now no longer serves this purpose and work associated with the sector has ceased to exist. Similarly, changes in technology mean that the work of hotel telephonists has faded and, in many cases, disappeared with the advent of automated telephones in bedrooms and guest mobile phones.

The technology challenge, particularly the consumer option to purchase and manage the booking of tourism products direct with suppliers such as airlines and hotels via the Internet, has reduced the need for and changed the role of travel agents, check-in staff and others involved in work in the sector in developed countries. Such change is dependent on the availability and quality of the technology and, in many developing countries, the role of the travel intermediary remains important in the absence of Internet or, at least, Broadband connectivity. A final example of changing or diminishing role is that of the tour guide whose work can, in part, be superseded by flexible, electronic alternatives at tourism sites, allowing choice of language and giving visitors a selection of perspectives on events and the site environment.

However, ICT in particular has also created new forms of work in tourism, notably through the application of ICT and its use in distribution and management of key functions such as yield. The advent of specialist Internet travel companies such as Expedia is clear evidence of this change, but the growth of specialist electronic distribution is complemented by website communications, marketing and booking options within virtually all "traditional" tourism companies so that the boundaries between them and e-companies has narrowed greatly.

These developments have created demand for technology specialists in the tourism sector and also for new marketing and management skills in a more general sense, allowing companies to maximise the benefits they derive from ebusiness. ICT has also changed the role of management information within the sector, allowing far greater depth and access to key information about guests and their behaviour. At the same time, it has revolutionised the management of pricing and yield so that human intervention is far less frequent than it would have been in the past. Technology has also changed the nature of work and skills required for many employees, not least in tourism. Many areas of work have been moved from relatively skilled levels to the routine or lesser skilled. A good example of such change is in the area of hotel front office where enhanced reservations and guest management systems have reduced the training and technical skills requirements of such work by up to 90% in terms of the time required to acquire full competency. As we shall see, the technical demands of such work have been more than compensated for by the wider bundling of skills requirements within such work.

Moving Beyond Technical Skills

Tourism work has, historically, been calibrated in terms of its technical skills demands. This is most evident in the approach adopted by the International Labour Organization (1979) in their Taylorian breakdown of hospitality work into individual, measurable micro-tasks that, in turn, can be re-built into a training curriculum and assessment instrument. On the basis of this, tourism and related service work has traditionally and widely been characterised as low skills although this stereotype is challenged in the context of hospitality by a number of authors on the basis that this represents both a technical and western-centric perception of work and skills.

In developed countries, the merging of family and working life has particular pertinence here in that many of the technical and interpersonal skills demanded of employees in tourism have close parallels with those learnt during socialisation in the home. Baum's (2006a) notion of social distance between the experience and behaviour of the tourist and employee is also of relevance here in that, in developed countries, there is considerable role crossover between the two in terms of transfer of experiences between the contexts. In less developed countries, such crossover is less likely.

Grugulis, Warhurst, and Keep (2006) talk about the evolution of what we understand to be a skill over time. In terms of tourism work, perhaps the first manifestation of change from a dominantly technical focus can be found in Hochschild's (1983) seminal study, which was one of the first to take our understanding of such work beyond the technical and professional domain, focusing on "the relational rather than the task-based aspect of work". Hochschild's work inspired recognition of what Westwood (2004) notes are commonly referred to as 'soft skills' and, in doing so, highlights less tangible dimensions in the bundling of skills and work in tourism. Hochschild argues that service employees are required to manage their emotions for the benefit of customers and are, in part, paid to do this. Likewise, Seymour (2000) considers the contribution that this notion of emotional labour makes to work in fast food and traditional areas of service work and concludes that both areas demand considerable emotional elements in addition to overt technical skills.

Bryman defines emotional labour as relating to Employment situations in which workers as part of their work roles need to convey emotions and preferably to appear as though those emotions are deeply heldy (emotions) that are supposed to make the recipient of the emotional labour feel good about the worker and the organization for which he or she works.

Sandiford and Seymour (2002) take this definition a step further in talking about the management of emotions for financial reward. This link between human emotion and commercialisation has not been without detractors such as Wouters (1989) and Newton, Handy, and Fineman (1995). The expectations of emotional labour add significantly to the skills demands of work in tourism. There are few areas of front-line or boundary spanning work in tourism that do not have a very evident and, in some cases, all important emotional dimension. In many respects, as Bryman notes with respect to Disney, employees are expected to give the appearance of enjoying their work as much as visitors are enjoying their time in the theme park. Maintaining this emotional facade in working conditions that are, often, anything but conducive to such behaviour takes its toll and requires skills and the outcome of extensive training in order to be maintained.

Blythman (2005) discusses the problems that such demands present in the context of supermarket work. After several hours at a time, any urge to be cheery or pleasant was overtaken by an all pervasive, mindnumbing blankness. I began to feel spaced out, as though dulled by drugs. Any energy I might feel at the start of a shift soon ebbed away. Even if you wanted to try to be pleasant with people, after only so long it was impossible to keep it up.

The demands that emotional engagement in the work place entails have not traditionally been recognised within skills hierarchies and have either been neglected or put to one side as of lower value and status than "real" productive activities. Bolton (2004) argues a strong case for the recognition of the skills dimensions within emotion work. She argues that emotional inputs are inherently skilled elements within the work routines, control processes and socially constructed demands that typify much service work.

On this basis, Bolton argues that "emotion work is indeed skilled work which contains recognisable elements of discretionary content, task variety and employee control". Ritzer (2005) extends this notion of emotional involvement in his discussion of "simulated people". Obvious examples are Ronald McDonald and the characters to be found in Disney theme parks but Ritzer notes that "Far more important, however, is the fact that most of the people we encounter in the new means of consumption are simulations, even if they are not wearing costumes". Ritzer argues that employers prescribe how workers look, what they say and how they behave in a more general sense with the result that "these positions can be filled by a wide range of individuals. There is little or no room for creativity or individuality".

Work with a strong emotional labour component is, however, not exclusively about theatre. Williams (2003) highlights the safety and regulatory context which trumps any considerations of service and emotional engagement with passengers in the work of airline attendants. Safetyrelated skills may be considered to be technical in nature and this illustrates that, while some areas of tourism work may focus almost exclusively on soft or ephemeral skills, the roles of government regulation and passenger concern are such that emotional engagement must always take second place to the hard skills demands of safety in the work place.

To the requirements of emotional labour in tourism can be added the skills demands of what Warhurst, Nickson, Witz, and Cullen (2000) describe as aesthetic labour, the skills required to look, sound and behave in a manner that is compatible with the requirements of the job and with the expectations of your customers. In many cases, aesthetic labour involves staff demonstrating the ability to respond to fashion and trend imperatives in the consumer marketplace in a way that can be socially exclusive of many groups and cultures within society. Aesthetic labour is about appearance but can also be underpinned by cultural cache, the ability of front-line staff to understand and engage culturally with their customers on terms dictated by the latter. Thus, service staff in some tourism contexts (luxury hotels, premium airline cabins, fitness centres, oneto- one personal training or other sports tuition) need to be able to make informed conversation with their guests or clients about politics, music, sport and almost any other imaginable topic, often from an international perspective. This requirement presupposes a certain level of prior education and cultural exposure as well as a commitment to remain up-to-date in these areas, what Nickson and Warhurst describe as the "gentrification of skill demand".

This implies a very significant change in the profiling of tourism skills in that work which has traditionally provided opportunity for those at the economic margins of developed country societies is, in part, now demanding a skills set that lies within the competencies of those with good general education and a more "middle class" cultural profile. This skills set is, therefore, beyond the reach of traditional recruitment pools for many tourism jobs. Warhurst etal's interpretation of the commodified aesthetics of labour clearly builds upon Tyler and Taylor's discussion of aesthetics and gender in the work place (in the context of flight attendants), which looks specifically at "those particular aspects of women's work which takes place outside formal, contractual relations of exchange, yet upon which formal, contractual relations of commodity exchange depend". Tyler and Taylor's interpretation of aesthetics in the work place draws on "women's attributed nature, femininity and sexuality the commodification of women's Otherness" (166). Thus, aesthetic skills can be seen as both an innate dimension of gender and as an area of skill which processes socialisation, education and training can develop and hone.

Westwood (2004) notes that in ascribing a 'soft skills' descriptor to labour with an emotional and/or aesthetic dimension, there is an implicit assumption that such skills are somehow less important than their 'hard' counterparts. This is a view disputed in Bolton's (2004) argument that emotional work has a clear high skills dimension. Of importance in wider human resource terms is Westwood's comment that such skills, whatever their level of demand, "are a very long way from the kinds of skills that the UK's education system is used to supplying" which persists in a focus on "the processing and supply of more academic skills". This indictment is applicable to many other countries and has particular bite in the context of tourism, pointing to a significant mismatch between education and training and the requirements of the contemporary industry.

Managing Diversity in the Work Place

Diversity in the tourism work place is not a new phenomenon, but full recognition of its impact and managerial implications in developed countries is relatively recent, driven by demographic, labour market and legislative change. Wood adopts an encompassing definition of diversity management when he talks of "a set of evolving philosophies and practices concerned with the utilisation of a variety of human characteristics, orientations and dispositions in satisfaction of ethical precepts and the pursuit of business goals". In the context of this paper, our main concern is with the consequences of diversity in the tourism work place that have arisen through mobility in the form of labour migration, but we will also acknowledge the significance of other forms of diversity to contemporary HRM within the sector. Indeed, as Adib and Guerrier (2003) rightly point out, it is rarely possible to consider the impact of any dimension within the diversity agenda in isolation in that, for example, ethnicity and disability are frequently closely associated with social class and economic status including labour market participation.

Governments in the developed world increasingly recognise the apparent benefits of labour migration to a country's economy.

Home Office research shows that in the UK over a single year, migrants (including asylum seeks and refugees) contributed £2.5 billion to the UK economy. Migrant workers can be beneficial to the economy in a multitude of ways: in particular, they are able to fill gaps in the domestic labour market and alleviate skills shortages as well as increasing the levels of employment which, in turn, helps to raise gross domestic product. Their age profile is such that they use less in the way of services but contribute to tax and national insurance payments which, in turn, help to finance future pensions.

The importance of labour migration to the work force of the contemporary tourism industry is well documented. Tourism businesses have long relied on a culturally diverse work force. Baum (2006a) traces examples of vocational mobility in the sector in Europe back to the 13th century and discusses the important role that, primarily, southern Europeans played in developing the culture and character of tourism operations in industrialised Europe in the 19th and much of the 20th centuries.

However, contemporary labour migration, within tourism in Europe, has received limited attention from researchers. Widespread labour shortages and other labour market changes resulting from the impacts of a combination of, among others, demographic, globalisation and economic factors in Europe are leading tourism companies to hire new employees from a wide range of less developed and transition economy countries. Traditionally concentrated in core, urban centres, multiculturalism within the tourism labour market is now a phenomenon that has reached geographically peripheral areas and has implications for the marketing of destinations such as Ireland which have depended significantly on images of people and place in their destination branding.

The numerical impact of migrant labour on the delivery of tourism services in these locations is particularly noticeable. As an example, it is estimated that there are over 250,000 non- Irish nationals employed in the economy of the Irish Republic or some 13% of the entire work force. This figure reaches 17% in the Irish tourism industry and is up to 25% of the work force in key areas of hospitality work. This growth was stimulated further in 2004 following the accession of 10 new Member States to the European Union. It is estimated that new arrivals to Ireland from within the

Union reached 50,000 in 2004, primarily from Poland. In addition, some 9000 work permits were issued to non-European Economic Area nationals.

The changing nature of labour markets in the tourism sectors of developed countries, as a result of increasing migration, raises issues that have been subject to analysis across a range of the social sciences. Conceptually, this discussion can be located within debate about different forms of mobility in contemporary society and their specific impact in the tourism context. The nature of mobility discussed here and its impact are less common in their analysis in that they are a form of migration (labour) that exists solely because of the presence of another form of mobility, that of tourism.

The issue under the microscope here also responds to Rosello's (2001) notion of the immigrant as guest in her consideration of hospitality and immigration in postcolonial France. If migrants are, themselves, guests in the communities in which they work, interpretative representations of the destination in that context may be provided for guests (visitors) by guests (workers). This context has the potential to place strain on understanding of working roles within the tourism sector and the nature of hospitality provided by those employed as front-line staff.

It is arguable that the widespread recruitment and use of migrant labour in the tourism industry of developed countries has acted to the detriment of real change within the sector's work place. The argument that the tourism sector cannot recruit to unfilled vacancies and, therefore, turns to external labour sources is predicated upon the assumption that the labour economics of the industry remain appropriate and need not change. There are exceptions, as evidenced in good practice examples across the sector, but much of the industry operates on the basis of a labour economics model that depends upon high turnover, low pay, poor conditions and minimal investment in training. Accessing low cost but untrained migrant labour is likely to act as a dead hand with respect to change within the work place economics of the sector. As a consequence, many tourism businesses do not perceive the need to change. They are not required to consider strategies designed to enhance labour productivity, notably through real investment in training and development, in order to reduce the numbers they need to employ at higher rates of pay because low cost employees remain readily available. This analysis accords with Riley and Szivas' comment that "by not recruiting fully trained workers, employers forego productivity in favour of lower labour costs". It is also consistent with Riley's assertion, based on conceptual rather than empirical evidence, but valuable here nonetheless, that "where unskilled labour is imported to fill a shortage, the effect is to deflate existing pay levels".

Notwithstanding the advent of minimum wage legislation in the buoyant tourism economies of countries such as Ireland and the UK, there is little doubt that the availability of migrant labour does allow tourism businesses to employ more untrained workers at lower cost than might have been the case had this source of employee not been available, thus imposing deflationary pressures on individual but possibly not total remuneration costs.

Our discussion thus far, in the context of diversity, has focused on culturally induced dimensions. The management of people in the contemporary tourism sector in many countries is increasingly either legally or morally bound to recognise diversity in terms of a far wider interpretation. These manifestations of diversity are not wholly new in tourism and there is evidence of their recognition, to a limited extent, in early analysis of the sector. However, highlighting such diversity in today's tourism work place is both functionally and ethically important. Dimensions that merit acknowledgement in this context include:

- Gender and the evident and continuing institutionalised disparity that exists in the status and pay of men and women in the services work place. Services work in most societies is highly gendered and this universal reality across national boundaries and continental divides is clearly evident in the range of contexts that are addressed by Sinclair (1997) and her contributing colleagues. Women, as Toynbee (2003) clearly illustrates, often undertake the least desirable and lowest status work in hospitality and other evidence from elsewhere in the services sector suggests that gender has an underpinning influence on rewards, achievement and status in the work place. Likewise the culturally induced absence of working women in the services sectors of some countries is tempered by evidence of gradual change in, for example,

Iran and Saudi Arabia. Some areas of gendered work in services can be seen to represent exploitation and degradation and, therefore, combating sex services, particularly in relation to children, has become a major concern of governments and NGOs in some countries. Some areas of services work have, historically, been a predominantly male preserve. Mills (1998, 173–4) notes, with respect to airline pilots that "In the first two decades of commercial flying the characteristics of heroism and experience came to form a unique type of organisational masculinity—the pilot. Indeed, British Airways' earliest corporate image was that of the experienced, heroic and supremely confident pilot." While gender balance on the flight deck has improved, Mills notes that it was the late 1980s before British Airways appointed their first female pilot. Progress towards gender balance, in this area of high status services work, has been varied across different airlines but female pilots are commonplace today in many countries. Ali Khan (2004) even reports the appointment of the first female airline pilot in Saudi Arabia. However, this area of work remains masculine in its operating culture so that the experiences of female pilots can be challenging and degrading at times.

- Sexual orientation is a theme that has been addressed in services in terms of consumer markets. The experience of gay employees in the sector is not widely recorded except in anecdotal form. This may be because, as Wood notes, "gays and lesbians are not always visible, indeed adopting invisibility as a strategy is one way in which homosexuals cope with organisational life and avoid the disapprobation of those who possess animus against homosexuals".
- Ability and disability is an area of increasing interest in services. The services industry is frequently portrayed as an industry for the young, beautiful and super-fit and this projection is used to create the image of vibrancy, energy and fun. The services sector can be described as one that offers opportunity to members of a society across much of its ability and disability range. It is a sector that can accommodate the expectations and abilities of those with exceptional talent (in culture, entertainment, sports,

technology, entrepreneurship as examples) as well as those in most communities who face challenges of a different sort in terms of physical or intellectual ability.

- Age in the sense that services work is frequently perceived to be an area for the young and historic data in developed countries certainly bears this out. However, changing demographics in wealthier countries means that traditional sources of labour are no longer so readily available, creating the potential of opportunity for more mature workers, returners to work and those retired from first careers. As we have already seen, this solution is, in part, countered by the availability of low cost and young workers from overseas.
- Social inclusion reflects the capacity of services, as a sector for employment, to provide opportunity to potential workers from across a wide social and economic spectrum. This capacity is not always delivered in what is a growing labour market contradiction within the sector, that of widespread employment vacancies in services existing alongside endemic and long-term unemployment within communities in both cities and in rural areas. A partial explanation can be drawn from the aesthetic demands of the industry in that some sectors of services impose implicit or overt entry barriers based on appearance, cultural cache and education upon those seeking work and many of those from socially excluded communities do not meet such criteria.
- Motivation and choice, in terms of why people choose to work and also factors that underpin voluntary, unpaid work in services.

Uncritical claims for the virtue and value of diversity in the work place must be put forward with some degree of caution. The aspiration of effective diversity management in the tourism work place can easily be blinded by what Wood calls "the worthiness of the concept" which belies the rather more pessimistic consensus of the research literature. Furthermore, as we have argued with respect to the employment of migrant labour in the tourism sector's of developed economies, their impact, while making sound short-term business sense, also has the effect of deflating remuneration, permit the continuation of variable working conditions and allowing employers to fudge investment in skills development. If this is true with respect to one form of diversity in the work place, may be necessary to question whether some of the other forms of diversity touched on here are also adopted with similar objectives.

Conclusions

We started this paper with a fairly damning assessment of work and working lives in tourism, arguing that, in many respects, Wood's bleak (1997) assessment of the industry remains substantially unchanged in many countries, both developed and less developed.

We have considered themes wherein wider contextual change can be identified that has a direct impact upon people and their management in the tourism sector and we have considered the consequences of such changes. The evidence points, unsurprisingly, to conclusions in the form of a curate's egg and, indeed, contradictions in terms of practice across the industry. For example, we have evidence of the gentrification of tourism skills from Nickson and Warhurst (2007) while, at the same time, ready access to low cost migrant labour, both legal and illegal, permits many tourism businesses to sidestep this trend and to ignore issues of productivity, skills development and general work place enhancement. As in other areas of work, it is clear that polarisation is taking place within tourism work, but the criteria of distinction relates to the branding and image of the work rather than to its technical or professional status.

"Cool" work is equated with style, fashion and consumer branding (bars, night clubs, boutique hotels, creative venues) while "uncool" includes the work of drudgery in the sector (cleaning, popular service) and also some glamour work from the past, airline cabin crew, particularly with some newer, lowcost airlines. Another example of contradiction is that vocational and educational opportunities for most young people in developed countries are such that many areas of tourism work are much less obvious and attractive longterm career options than they might have been 20 years ago.

At the same time, growth in tourism in developing countries means that the sector has become an important source of employment for those previously dependent on subsistence living so that what is, ostensibly, the same work in a technical sense is constructed in very different ways across social, cultural and economic contexts.

It is true that, at an organisational level, human resource practices in tourism have changed in many developed countries and in most larger operations. This change has been driven by a combination of the effects of commercial, legislative, ethical and external environmental pressures. At the same time, tourism remains a sector within which, worldwide, very poor employment practices persist, incorporating both minimal compliance with the law and transgression beyond legally accepted behaviour.

Some of the changes over the past 20 years that are considered here, notably the mass mobility of economic and political migrants from the world's poorer countries, have allowed tourism work and employment to remain firmly located at the margins of many societies in terms of benefits and status and has acted counter to attempts to reform and modernise the sector with regard to its employment practices.

In the final analysis, the conditions of work in tourism are attributable to the outcomes of market force pressures, temporised in part and in places by government and wider societal interventions. In parallel to our bleak assessment of the work environment, it is important to recognise that insatiable and growing demand for low cost tourism services, across the globe, means that consumers must also take responsibility for pressurising operators into undesirable, marginal or even illegal employment practices. It is self-evident that downward pressures on the overall cost of tourism (low cost airlines, aggressive tour operators, electronic distribution, deregulation) encourages the use of low cost labour and, to an extent, may also deflate expectations of service and product quality. Growth projections for tourism, over the next quarter of a century, are such that it appears unlikely that we will see fundamental change in this environment in the foreseeable future.

Human Resource Module of the Tourism Satellite Account, Update to 2006

The aim of the Human Resource Module (HRM) is to provide timely and reliable statistics on the human resource dimension of tourism. It serves as a useful planning and forecasting tool for policy makers in the tourism, employment and training areas. Various tourism-affiliated agencies, academics, and decisionmakers in tourism will also be able to use it for research and analysis, planning and development. Travel Services accounted for 47 thousand jobs in 2006, up 1.3%, following a 5.9% gain in 2005. This industry group accounted for only 2.6% of all jobs in tourism. The average hourly compensation for jobs in this industry group was above average ($21.56 per hour versus $17.95), as were the hours worked (1,805 hours per year versus 1,559). Travel counsellor was the predominant occupation, accounting for 42% of the industry's employee jobs.

Jobs, Hours and Earnings in Tourism Industries

A total of 2.8 billion hours was worked in tourism industries in 2006, accounting for 9.7% of the 29.1 billion hours worked in the economy overall. This reflected an average 1,559 hours of work per year, somewhat less than the economy-wide average of 1,738 hours. The lower hours of work reflected the higher proportion of part-time jobs found in tourism. It is interesting to note that the average annual hours worked increased slightly in 2006 in tourism industries, but were unchanged for the economy overall. In Retail Trade, a sector characterized by a high proportion of part-time jobs, like tourism, the average annual hours of work per job fell from 1,584 hours in 2005 to 1,566 hours in 2006.

Profile of Employees in Tourism Industries

The HRM includes details on three characteristics of employees namely, gender, age group and immigrant status. The following highlights some of the HRM results according to these demographics.

Women held 920 thousand employee jobs in tourism industries in 2006, an increase of 22,000 from 2005. These gains were mostly full-time and accounted for nearly half the job gains in the sector. Among women, the number of employee jobs held by those aged 45 and over increased the most in 2006 (+3.5%). Among men, on the other hand, jobs held by those aged 25-34 increased the most (+3.9%). The number of jobs held by women and men aged 35 to 44 hardly changed. Women were notably under-represented in Other Transportation, holding only 26% of the employee jobs.

Conversely, 68% of jobs in Travel Services were held by women. Women were more likely to be working part-time than men. They also earned less. Women working in tourism industries earned $19,100 in 2006, compared to $30,500 for men. There was significant variation in women's wages and salaries, with jobs in Air Transportation paying the most ($42,269) on average, and jobs in Food and Beverage Services paying the least ($14,632).

Youth aged 15 to 24 years held 658 thousand employee jobs in the tourism industries in 2006. These young workers were more likely to be working in part-time jobs than other tourism workers, accounting for two-thirds of all the part-time work in the sector. Their wages were also considerably lower.

For example, the average hourly wage among workers aged 15-24 was $8.82 in 2006, just over half the average across tourism industries. Over 1997 to 2006, the number of jobs held by younger (15 to 24 years of age) and older (45 + years of age) employees in tourism has grown significantly, averaging 2.8% and 4.8% per year, respectively. Over the same period the number of jobs held by 25 to 44 year olds has declined.

Immigrants (persons born outside Canada) held 344 thousand jobs in tourism industries in 2006, or 20% of employee jobs. They were more likely to be employed in Travel Services and less likely to be employed in Recreation and Entertainment compared to non-immigrants. Immigrants were also more likely to be older: 18% were between 15 to 24 years old, compared to 44% for non-immigrants. Over 40% of immigrant workers belong in the 45+ age group.

Immigrants working in tourism industries were more likely to be men (53% versus 43%) and more likely to be in full-time jobs (72% versus 58%) than their non-immigrant counterparts. These results have been quite stable over 1997 to 2006. On average, immigrants worked longer hours than their non-immigrant counterparts, 1,755 hours per year versus 1,485 in 2006. This was the case for both men and women and for full-time and part-time jobs, across the period covered by the HRM. Immigrants also earned higher annual wages and salaries on average ($28,769 versus $23,112 in 2006), although this reflects the fact that the immigrant labour force in tourism industries is older and that older workers earn more than younger workers 6: Human resources for travel and tourism Learning outcomes. By completing this unit candidates will develop knowledge and understanding of human resources procedures and issues relevant to travel and tourism organisations.

They will also develop an understanding of the recruitment process and the skills required in an interview situation. Candidates will produce evidence to meet the unit assessment objectives in order to show that they understand:

- the responsibilities of the human resources department in a travel and tourism organisation
- how travel and tourism organisations manage their human resources
- the recruitment process.

Candidates will also demonstrate their practical skills in interview techniques.

Assessment Objectives Knowledge, Understanding and Skills

Describe the responsibilities of the human resources department in a travel and tourism organisation Human resources department responsibilities:

- human resources planning
- recruitment and selection
- training and development, eg induction, mentoring and coaching
- internal and external training
- dismissal, redundancy, promotion, demotion, transfer
- support and advice, eg staff and line managers
- policies and procedures, eg grievance, disciplinary, equal opportunities, maternity, paternity, sickness
- contracts, terms and conditions, holidays and hours of work
- adherence to legislation, eg race, religion, gender, gender identity, sexual orientation, disability or age (equality and diversity)
- staff welfare
- ethical issues

Explain how travel and tourism organisations manage their human resources Organisational structures:

- flat, tall Management styles
- formal, informal Motivation of staff:
- motivation theories
- job enlargement, enrichment, rotation
- pay, bonuses, benefits
- appraisals

Leadership:

- styles (democratic, autocratic, laissez-faire)
- importance of clear targets
- communication channels

Explain how travel and tourism organisations manage their human resources

- line management Teamwork:
- team roles
- targets
- importance of effective communication

Chart the Recruitment Process

The need for staff:

- staff turnover
- organisational growth
- internal change

Examples of recruitment:

- internal
- external
- use of agency
- headhunting
- advertising

Stages of the recruitment process:

- job analysis (production of job description and person specification)

- attracting candidates (timing, different methods and their benefits)
- short listing (from CVs and application forms)
- selection interview (planning, the panel, good techniques)
- testing (psychometric and aptitude)
- appointing (contracts, terms and conditions)
- evaluation of process
- equal opportunities issues
- induction

Costs:

- of poor recruitment
- poor performance
- impacts on team
- advertising, staff time

Demonstrate interviewer and interviewee techniques Interviewer:

- planning
- questioning techniques
- format and style of interview
- use of interview record sheets
- awareness of legislation regarding equality and diversity

Interviewee:

- production of curriculum vitae
- planning and preparation for interview
- knowledge of organisation and job role
- awareness of dress code
- non-verbal communication
- dealing with questions
- asking appropriate questions

Assessment

This unit is centre assessed and externally moderated. In order to achieve this unit candidates must produce a portfolio of evidence showing that they have met all of the assessment objectives. Portfolios of work must be produced independently. They will need to be made available, together with witness statements and any other supporting documentation, to the OCR Visiting Moderator when required.

Centres must confirm to OCR that the evidence produced by candidates is authentic. An OCR Centre Authentication Form is provided in the Centre Handbook and includes a declaration for assessors to sign. It is a requirement of the QCA Common Criteria for all Qualifications that proof of authentication is received.

Guidance on Assessment and Evidence Requirements

This unit aims to develop candidate's knowledge and understanding of the role of the human resources department and its importance within the organisation. The unit also aims to develop the skills required to perform effectively in an interview situation.

This unit has links with Unit 4: Customer service and selling skills in travel and tourism, Unit 8:

Planning and managing a travel and tourism event, Unit 9: Living and working overseas, Unit 11:

Career planning for travel and tourism, Unit 12: Developing skills through work experience in travel and tourism, Unit 13: Working as an overseas resort representative, and Unit 27: Working as airline cabin crew.

Links with a selection of travel and tourism organisations are encouraged for the delivery of this unit. Centres may wish to establish these. Alternatively, candidates may be able to research organisations, either individually or in small groups, share information and make comparisons. Information may also be provided through a case study, visits, talks, work experience or alternative. Ideally, organisations from different sectors of the industry and different types of organisation will be used to highlight different procedures and practices.

It is envisaged that such links with organisations will highlight the fact that the role of the human resources department varies from organisation to organisation and that management techniques and recruitment practices vary enormously. Classroom discussion of the different practices should be encouraged. However, it is recommended that underpinning knowledge of all areas is provided prior to organisational visits. This will enable candidates to make comparisons and comment on good practice. There is a wide selection of printed and video material available on all aspects of human resource management.

When developing candidates' understanding of management techniques, tutors should draw upon candidates' experience of being 'managed' at work experience, within a work place and even within the classroom. Where candidates have worked in teams, they should be encouraged to consider whether the teams worked well and if so why. Tutors may wish to use the Belbin questionnaire to demonstrate the different team roles and the fact that a range of roles within a team is important.

It is envisaged that this unit will be used to develop candidates' awareness of the recruitment practices and the necessary preparation needed to gain employment within a travel and tourism organisation. Candidates should chart the stages of the entire recruitment process, with explanatory notes of each stage. Again, contact with organisations will highlight differences and possible 'short-cuts' taken by organisations. Candidates should be encouraged to discuss these and comment on good practice. An understanding of the recruitment process can be used to encourage candidates to consider the need for their own applications to be professional and the costs involved in recruiting one person.

When preparing for Assessment Objective 4, candidates should be encouraged to produce curriculum vitae and complete job application forms to a professional standard. They could collect and evaluate job descriptions and person specifications. The paperwork used to shortlist candidates should be made available to candidates. Candidates should develop an awareness of their own body language. Self-reflection on skills gained and those requiring further development should be encouraged. It is anticipated that the practical activities used to develop candidates' interview techniques both as an interviewer and interviewee will help their preparation for their own interview situations, on completion of the course. Candidates can work in pairs or small groups for the assessment of Assessment Objective 4, with each candidate taking a turn as the interviewee and interviewer or interview panel member. Tutors are encouraged to video these interviews and candidates should be encouraged to self-evaluate. This could be cross-referenced with Unit 11: Career planning for travel and tourism.

Candidates may provide portfolio evidence for all of the assessment objectives in this unit using a range of presentation techniques. This may include assessor testimony/witness statements logbooks, diaries, the use of video, audio and presentation software, posters/charts, written work. Where video and/or audio evidence is provided this must be supported by assessor testimony/witness statements. Where candidates demonstrate competence, centres should record skills demonstrated on appropriate recording documentation.

3

Employment in Tourism Sector

Introduction

Employment in the travel and tourism industry in Africa. About 6.3 million people work in the travel and tourism industry in Africa, where tourism is highly dependent on natural and cultural environment. However, since travel & tourism touches all sectors of the economy, its real impact is even greater.

Preparing for Employment in Travel and Tourism

Activity

In the last session, work was focused on how recruitment and selection is used in organisations to attract effective people into jobs in the travel and tourism sector. Building on an understanding of how people in the real world make progress through their careers in the sector, you will have learned from completing work on a series of tasks:

- The stages involved in recruiting staff into jobs that you selected
- That you can produce a flowchart of the process
- The documents needed, such as a job description and person specification
- The strengths and weaknesses of your chances of getting into the selected job

Higher grades were available if you started an action plan for getting the job you want in the industry. In this session, you're going to start looking at the skills you will need to develop in order to promote yourself in a positive fashion during a job selection process. That means analysing someone's interview performance and then showing that you could do better by using self-selling skills.

If you've made it through the initial pre-selection stage to be invited for an interview, you know you stand a chance of getting the job if you perform well at interview. Some people complain that interviews are too highly pressured situations for them to show themselves in the best possible light. But in truth, good interviewing skills are very rarely natural-they have to be learned and then sharpened by experience. Let's see how one individual handled a particular interview.

A Dream Job and a Nightmare Interview

Tarjani felt nervous. She had been looking at the email she had received from the airline, saying she'd got through to an interview for her dream job: member of cabin crew on the London to Singapore long-haul service. But she hadn't found out much about the airline or the country she would be visiting regularly.

Her friend Murali had warned her that she had better be well prepared for the interview, as he knew that the company were pretty hot on getting the right people in as cabin crew. But Murali had gone off with his mates for the evening and Tarjani didn't really know where to start.

Unfortunately, the interview was the next day and she still hadn't done much preparation, expect for re-reading the job advert. She hadn't kept a copy of her application, or the documents the company had sent through-the job whatsit and person thingy-as she had been in too much of a rush to get the application sent.

She was still going through her wardrobe, deciding what to wear for the big day tomorrow, when it occurred to her that she would have to catch the bus to the place where the interviews were being held. Murali wouldn't be able to give her a lift-he wouldn't be back at his place until well after she had to leave to get to the interview.

Suddenly, she remembered that she didn't have any credit on her mobile, so couldn't check the bus times or order a taxi if she needed one. That phone box down the road was still out of order, so she'd have to spend all her time this evening going through the timetables online. That took ages, because she always forgot to favourites the right Web site.

She was in a right state and had to stay up really late, as there was no way she could sleep with all the stuff she hadn't done on her mind.

The next day was one that Tarjani would like to forget, but didn't think she would be able to for a while. Later, when she talked to Murali, the sorry tale emerged:

- She'd overslept and missed the bus that would have got her to the office where the interviews were happening.
- Although in the end she was just in time, she was so flustered that she barged into the wrong office, interrupting another interview that was going on. So embarrassing!
- She'd thrown on some clothes which would have been OK if they weren't so creased they looked like she was on her way back from a festival.
- The first question in her interview asked her to say what she knew about the company: doodly squit, as it turned out. She couldn't even get the name of the airline right.
- The other questions weren't much better. She hadn't realised that they would be so in-depth. "What would you do if a passenger was rude to you because for safety reasons you wouldn't allow him to see the flight deck?" She hadn't seen that one coming.
- She thought she was on firmer ground with her answer about her qualifications. But she'd forgotten the name of a couple of modules on her college course. Well, it was nearly a year ago. And surely they'd got it all on her application? That didn't go down too well.
- To cap it all, she caught her heels in the hem of her skirt as she got up at the end of the interview and nearly fell over. She felt such an idiot and the four interviewers all had a good laugh about that. She'd just scowled at them as she left.
- As she left the offices, it started to rain. Disappointed and soaked, she eventually got home after missing another bus.

Murali agreed with Tarjani's analysis: she wouldn't be hearing from them again. "Next time you'll be better prepared," he said. She couldn't help feeling angry with him for deserting her just before her big moment. I mean, if you can't count on your best friend to help you through that, who can you rely on?

Task

Using the experience of Tarjani, who quite clearly blew her big chance at the job of her dreams, write a script for an interview that goes somewhat better. Base the interview on your own choice of job, selected in an earlier session, or one that you have only recently identified.

Track the progress of how you would prepare for the interview, making sure you cover the following important aspects of promoting yourself positively.

About the Organisation

- How is it structured?
- Where are the teams of staff located?
- How is the organisation presented in the media?
- Why do you want to work for them?

Practical Points for the Day

- Have as normal an evening as possible before the interview day.
- Don't stay up late the night before. If you've prepared well, you've got nothing to fear.
- Eat a meal before leaving for the interview.
- How will you get yourself ready for the interview?
- Prepare clean, ironed and appropriate clothes to wear.
- Plan your journey to and from the interview.
- Make sure you get to the interview with plenty of time to compose yourself.

Revise Your Application

- Read through what you said about yourself in your application.
- This means always keeping copies of everything you sent.
- Interviewers only have this information about you, so make sure you know what you said.

Anticipate Questions

- Think about the likely questions you are going to be asked.
- How will you answer them?
- Ask someone beforehand to think up some really tricky questions and work out what you might say in response.

Practice What you will Say

- Practice your interview technique by writing a script of things you might want to say.
- Read these through (in private or with someone you trust!) and listen to how you come across.
- Make sure that you can make your key points fluently, by concentrating on practicing them out loud.

Use the Opportunity

- Remember that an interview is not just about an organisation finding out about you.
- It's also an opportunity for you to find out if you'd like to work for an organisation.
- Think up some really good questions, which will show that you've really thought about the job and where it could lead you.
- Practice asking these out loud before the interview itself

Tourism=Employment: Is India Capitalising?

At several trade and global events over the years, the travel and tourism industry has been highlighted as an important economic employment generator. Veterans have voiced their opinion on the same. It is certain that travel and tourism, if properly encouraged can play an important role for economic stimulus and building consumer confidence. Travel fuels business growth, makes entertainment possible and sustains rural destinations.

It also strengthens trade by boosting income for the poorest countries, as well as for global suppliers. Taking all these factors into consideration we need to recognise the value of travel and most importantly its capacity to generate jobs. The tourism sector in India did witness an increase in employment numbers from 44.7 million to 51.1 million during the period 2004-05 to 2006-07 however, we need to cash in more on this potential.

Taking India and its cultural diversity into consideration, we have diverse offerings and also the talent of the youth and artisans which need to be tapped. Every state has diverse tourism opportunities but still the focus is on the regular. This gives us an opportunity to augment the much talked about domestic tourism, which certainly needs a short in the arm. Apart from a few players in the industry who have tried to bring a new flavour to domestic tourism, this sector yet needs to be aggressively marketed.

Encouraging domestic travel is good for consumer confidence; international travel has the added value of strengthening trade flows. Action to boost trade promotion, simplify regulation, build infrastructure and rationalise taxes, in turn incites companies to invest, innovate and stimulate demand. This kind of public–private sector collaboration should be strongly commended within and between all states, as it can help build resilience and buoyancy across economies

Tourism Employment & Opportunity

CDS' innovative TEMPO model is a collaborative system organized to build the capacity of micro, small, and medium size enterprises to access new markets and B2B linkages, more fully participate in public sector planning, and more convincingly sell the assets they have to offer to the tourism industry.

TEMPO is an 'intrapreneurial' model, and programs that follow it focus on assisting local businesses to provide services demanded by tourists at market rates and international standards. The programs utilize donor funding to build capacity of local businesses and perform asset audits and value chain analyses to determine the goods and services on offer versus market demand from tourists. They then become collaborative non-profit enterprises that link high-performing local businesses into international booking and reservations systems.

This combination of services that provides capacity building for businesses in the tourism industry and facilitates entry into real-time reservations systems is the stand out added value of TEMPO versus other tourism development programs.

Activities within the TEMPO model that create sustainable and sustaining tourism enterprises include:

- Demand Surveys
- The CDS Inventory and Asset Audit System
- The CDS Tourism Products Registry™
- Value Chain Analysis
- Strategy and Action Planning
- Capacity-building and Partnerships
- Competitive Grants
- Product Development
- Digital Content Development for Marketing and Sales
- Linkages to Wholesale and Retail Tour Operators and Other Channels

Tourism Employment

Overall View

On average, 1.1% of persons employed in the EU work in the tourist accommodation sector.

In 2007, more than 9 million persons were employed in the hotels, restaurants and catering (horeca) sector in the EU; this equals 4.2% of all persons employed. The highest number of jobs in this sector was observed in Spain (1.45 million), followed by Germany (1.43 million). However, when taking into account the size of the labour market, the largest shares employed in the horeca sector were found in Malta (8.3%), Spain (7.1%), Greece (6.9%), Austria (6.4%) and Cyprus (6.3%).

About one out of every four persons employed in the horeca sector works in an enterprise providing tourist accommodation (hotels and similar accommodation, campsites, etc.), giving a total of 2.3 million employed in 2007. At the height of the tourist season, i.e. in the third quarter of the year, the number of persons employed climbs by an additional 10 percent to an estimated 2.5 million. In relative terms, this means that 1.1% of all the employed in the European Union work in the tourist accommodation sector. The Member States showing the highest share of employment in tourist accommodation were Malta (5.3%), Cyprus (3.2%) and Austria (2.3%). Not surprisingly, these are also the top three Member States in terms of tourism intensity, i.e. the number of nights in collective tourist accommodation divided by the number of inhabitants. The sections which follow take a closer look at the pattern of employment in the tourist accommodation sector, compared with the horeca sector and the labour market as a whole.

By Gender

The share of female employment in the tourist accommodation sector is high at 60%. The share of full-time employment in the tourist accommodation sector is not much different from the share in the EU-27 economy as a whole. About four out of every five persons are employed on a full-time basis. Looking at the hotels and restaurants sector as a whole, this is the case for only 72% of the persons employed (or 69% when excluding the tourist accommodation subsector). Only in the Czech Republic does part-time work tend to be slightly more common in tourist accommodation (8%) than in the horeca sector as a whole (7%).

Looking at the country data, big differences can be seen, ranging from almost no parttime employment in the tourist accommodation sector in Bulgaria or Romania to a rate of 60% in the Netherlands. In general, the figures for this sector reflect the full-time/part-time breakdown in the economy as a whole. Countries with a high share of part-time employment in short-stay accommodation, such as the Netherlands, Denmark (44%), Norway (38%), Germany (32%) or Sweden (30%), also have around 25% or more part-time workers in the whole labour market, compared with the EU average of 18%.

The tourist accommodation sector is a major employer of women. On average, 60% of the EU labour force in this sector consists of female workers, who make up only 45% of the persons employed in all economic activities in the EU. In terms of creating job opportunities for women, the accommodation sector scores even better than the hotels and restaurants sector as a whole – where female employment stands at 56%.

The differences across the European Union are relatively small, although slightly more pronounced than for the economy as a whole, where in nearly every country the share of female employment deviates from the EU average of 45% by no more than a few percentage points.

Among the countries for which data are available, more than two out of every three persons employed in the tourist accommodation sector are female in Romania (72%), Norway (71%), Poland (70%), Finland (70%) and Germany (69%). Malta (38%) and Italy (49%) are the only countries where women do not take the majority of the jobs in the tourist accommodation sector. But, together with Greece, these two countries also have the lowest female participation rate in the economy as a whole.

The analysis by gender with the full-time/part-time breakdown. The proportion of women working full-time is much higher in the accommodation sector (75%) than in the rest of the economy (68%) or, more specifically, than in the hotels and restaurants sector as a whole (64%). Among men working in this sector, 90% have a full-time contract, which is slightly less than the overall average for men (92%).

Only in the Nordic countries – Denmark (50% versus 36%), Sweden (51% v. 42%) and Finland (27% v. 19%) – are significantly more women working parttime in the tourist accommodation sector than in the economy as a whole. On the other hand, a significantly higher proportion of women are working full-time than in the economy in general in Austria (69% versus 59%), Portugal (96% v. 83%) and Switzerland (59% v. 41%).

The lowest rate of full-time employment in the EU can be observed in the Netherlands, for both male (59%) and female (28%) workers, but this Member State also registers the lowest overall average rate across the EU for both men and women.

The shaded/patterned sections of the pie charts, the share of part-time employment. In both the tourist accommodation sector and in the labour market as a whole, slighly less than 20% of persons employed works on a parttime basis, 19% and 18% respectively. In both cases, women account for around 80% of these part-time jobs. Out of 100 persons employed in the EU, 4 are part-time working men while 14 are part-time working women. For the tourist accommodation sector this is 4 and 15 respectively.

The situation with full-time employment is more pronounced. Women occupy 56% of full-time jobs in the accommodation sector. Indeed, out of 100 persons employed in this sector in the EU, on average 81 work full-time, of which 45 are women and 36 are men.

On average in the economy women account for only 37% of full-time employment.

By Age

43% of those employed in the tourist accommodation sector are under 35 years old. Both the hotels and restaurants sector as a whole and the tourist accommodation sector offer job opportunities to a young work force.

Indeed, with 48% of persons employed in hotels and restaurants and 43% in the tourist accommodation sector younger than 35 years, both have a much younger age profile than the rest of the European Union labour market, where only about one in three of those employed is under 35.

This observation at EU level also applies to most of the Member States for which data on the age profile of employment in tourist accommodation are available. In most of these countries, the share of the two youngest age groups taken together lies 10 or more percentage points above their average share in employment in the economy as a whole. Under-35s make up more than half of the employees in the tourist accommodation sector in Slovakia (58%), the Netherlands (56%), Sweden (56%) and Norway (56%). In all four countries, this share exceeds the average for the whole economy by around 20 percentage points.

Cyprus is the only Member State where the age profile of employees in tourist accommodation is less young, with under-35s taking just 28% of the jobs in the tourist accommodation and 33% in the horeca sectors, whereas their share in the economy of Cyprus as a whole stands at 37%. Only in Greece and Spain, two countries with a big tourism industry, does the age profile in the accommodation sector appear to be not significantly different from the age profile in all economic activities taken together.

At the other end of the age distribution, employment opportunities for persons aged 55 or more tend to be more limited in tourist accommodation (11%) than in the labour market (14%) overall. However, it must be underlined that reliable data are available for only a few countries, partly due to the low probability of including older persons employed in this sector in the sample for the survey used to collect the data.

By Education Level

More than one third of tourism accommodation employees has lower level of education.

The data in the previous sections revealed that tourist accommodation in particular employs younger and female workers. A third socio-demographic group strongly represented in this sector are persons with a lower level of education, i.e. persons who completed lower secondary education at most. That 36% of employees in the tourist accommodation sector did not complete upper secondary education, compared with a general labour market average of 25%.

For all countries where data on employment broken down by educational level are available, the conclusion that the tourist accommodation sector employs relatively more persons with a lower level of education holds true. The biggest deviations from the average for the economy can be observed in Switzerland, where the share of lower educated persons in tourist accommodation is more than double their share in the whole labour market (36% versus 16%). Other countries where – compared with the entire economy – this sector offers jobs especially to less educated persons are Germany, Sweden, Norway and Denmark. Portugal (71%), Cyprus (24%) and Hungary (14%) are the only countries where there seems to be no noticeable difference (Portugal being the country with the highest share of employees with a low level of education in the European Union).

These findings are in line with the statistics on ICT use in enterprises, which indicate that the tourist accommodation sector does not require a high level of e-skills from most staff. Instead, only 36% of the employees in this sector use computers in their daily work, compared with almost one out of every two employees (49%) when considering all economic activities. Among the branches covered by the Community survey on ICT usage and e-commerce in enterprises, only the construction sector has a lower penetration rate for ICT at the place of work than the hotel and accommodation sector.

By Job Status

A high share of temporary jobs and limited average stay with the same employer.

The accommodation sector does not differ significantly from the rest of the economy in terms of full-time/part-time breakdown. However, considering the duration of the jobs and the average stay with the same employer, the sector appears to offer less stable jobs than the rest of the labour market.

The proportion of those having a temporary job rather than a permanent job is more than twice as high in the tourist accommodation sector (where 30% of the jobs are temporary) than in the economy as a whole (14%). In all the countries for which data on the duration of jobs are available, the accommodation sector performs relatively poorly. The largest discrepancies between this sector and the economy as a whole can be observed in Greece (59% permanent jobs v. 89% in the whole economy), Italy, Sweden and Bulgaria. The more limited availability of permanent jobs can be linked to the seasonal nature of tourism. Indeed, Greece, Italy, Bulgaria and Malta also appear to have the largest variation in number of persons employed between the peak and the trough quarters. The discrepancy in terms of share of permanent jobs between the tourist accommodation sector and the economy as a whole is particularly small – not more than 3 percentage points – in Hungary, Finland, Denmark and Spain.

The lowest shares of permanent jobs in the tourist accommodation sector can be found in Poland (58%), Greece (59%) and Sweden (61%). In the case of Poland, however, this is not exceptional, as this is also the Member State with the lowest proportion of permanent jobs in the economy as a whole (72%).

Another indicator of stability of employment is the average stay with the same employer. That staff turnover is much higher in the accommodation sector – with an average stay with the same employer of slightly over 6 years (76 months) – than in all economic activities taken together (121 months, in other words more than 10 years). Comparing the accommodation sector with the rest of the economy at the level of the Member States, the average stay is less than half as long in Greece and Sweden. On the other hand, the discrepancy seems to be smallest in Portugal and Spain.

Seasonal Variation

The tourist accommodation sector has a strong seasonal component.

Tourism activity varies strongly in the course of the year. In every Member State, occupancy in collective accommodation (expressed as number of nights spent by tourists) is at least twice as high in the peak tourism month as in the quietest month. Logically, the countries with a short tourist season have the highest seasonal variation in nights spent. In Greece and Croatia, the number of nights spent in collective accommodation is respectively 13 and 35 times higher in August than in the low season in January.

The quarterly data, that the number of tourism nights is 2.5 times higher in the third quarter (the peak quarter) of the year than in the first quarter (the trough quarter). With a ratio of "only" 1.2, employment in this sector tends to be far less affected by seasonal influences. On average, the seasonal variation is only half as pronounced in the hotels and restaurants sector as a whole as in the tourist accommodation subsector. In only four countries (the Czech Republic, Denmark, the Netherlands and Norway) employment in the latter subsector seems to be less volatile over the year than in the horeca sector.

In the economy as a whole, seasonal fluctuation is relatively limited – but this robust aggregate can, of course, hide strong seasonal variations in certain branches of the economy. Within the tourist accommodation sector, the highest seasonal fluctuations in employment are observed in Greece and Croatia. In both these countries, the level of employment in the peak quarter of the year is nearly double the level in the trough quarter and 30% to 35% higher than the annual average. At the other end of the spectrum, there is no significant seasonal variation in employment in Denmark, the Netherlands and Norway, although the number of nights spent by tourists is two to three times higher in the peak season than in the low season.

Based on data for ten Member States (accounting for 65% of employment in the tourist accommodation sector in the EU), the seasonal variation in employment separately for full-time and part-time jobs. The two types of employment contract tend to have a different seasonal pattern. While both are relatively low in the first quarter, part-time employment seems to be the main contributor to the seasonal needs in the second quarter. In the third quarter, full-time jobs appear to fill the additional needs on the tourist accommodation labour market (although it is not clear from the data whether these are additional full-time posts or an increase in weekly working hours to bring existing part-time posts up to full-time level).

By Region

Regions with high tourist activity tend to have lower unemployment rates.

Tourist activity can have a negative impact on the quality of life of the local population in highly touristic areas. However, the influx of tourists can also catalyse the local economy, including the labour market.

The top regions (at NUTS 2 level) in the European Union in terms of number of nights spent by tourists per capita of the local population and takes a look at the unemployment rates in these regions. In order to take into account structural differences across the EU, the regional unemployment rate is compared with the unemployment rate at national level.

Although tourist activity will, of course, not be the only factor affecting the unemployment figures, That in all but three of the 20 most popular tourist regions listed, the unemployment rate lies below the national average. Two of the three regions where this does not hold true, namely the Canary Islands and Corsica, are island regions relatively remote from the mainland.

The Community statistics on tourism provide no data on occupancy of collective accommodation below the NUTS-2 regional breakdown. However, at a more detailed regional level the number of bedplaces in tourist accommodation in comparison with the local population figures can be used as a proxy for the intensity of tourist activity in the region – assuming the capacity eventually accommodates tourist visitors. That in most of these tourist areas the unemployment rate is lower than the national rate. Two of the most significant exceptions to this finding are the Greek islands Zakynthos (Zante) and Kerkyra (Corfu), both part of the Ionian Islands. As shown above, Greece tends to have a highly seasonal tourism industry. This seasonal component possibly distorts the comparison as the unemployment figures are an annual average. In Rügen, Germany's number one region in terms of tourism intensity, the unemployment rate is nearly 10 percentage points higher than the German average. In this specific case, the comparison is affected by the fact that Rügen is in Mecklenburg-

Vorpommern, the Bundesland with the highest unemployment rate.

Total Employment

Tourism industry in EU occupies about 13 million persons.

The analysis in this paper mainly focused on the tourist accommodation sector, not on the entire tourism industry. In general, the breakdown into economic activities used in official statistics does not single out the tourism sector as a whole. In particular, apart from a few core tourist activities such as tourist accommodation or the activities of tour operators and travel agencies, most tourist activities can be filed under sectors of the economy of a broader nature. For instance, restaurants can cater for both tourists and locals or transport companies can provide services to tourists but can equally well run freight or commuter operations. To overcome this measurement problem, the European Union, together with international organisations active in the field of tourism statistics (the UNWTO, UNSD and OECD), has been fostering development of a framework that will allow accurate measurement of the tourism industry and comparison with other branches of the economy.

Taking the concepts, definitions and aggregates of the System of National Accounts as a starting point, this statistical instrument called "Tourism satellite accounts" (TSA) should allow valid comparisons with other industries and also between countries or groups of countries. Part of these TSA cover employment in the tourism industry. Unlike the analysis in this paper, the TSA figures are not limited to the tourist accommodation sector, but also include tourism-related activities of other branches, such as the food and beverage serving industry, passenger transport or culture, sports and recreation.

Currently, national, non-harmonised data are available for a handful of Member States. These estimates for 10 Member States. The contribution made by the tourism industry to total employment ranges from 3.4% in the Czech Republic to nearly 10% in Slovenia. In Spain the tourism industry accounts for almost one out of every eight jobs (12.0%) in the economy.

Based on the aggregate data for these 10 Member States, the share of the tourist industry in total employment appears to be around 6.2%. Employment in the accommodation sector accounts for around 1.1% of the labour market, or approximately 2.3 million jobs.

From the TSA estimates, total employment in the tourist industry can be estimated to be five to six times higher, with somewhere between 12 and 14 million employed in the EU. Once again, it must be stressed that these preliminary figures are based on non-harmonised national data from only 10 Member States.

Data sources and availability

- ":": no data available;
- ".": unreliable figures that cannot be published;

Classifications

- The economic activities are classified in accordance with

NACE Rev.1.1, the statistical classification of economic activities. "Hotels and restaurants" correspond to division 55 of NACE Rev.1.1, whereas the "Tourist accommodation sector" covers only two classes of this division, namely 55.1 (hotels) and 55.2 (other short-stay accommodation).

Data Sources

The data used in this article were generally collected by the national statistical institutes of the EU Member States, under Council Directive 95/57/EC of 23 November 1995 on the collection of statistical information in the field of tourism and under Council Regulation (EC) No 577/98 of 9 March 1998 on the organisation of a labour force sample survey in the Community. However, the data on employment in the tourist accommodation sector were provided to Eurostat on a voluntary basis, outside the legal framework.

China to Boost Tourism Employment to 100 Million by 2015: Report

China's tourism industry is expected to employ 100 million people by 2015, state media reported Thursday, meaning one in every 14 Chinese will work in the sector then. The government will introduce various policies to help the industry reach the goal, which marks a steep increase from the 60 million currently employed in the industry, the People's Daily said.

Authorities will adopt measures to facilitate job hunting and subsidise training of new staff, according to a statement posted on the National Tourism Administration's website Wednesday.

They also plan to launch a campaign to expand tourism infrastructure in less developed areas, the administration said.

Labour Minister Tian Chengping said earlier this year that the employment...

Employment in the tourism industries

- Two possible points of view on Employment
  - from a perspective of supply (persons employed) and
  - from a perspective of demand (jobs)
- A person might have more than 1 job
- A job might be occupied by more than 1 person
- No one to one relationship between jobs and employed Persons

Tourism Employment vs. Employment in the Tourism Industries

- Labour is a factor of production, and as such, related to a production process, not to a product, and even less so to the consumption of a product by certain category of consumers (a visitor);
- Employment in an establishment, and thus in an industry, can be observed and measured:
- Employment associated with tourism consumption can only be estimated via an explicit or an implicit model.

The basic recommendations: measuring employment in the tourism industries.

The Units of Measurement

- Number of jobs,
- Number of employed persons
- hours worked (which should be included???)
- Equivalent full time job

What do we want to know?

- For each tourism characteristic activity:
  - Number of jobs (monthly? Yearly? Peak and low?) by

- Gender
- Status in employment
- Qualification
  - Number of employed persons
  - "Quality of the job"
- Permanent
- Seasonal
- Direct contract/through an employment agency
- With/without social insurance

Sources for measuring employment in the tourism industries;

- From the supply side: household surveys; main difficulties
  - Significance at the detailed level of activities
  - Comparability of measurements overtime
  - Geographical coverage; issue of rural area or small villages
- From the demand side: surveys of economic activities; main difficulties
  - Snapshot at a given moment in time
  - Relationship of this snapshot with supply statistics
  - Non permanent activities; seasonality
  - Use of employment agencies

Tourism Creates Employment Opportunities

Culture

Tourism creates opportunities of employment in the smallest and most remote communities. The Eastern Cape is one of the privileged provinces which has been awarded such an opportunity. This task of alerting people to the possibilities is led by a non-government organisation called Fair Trade in Tourism South Africa (FTTSA) which is working towards a fairer, participatory and sustainable industry in South Africa.

One of its specific objectives is to contribute towards the Black Economic Empowerment programme and also to assist community-based and other emerging tourism enterprises to access niche markets.

Projects in the Eastern Cape include the Mehloding Community Tourism Trust in the northern Alfred Nzo District Municipality; Pondoland Community Trust and Tshezi Trust in OR Tambo District Municipality; the Kwam Emakana township homestays in Cacadu District Municipality, and the Nqileni Community Trust in Mbashe Local Municipality.

The Mehloding trust is one of the successful projects led by the NGO. The community owns the Mehloding adventure hiking trail and some home-stays for tourists. This was an underprivileged community due to the lack of employment opportunities but FTTSA has sprinkled some nourishing water on the economic and social condition of the community.

Thozamile Xaki, a community tour guide, said: "We learn more about the environment and we gain entrepreneurship skills. This gives us as the community the urge to plough and preserve clean water for our tourists and it encourages us to start our own businesses."

The projects have created job opportunities to impart skills to those who lack them and also recognition for Mehloding but above all the activities draw tourists to Mehloding.

The beautiful nature-preserving community has caught the attention of many tourists throughout the many years of its existence.

Nomthandazo Mnyameni, another community tour guide, said she has witnessed change in her community in terms of recognition and their knowledge on how to approach other NGOs when they need any kind of assistance. Even though this project is alive and advantageous, it does not really cover all the community's needs in terms of giving all of them suitable jobs, nor has it employed all the jobless.

Jabu Manyathi is not employed in this project. She said the project had given jobs to some and imparted skills for those in need. One still has to stand up and do something for oneself in order to survive. Jabu said she was not satisfied with the communication channels between the organisation and the community members that are not employed on the project.

4

Academic Learning and Teaching in Educational Tourism

Summary of Key Findings

Educational Tourism as Lifelong Learning

- Intentional, experiential, and structured learning are perceived by scholars, clients and companies as the defining features of educational tourism.

Evidence from Academic Scholars Indicates that: :

- Over half of those surveyed have already engaged in a form of educational tourism.
- Three quarters of those surveyed would do so in the future.
- Participation in educational tourism changes the way they think about their work.
- Participation in educational tourism enhances their communication and teaching skills in and beyond the classroom.
- Participation in educational tourism enhances their research both directly and indirectly through securing funds, accessing unique or important sites, and engaging with a learning community.

Evidence from Educational Tourism Providers Indicates that:

- Participation by academics is highly valued.
- Participation by academics can occur in a variety of ways, not just leading tours.

- Cutting edge knowledge content created by academics creates a marketable educational tour product.

Evidence from Educational Tourism Clients Indicates that::

- Group learning is preferred over independent learning.
- History, cultural heritage, and natural landscapes were the most highly valued content of educational tours.
- Meaningful contact with the local communities is a highly valued experience in educational tours.
- Clients rate prior educational materials for their research highly and like to research their trip in advance.
- Maps and handbooks are the educational aids most highly valued by all respondents, before, during and after the tour.
- Novels and informal meetings are also highly valued as post tour educational aids.

Background

In July 2007 Associate Professor Susan Broomhall, Mr. Tim Pitman, and Dr. Ela Majocha from The University of Western Australia (UWA), funded by a grant from the Australian Learning and Teaching Council (ALTC) commenced a study into educational tourism in Australia: "Articulating Lifelong Learning in Tourism: Dialogue between humanities scholars and travel providers". The aims of the study were to:

- Improve communication between scholars and the tourism sector, with a particular focus on the adult educational tourism market and Arts and Humanities scholars;
- Support the development of educational tourism as a facilitator of lifelong learning;
- Equip scholars with the skills necessary to contribute to educational tourism; and
- Improve the learning experience of tour participants on educational tours.

The project commenced in July 2007 and will be completed in June 2009. A full project time line is available at. This interim report details the analysis of literature, interviews, and on line surveys. It is disseminated in its current form for feedback from academic stakeholders. Data used in this analysis come only from publicly available documentation, and from interview subjects and survey respondents who have given express permission to have their data circulated to this readership.

This consultation discussion paper is a work in progress, and feedback received will shape the final report to be submitted to the ALTC and made available for public release. Please do not cite publicly from this document. A final report will be made available to all stakeholders at the end of the project.

Support for this report has been provided by the Australian Learning and Teaching Council Ltd, an initiative of the Australian Government Department of Education, Employment and Work place Relations. The views expressed in this report do not necessarily reflect the views of the Australian Learning and Teaching Council. The project team gratefully acknowledges the participation of the following organisations:

- Academy Travel
- Alumni Travel
- Australians Studying Abroad
- Centre for Continuing Education, University of Sydney
- Odyssey Travel
- Renaissance Tours
- UWA Extension

Data Collection Methods

Educational Tour Provider Literature

Qualitative and quantitative content analysis was conducted on a range of publicly accessible forms of documentation that is produced by educational tour companies. These texts included website material, advertising flyers and brochures, specific tour itineraries, and detailed tour handbooks. This literature was collected during late 2007 and early 2008.

Online Surveys

Responses for this aspect of the study were collected via an online survey. Two surveys were conducted. The "client survey" collected data from individuals who identified themselves as having had previous experience of educational tours as well as from those who had not. These individuals were approached via an email invitation to a combination of existing company client records, from the UWA Extension database, and from an open invitation on the travel/place website.

Because of the last category, it was not possible to determine the total number of people who were contacted. A total of 612 participants and potential participants completed this survey, of which 465 agreed to share their responses with educational tourism providers. A second survey was constructed for academic scholars in the Arts and Humanities fields in Australian universities. 1552 academics were invited by email to complete the survey. 228 completed the survey, and 183 agreed to share their responses with educational tourism providers. Responses to all questions were optional, in an effort to encourage people to complete the survey. This explains the varying sample sizes across the questions.

Interview Data

Six Australian educational tour providers were approached for interviews. Personnel from five companies agreed to recorded interviews. Detailed interviews were conducted, including company directors, tour program developers, tour leaders, tour managers and trainers, operations managers, marketing and sales staff. A range of academic scholars, currently employed in Australian universities, were also interviewed in depth. Some had extensive experience as tour leaders, program designers or course material designers, while others had experience of organising study tours and volunteer tourism for university students. Finally, some academic scholars were interviewed as interested future leaders.

Work place Observation

The project team visited the offices of all six companies and observed working practices and structures. Project researchers also observed tour leader training and discussed the research themes with prospective and current tour leaders.

Defining Educational Tourism

Clarifying academic, provider and client understanding of what educational tourism is and can be, was a fundamental starting point for the project, as well as a springboard to the team's other research questions. The idea that learning occurs in non formal environments, such as travel, is not new. Putting aside discussions in Herodotus, or the role of the Grand Tour in eighteenth and nineteenth century Europe, one can look at seminal discussions of the role of education that played out in the 1960s and 1970s.

Global education lobby organisations such as UNESCO and the OECD observed that education should be dispensed through a multiplicity of means; what was important was not the path that an individual had followed, but what learning had occurred as a consequence.

The general increase in leisure time since the Second World War, plus the increase in disposable income and relative decrease in the cost of travel has given many more people the opportunity to engage in "intellectual improvement". With a widening in people's interests and appreciation of cultural values, many individuals have come to look upon vacations as a means of developing these interests (ibid). Tourism is, arguably, one of the few contemporary sites outside of the education industry where explicitly designated, non vocational learning about other times, places, and peoples takes place.

The 1980s witnessed the appearance of new tourism designs that both recognised tourism's negative impacts and imagined a more positive role for tourism. These new designs include ecotourism, ethnic tourism, nature tourism and adventure travel. The informal learning that occurs in these environments can often be translated back into a formal curriculum. Sesow and Wunder (1995) have explored how teachers have been able to use their travel experiences to enhance their students' learning.

Much of the discussion has centred on theories of experiential learning, such as those expounded by Kolb (1984) and Mezirow (1990, 1991). Guy, Curtis and Crofts (1990) explored the factors influencing the rate and degree of environmental learning of first time visitors to an international destination. The relative contributions of direct experience and direct and indirect sources of information were examined. Their empirical study concluded that the immersive experience of travel was the primary correlate of learning in terms of scope, accuracy, and detail. Similarly, Schmeink and Thurston (2007) found that travel experiences enhanced the ability of children with spatial cognition. However the power imbalance inherent in many tourist/local interactions means that usually it falls to the traveller to choose who to interact with, where to go, and what to consume. Consequently, the validity of what is learnt is always contestable. Yet there is evidence that learning and benefit can occur in both directions. For example, the almost accidental development of tourism in the Longsheng county of Guangxi, China, has resulted in the revival of previously vanishing aspects of local culture and the strengthening of community education programs for the local community.

Much of the analytical interest in educational tourism to date, particularly in the form of mature age tours, has come from practitioners and the market. The most significant in depth studies of the field stem from research commissioned by companies themselves about their client markets and their learning needs, as well as influential intellectual investigations into their ontology conducted by company personnel. Although a relatively under researched scholarly field, establishing a theoretical framework for touristic learning could assist in the development of products that better fulfil both consumers' needs and providers' objectives and perhaps illuminate our understanding of forms of learning which are more incidental. Beyond this, a greater understanding of touristic learning may also provide new insight on why people travel at all.

Academic research into educational tourism, however, has been slow to emerge. A recent collection of scholarly papers in contemporary niche tourism does not include adult educational tourism. This may be because it requires synthesis of two areas of scholarship: education and tourism. Scholars are increasingly observing that education facilitates mobility whilst learning has become an increasingly important part of the tourist experience. Using broad definitions, their work has allowed for the analysis of people not usually classified as tourists travelling to seek an educational experience.

For example, Cooper and Latham (1988) consider schoolchildren visiting a museum to be potential educational tourists. Cushner (2004) considers the "travelling teacher" to be the master of experiential learning, by using his or her travelling experiences (as well as encouraging this intrepidness in her or his students) as the ideal way of acquiring multicultural skills. In fact, anyone combining travel with their normal duties (soldiers, diplomats, spies, journalists, politicians) could be said to be undertaking educational travel. Ritchie has argued, "the concept of travel for education and learning is a broad and complicated area, which explains why tourism academics and industry have to date largely ignored this field."

As such, definitional issues dog the field. Hecht, Starosielski and Dara Abrams (2007) use the term "information centric" tourism to describe a range of touristic experiences that are motivated by a desire or need to learn.

This includes "alternative" tourism: a touristic activity that attempts to negate negative aspects whilst retaining the positive ones; "heritage" or "cultural" tourism; "literary" tourism or "eco tourism". This project analysed provider literature and websites to assess the use and meanings of the term in current Australian practice. Surveys canvassed the perceptions of a broad range of potential clients and academics. Finally, our more detailed follow up interviews directly posed the question of defining this term to educational tour directors and employees, and to the academics with whom they worked.

Educational Tourism and Learning

The Australian tourism sector that identifies itself as providing educational tourism offers many kinds of educational experiences through travel, from a broad range of mature age study tours and programs, to participation in academic research programs such as archaeological digs and ecological fieldwork, for credit on site university units, school group tours, and professional development tours.

Provider literature identified learning or enquiry as a key differentiating point of its niche in the tourism market: from the passive "audience interested in travelling to learn", to the more dynamic "enquiring minds" which focus on "stimulating ... the active, inquisitive traveller". Companies' advertising material promoted the notion of an in depth engagement with other cultures through the opportunities they provide to gain contextualised knowledge as well as a deeper (often longer) appreciation of particular sites. One company proposed a quote that summarised its target audience identity: "I want to have time to absorb the environment and to learn something about what I'm seeing."

Similarly, learning was unmistakably the dominant outcome defined by survey respondents who returned 609 responses to the question "What does the term 'educational tourism' mean to you?" The responses ranged from the succinct to the expansive: A holiday with a strong learning component.

Travelling so as to learn more about a place, culture, activity, period of history, rather than just have fun or relax. It can be guided by people &/or books &/or lectures etc, before, during & after the actual travel. It is primarily for personal pleasure rather than formal education, though that could be a component in some tours. Ideally it demonstrates great respect for the people who live in the place & their environment eg by them owning the tour company, being specialist guides etc. It involves a relationship, not just looking at people.

The concept of learning appeared in more than 83% of the definitions. For example: Travelling with the aim of learning rather than just having fun alone. Seventeen definitions identified all tourism, indeed travel in general, as being educational: I guess that all tourism has something of an educational dimension to it.

Visiting other 'places' either physically or virtually where you will encounter 'different' perspectives, experiences, cultures, countries and projects for the purposes of learning and reflection.

The definitions expressed three key ideas about the form of learning in educational tourism:

1. It is intentional (e.g. "Taking a trip specifically to broaden my horizons or enhance my knowledge."; "Travel with a purpose; an enriched travel experience that provides food for your brain"
2. It is experiential (e.g. use of word/phrases such as included "immersion", "hands on", "vivid" and "evidence", "engaging with ideas in their original context" and "being exposed to politics, society and economy")
3. It is structured. (e.g. "It is the combination of travel with a structured educational program." "Going overseas to learn something in a structured way."

These three elements were also highlighted in definitions provided in interviews. One director saw his company's focus as " travel experience through learning for fun." Academics defined the provision of an explicit structure to pursue learning as the significant feature of educational tourism. One academic tour leader expressed it as: "Tourism, or travel which is structured, has a theme to pursue and requires some background knowledge of the sites being visited and some attempt to analyse on the spot." Another highlighted "the desire to acquire information about that place and that information can be on, you know, I think anything to do with architectural history, art, it can be broader history. It can be to do with laying out of gardens, it can be cookery, it can be all sorts of things. It's the sense of information." One experienced female academic leader offered: "education tourism is for those people who want to take it seriously, who want to learn from it, rather than those who just want to come along for a holiday." Statements such as these emphasised the intent required by clients to learn on such tours as an important definitional feature of educational tours.

However, a marketing manager of an educational tourism company highlighted one of the challenges of marketing this form of tourism as learning: "From the client's perspective you have to be careful how you approach educational tourism because some people think that they're not smart enough." Indeed, experienced tour leaders recognised that clients wanted different types and quantities of information, as one male academic leader observed: "they all want to learn ... but there's a certain amount that they want to learn".

Another reflected: "I don't know how serious some of these people are, they like to think that they are interested in educational tours, they're interested to a degree." Others emphasised the importance of the traveller identity that participation in such a tour might convey for clients. One academic tour leader surveyed for this study considered that: people [who] go on an educational tour want to see themselves differently from normal tourists. In fact they may not be that different, you're still travelling on buses, you're still staying in quite fancy hotels and so on. It's not that different from all the other tourists but they want to see themselves as there for a different purpose. And they, I think, have a genuine interest in engagement with the local culture.

Educational Tours and Personal Development

For most survey respondents, educational tourism suggested the idea of an intentional, structured, *in situ* learning experience. Overwhelmingly, both academic and client respondents' definitions pointed to the need for a conscious or deliberate learning component as part of this form of travel. So how was learning described in company literature? As seen above, explicit references to provision of an educational component, in depth information, cultural contact, and mental stimulation were central to the marketing strategies of educational tour organisations.

Several companies indicated that their tours could be claimed as professional development or used for academic credit, however the generally accessible educational tours are typically designed for the satisfaction of individuals rather than professional or scholarly requirements. "Experience", "explore", "discover" were the key descriptors of the educational experience within company literature. "Learning" was not commonly used and was often replaced by less directed (and less quantifiable) verbs such as "enquiring".

In general, the learning described was implicitly about personal development rather than testable information. Companies emphasised that no specific academic qualifications were necessary to participate in a tour – rather a willingness to explore another culture in detail. Attitude rather than qualifications was thus a key requirement for clients. The degree of knowledge attainment was up to the individual, with phrases such as "broadening your knowledge" conveying learning that was measurable only at the level of each participant.

Educational tours contributed to a participant's personal and intellectual lifelong learning. Because of the individual nature of the learning, and the need to avoid quantifiable knowledge outcomes that cannot be guaranteed for each participant, there was in general no attempt to provide specific learning outcomes for an individual tour.

The humanistic perspective of lifelong learning contends that learning throughout life, and via varied fora, is a means by which individuals develop personally and socially. Lifelong learning, travel and personal development are linked by the acknowledgement that the experientially based, informal learning that can occur in touristic events can be beneficial in these terms. At the level of the individual tourist, the primary goals of a leisure trip are likely to be experiential. Lifelong learning via tourism is becoming increasingly important to many individuals:

But it is not only older people who are going on tours and overseas holidays—it is people of all ages who travel abroad for holidays and not all just seek the sun and the sand, many do go to places of historical and cultural interest and seek to understand more of this cultural heritage. But it is not only a matter of understanding but preserving this heritage that is important and as concern for the planet grows, so this role becomes more important. Tour guides and guides to sites of such interest and importance are playing a significant liberal adult educational role.

Events experienced whilst on a leisure trip can not only cause individuals to change their perception about the country being visited but also the way in which they view their own country. Some forms of tourism place a specific emphasis on lifelong learning as a focus of their activities. Moscardo (1996) explores the idea of the "mindful" tourist and argues that their experiences with heritage tourism allow them a greater understanding of the wider environment. Thacheen and Lauzon refer to learning tours as "organized conversations" in which an individual's experiences can change his (sic) life as well as those around him. Elderhostel, an American tourism provider to the over 55s ("baby boomers"), has conducted research on learning habits of the over 55 age group. The research concluded that "a sustained commitment to learning" was seen as a way of achieving successful aging by the baby boomers. Furthermore, the learning combined "blending intellectual stimulation, social engagement, physical activity, and creative expression". Participation in an educational tour meets at least the first three of the four criteria of lifelong learning for some seniors.

Australian tour company personnel interviewed for this project saw explicit learning objectives as off putting to clientele who might be of different educational levels and experience. These were also perceived to be hallmarks of degree or university study. With educational tours, they insisted, learning must be progressed in an enjoyable way.

The director of one educational tour company described the learning that they provide as "what we're about is continuing education, lifelong learning. So it's about learning for fun without examinations attached." As one tour designer articulated for her company: We do think of them as educational experiences because they do come away from it having learnt something and having very special experiences that I think helped aid their learning and ... the sort of experiences that we provide really enhance their whole travel experience.

Educational Tourism and Expertise

Explicit academic connections matter to educational tour company marketing. Provider literature, such as tour programs and brochures, make clear the academic qualifications of its personnel. The previous teaching appointments at secondary and tertiary level of employees, from directors and office staff to tour leaders, were typically provided in website and brochure literature. Previous tours led by the staff members were commonly noted as a form of recognition of prior experience in this domain. The use of tertiary scholars as leaders was frequently noted in addition to other forms of expertise (although how this would be identified was unspecified): "led by academics or experts in the focus of the tour." Companies defined their tourism therefore as one engaged with academic or other expertise.

Most definitions offered by clients and academics in the survey did not include an aspect of the facilitator, guide or leader of the learning experience, but where the leader was mentioned, they were most commonly described as being an "expert":

The opportunity to learn more about areas and places through visits accompanied by expert guides.

Importantly, one marketing manager in an educational tourism company saw the involvement of academics and experts as crucial in the distinction of their company from other tourism providers: "we believe educational tourism is having group leaders that know more about the place and can put it into a sense of its era and the perspective of where it's come from."

One experienced male tour leader reflected that it was the careful structure, unique locations, as well as the expertise of the leader expertise that attracted clients: "because you have worked there for 35 years and also because you are a professional'. He reflected on feedback from tour participants that indicated that: they want to be informed by someone that they think they trust knows the material. And I think that's the reason they look at them and say okay, this person's worked there that long, they lecture at this university so we can rely upon what they say.

Educational Tourism or Travel

Educational tourism providers did not generally refer to their activities as tours and the participants as tourists. The preferred terminology includes travel, travellers and programs. The tourist traveller dichotomy goes back at least to the end of the eighteenth century and first quarter of the nineteenth century, when travel both domestic and foreign gained popularity. Previously, the experience of travel by young aristocrats in the seventeenth and eighteenth centuries was described as "tour" derived from the Grand Tour, and those who participated were called "tourists". With the emergence of a broader section of the population able to participate in tourism, the nineteenth century saw vigorous debate on the subject of the true "Traveller" as opposed to the "Vulgar Tourist".

While the words "tourism" and "travel" are used by some scholars interchangeably, for others they are quite distinct. Russians use the same word (tourist) to describe both the broad and the narrow: a tourist can be either a traveller for pleasure, enlightenment or excitement, or simply anyone who travels, for a purpose, using their own physical powers.

Similarly, in his examination of sustainable tourism in Nepal, Zurick (1992) uses the terms "adventure travel" and "adventure tourism" interchangeably. Yet for Daniel Boorstin tourists are a particular – and inferior – type of traveller, who have shifted their gaze from authentic travel to unauthentic tourism.

Most of us aren't travellers at all – we're tourists, vulnerable to the process of commodification as the places we visit. A homogenous group of dopey beasts, who take cattle class flights at 3am, organise stag nights in Prague, and demand egg and chips and a beer whose name we can easily pronounce on a sunny beach in Spain. The smaller the world gets, the more we seem to want it to be as much like home as possible.

Gorusch (2003) suggests that tourism often implies a controlled experience driven by a hidden agenda and uses by way of example the promotion of domestic tourism in post war Russia to advance the Stalinist regime's own xenophobic interpretation of world events. Others link definitions to the behaviour of the individual: whereas the act of taking a photograph is likely to signify a tourist, that of writing is more often associated with travellers, perhaps due to it being more commonly linked to professional activities such as journalism. Consequently the terms travel and tourism can be synonymous for some scholars and conflicting for others. This is in part a consequence of definitions being driven from both the demand side (consumer) and supply side (industry) of tourism. Whilst some definitions describe those with whom the industry wishes to engage, others reveal how individuals wish to perceive themselves. Researchers themselves often construct definitions of tourism in order to define their own, specific subject of enquiry.

It is notable that a significant number of both academic scholars and education tour company practitioners appeared to display some aversion to use of the word "tourism". Feifer, succinctly observes that "no one wants to be called a tourist". Generally within the travel provider literature terms such as "travel," "journey" or "adventure" were preferred – seemingly, as a broader, more intellectual and less explicitly commercial definition of their practices.

One brochure used a quote from a participant: "The program contained a good mix of information and activities meaning that I felt like a traveller rather than a tourist." In particular, in defining the identity of a typical company client, tour provider literature highlighted the distinction between travel (what they do) and tourism (what something else unspecified – perhaps mass tourism does). This was achieved by the choice of adjectives to describe tour principles and clients, by implication indicating what it was not. Thus, there was the perception that something was wrong with being a tourist.

The description of tours emphasised the provision of more detailed information and cultural engagement than was possible in "mass tourism". Clients should therefore have the desire to have "greater involvement in another culture, than merely observing it from a coach window" and were "those who want more out of travel than simply a catalogue of places." Features included "extended stays" to "get to know the places you visit".

Mass tourism was portrayed either as the absent other against which comparisons were made, or through phrases which critiqued other modes of touristic engagement: spend your time actually looking at the things you've travelled to see, rather than straining to listen to a local tour guide. Through the background talks you'll also build up a coherent understanding of the country you're visiting, not just a fragmented set of facts.

Educational tourism, these brochures claimed, was for "those who want to move beyond mass tourism" or "beyond the worn tourist trails." The experience that these tours provided was perceived to be "unique and privileged" and might sometimes involve "some unusual sectors" as well as "all the classic travel experiences".

This notion of a deeper and intentional effort to form a richer or deeper understanding of a place or culture echoed survey responses. One marketing manager explained: "while we offer similar… destinations, we tend to offer a more comprehensive approach to the history and the sense of place". An employee in one educational tour company described his company's niche learning approach in the following terms: "it gives tourists an opportunity to step outside the regular old box of a tourism experience and gives them an insight into educational aspects and certainly would... develop knowledge and satisfaction of visiting a destination instead of just seeing the elementary sights and sounds."

Moreover, the organised tour structure could itself be advantageous, as a content developer at one company identified: "we offer very good value for money because the experience that people are paying for is something quite unique, and something they most certainly couldn't achieve on their own." For the following phases of the research, we elected to keep the term "educational tourism" in order to make the direct connection to the format of the educational experience we were most commonly analysing in this study – both in the sense that it concerns the organised tour, and to reflect the fact that these are commercial operations. Our interviews with academic scholars and educational tour company representatives suggested diverse views both within and between these groups about the meaning of this term and its coverage of 'paid for' tourism practices in Australia.

Indeed, within the interview context, directors of companies referred more commonly to intellectualised notions of travel as mind broadening, eschewing the explicit commercial dimensions of their company practice. Moreover, one director of a not for profit company had consciously rejected the terminology of "a tour" for the following rationale: "we run programs, educational programs, basically, instead of tours. It's to differentiate a little bit what we do from what the commercial world does". The use of participant feedback statements as above which distinguished between travel and tourism served to reinforce a difference in these modes of practice.

When asked the same question, some scholars perceived the use of the term "tourism" to be problematic or conceptually incompatible with education. In the survey, several respondents – all academic provided negative definitions of educational tourism, centring either the quality of the learning experience or a belief that tourism itself was negative: Travel can be educational, but tourism per se is not educational Sounds a bit sus. The exploitation by the tourist industry of peoples better instincts toward the planet. A marketing ploy When asked about their engagement with educational tourism, some scholars explained their disinterest in terms of perceived exploitation of the tourist mode:

The idea of "tourism" has negative connotations for me; it signifies to me a type of intrusion. I realise that some places rely upon tourism economically, but I feel suspicious about claims made about the type of learning that can occur as a tourist. Because I don't think mediated encounters with living people or places that are pre defined as "other" will conduct to those peoples' or places' welfare. This perception has been noted in scholarly literature. Werry (2008, 14), for example, refers to the "paradox of tourism":

The more cultural capital the travel consumer wields and accrues (through tourism), and the deeper her belief in travel's potential to inform and transform, the more deep seated her prejudice against tourism as a "bad cultural object" is likely to be. For such consumers, tourism is a byword for superficiality, in authenticity, wilful ignorance, political irresponsibility, exploitation, and cultural prostitution.

In interviews, while one academic linked educational tourism to the tradition of the Grand Tour, a number of other academic responses saw tourism as a limited or limiting term. As one male academic and tour leader argued: "by using the word tourism, you're limiting yourself to one part of the phenomenon. If you use the word "educational travel", you would be widening that." As another explained: "there is also, almost a contradiction in terms: educational tourism, isn't there? Because tourism often necessitates a sort of blinkered view of the world, what I call cocooned existence we've all seen tourist buses with people who seek to stay within their comfort zone... You're in a bus, you're in a nice hotel, you don't have to learn the language." Yet the same academic concluded his response by reconciling the possibilities of learning within a commodified genre: "I think educational tourism, if it's to be packaged as a commodity, is tourism with a particular focus and the focus is to engage with aspects of the place where you are touring. In other words, it's beyond looking."

Educational Tourism Knowledge

To examine educational tourism learning further, survey respondents were presented with a series of statements concerning factors contributing to knowledge acquisition and were asked to indicate the degree to which they did, or did not, agree with the statements. Some of the statements were contradictory and others similar, to allow triangulation and cross checking of answers. Respondents scored the statements from 0 to 5: with 0 meaning they thought the statement not applicable, 1 meaning they disagreed strongly and 5 meaning they agreed strongly. Clients were asked to think about themselves, as an educational tourist, when considering the statements. Academics, however, were asked to respond as educators. Some statements were unique either to academic or client surveys.

A series of statements tested the importance of elements such as repetition, novelty and reinforcement in the learning involved in educational tourism. New experiences (which could be either a new subject matter or destination) were clearly preferred by tour clients, over reinforcement of destinations or content with which they were already familiar. Female clients displayed a stronger preference for new experiences than males. Academics appeared ambivalent as to whether new experiences or repetitive ones were superior in terms of learning.

Respondents were also asked what sort of experiences and knowledge were important in an educational tourism experience. The answers reveal responses to two different aspects of the question: the kinds of experiences and the type of knowledge desired. Experiencing a different culture was seen by some as a means of understanding, or re examining their own or themselves: Travel that extends me physically and mentally so that I learn both about myself and the area of travel.

Some respondents were careful to express the difference between overt, touristic cultural experiences and engagement with the daily life of the country being visited: For me, educational tourism could hold two meanings: Tourism while discovering the Culture Tourism while discovering the culture (living with people from one specific culture, sharing their table, etc) Understanding contexts was seen to be the type of knowledge to make sense of that. In terms of concrete knowledge genres, history and cultural heritage were the preferred elements of an educational tour. Understanding natural landscapes also rated highly.

It enriches tourism by providing travellers with a greater appreciation for the histories of the locations that they visit. These histories can bring to life otherwise overlooked aspects of a location, and create connections that enrich the experience of visiting a place When I travel, I always want to learn more about the place I am in and the way that present is informed by the past. 3.7 Conclusions Although academics tended to hold more diverse ideas of what educational tourism could be than did clients, a number of key findings were apparent between the groups:

- The primary outcome of the educational tourism experience is learning and furthermore, that the learning is intentional.
- Tour operators contend that they will provide particular knowledge, expertise or experience so as to distinguish their product within the broader tourism sector.
- "Tour" and "tourism" appear problematic terms because they can convey mixed messages to both tour clients and academics.
- "Travel" is frequently substituted to connote both the exploration of physical places and the personal development journey.

Engaging with Educational Tourism

In what ways do academics currently engage with this form of education to communicate with new audiences and to develop their knowledge? Why do they do so? How does it challenge them intellectually as teachers and researchers?

Approximately half the academic scholars surveyed (92 out of 183) had previously participated in some form of educational tourism, according to their own definition of the term. Almost half of these had participated as either a guest lecturer or tour leader. A sizeable proportion had also presented information sessions, or authored educational tourism materials.

Other forms of educational tourism experiences included:

- Acting as an impromptu tour leader for visiting family, friend, students or colleagues.
- Program coordinator.
- Using travel to further one's own teaching and research.
- Lecturer in a course with tourism related material.
- Giving adult courses.
- Lecturing on study (credit) tours.
- As a participant themselves.

Embedded Knowledge Experts

A well qualified tour leader was clearly an important part of educational tour marketing. Travel company literature emphasised the care and consideration of tour groups in "sourcing" an appropriately trained program leader. But what does qualified and trained mean in this context? Content expertise or knowledge was the most commonly discussed feature of tour leaders.

They were "informed", "experts", and "specialists" with "extensive knowledge". As noted above, the academic qualifications of tour leaders were frequently highlighted in company literature and their academic titles commonly used. Leaders' current or present positions within higher education institutions were noted, as well as other work roles relevant to the tour content.

Surveyed academics and clients were asked "When taking part in educational tourism, what are the qualities that would make a person a good tour leader?" There were 427 free form responses to this question. Knowledge was clearly the most sought after quality of a tour leader (included by two out of every three respondents). However, most respondents did not expand upon their definition of knowledge skills. Close examination of the responses revealed that underlying the vast majority of definitions was the assumption that the tour leader will be appropriately qualified to speak on the subject matter of the tour:

Friendly, welcoming, I would take for granted that they would be qualified Where survey respondents did clarify what qualified might mean, most sought experiential knowledge in a tour leader, defining it as knowledge stemming from first hand experiences of the tour content, including local integration, language skills and personal connections.

Interviews with educational tour personnel were consistent in their agreement that the involvement of knowledge experts was a key feature of their ethos, and marketing edge. Academic qualifications were widely considered to signal knowledge expertise (although not exclusively). Experiential knowledge of a location was also highly valued, matching the views of survey respondents above. A manager at one educational tour company defined a good leader as having "an expertise either in a particular country they are going to, they will know the local language, they can speak the local language, they've had either study of that particular country or lived in that country so it's not just someone who is a tour expert as such. They're someone with far higher qualifications." The director of one educational tour company did connect expertise to academic recognition: "Our tour leader for our tours has to be an expert in his or her field so they must bring with them an educational standard of some level. ... they have to be an expert in that field, recognised expert, not a self proclaimed expert."

In addition to the leader, tour companies provided a suite of other knowledge experts such as "local guides", "local lecturers" or "on site experts", who were responsible for "enhancing" the tour experience. Tour literature suggested that these personnel were "authoritative" typically because they either provided scholarly knowledge or possessed unique professional expertise. This gave participants a particular, in depth or unusual insight into the locality because of the guide's access to off limit or off the beaten track sites, or the perspective of a well informed local on the tour's theme. One leader saw the inclusion of local experts as an important way in which educational tourism could foster local communities and knowledge development: when it actually comes to walking around and looking at things, whether it's inside an art gallery or whether it's on site, whatever it might be, ... the main interpretation automatically is left to the local person.

It's part of their employment, it's obviously a very good thing for them to develop those skills and they bring, I would have to be honest, not just more detailed knowledge of their local political and social context, they also may visit a site a hundred times and I may have only visited it four times and so they may know more recent excavation, more interpretative history. And it's their right to talk about their country of course. But what I will do, will be to add some comments of what we're looking at, with their permission of course and we try and do it in a very friendly way.

Leaders drew distinctions between their role and that of local experts in terms of the material and contexts they provided: The local guy, if we have one travelling with us, might talk about social, gender, political issues of the current day which are things which he or she would know in more detail than I would. Then I might talk a bit about the sites that we're visiting and their cultural impact. So I will try and do that every couple of days on the bus. ... Certainly the interpretation of that I can bring, and hopefully it's appreciated, is by putting these things in a much wider cultural, political, historical context which you know which is, I would imagine, beneficial for people to enjoy hearing in that sort of way.

Academic engagement as knowledge experts on tour was perceived to add value not just by tour providers and their clients, but also by scholars. One male academic reflected: I think you could say therefore there's an onus upon us to put that back... into the community. But I think there's a lot of people in the community who are really interested in this so it's not like oh well, we have to do this. I think there are people out there, lots of people, who are interested in all sorts of things... I think it's enjoyable.

Moreover, by providing his expertise on tour, one academic leader felt: "I'm able to pursue what I'd say is my personal interest which is the same as my professional." Participation in educational tourism assisted scholars' own understanding of their teaching strategies and research. One male academic reflected: "not all that I do personally in my research leads into my teaching... but a lot of it does". More than one academic explained their involvement in terms of advancing their own research agenda through the opportunity to explore new or unique destinations, or to revisit sites of interest. Practically speaking, involvement with a tour company had enabled some scholars to develop their research interests with the funds the company provided. One academic indicated that the company had donated funds to his team's ongoing excavation. One company involved in this study is in fact a not for profit organisation, comprised of 25 members universities and colleges, part of whose income is allocated to support university based research programs.

Learning Facilitators

Enthusiasm was another quality of note for leaders. They had "passion" for their subject and "love" for the places to be visited; indeed these were "their favourite places". They possessed "skills in communicating this knowledge to an interested audience". This signified an important facet of educational tourism as it was marketed by companies: that the learning should be made both accessible and fun.

It was not surprising therefore that companies also highlighted the people skills of their leaders. They were "caring" and "willing to adapt to the pace of the group". Leaders' sensitivity to the diversity of knowledge and experience of tour participants could be emphasised in the lifelong learning market of educational tourism. This was reflected in the personal qualities desirous in a tour leader rated in the survey: A good sense of humour... very perceptive so they can read the mood of the group and understand what is required for that particular session.

Knowledge was considered by survey respondents not as a quality, but as a non negotiable pre requisite for a tour leader. No company staff member referred to knowledge expertise independent of communication and social skills. One director summarised the best tour leaders as: "Excellent qualifications, be good at their tour leader experience and social coordinator." Indeed, communication rated as the most valued personal skill in a tour leader, across all respondents: Good at communication i.e. also in eye contact and rapport with people. They don't sound like they are bored and have said the thing a 1000 times, but genuinely interested in what they do, teach.

This passion to communicate knowledge defined the excellent tour leader, as the director of one educational tour company observed: "somebody who is deeply involved, intimately involved with the country or the theme of a particular tour, who can share that enthusiasm with others but who also has an empathy for travellers who may not be experienced". These qualities marked those who were "the best in their field," an employee of one company commented: "the knowledge of their subject, their confidence in their subject... They have to be able to impart the knowledge to their clients in a way that people are going to appreciate while they're away". One male academic reflected: "For teaching I would say because it broadens your communication skills."

To cater for the range of skills required in tour leader, some companies have created a division between an organiser/manager role and the accompanying expert. This is in addition to the on site guides who might also be provided. As one designer put it: "the tour manager is really somebody who assists with the tour arrangements. The tour leader is responsible for the educational and the social aspects of the tour really. ...what we've done is divided the expectation and the needs of tour members." However it is notable that the social aspects of group cohesion and dynamics (if not practical arrangements) were seen as the role of the intellectual expert. One academic leader described his input as leader on a photography tour in the following terms:" I was there as a kind of creative mentor, I suppose, that is the term that I like to use. And that worked very well."

Leaders were defined as flexible thinkers. When asked to consider how they delivered content on tours, leaders' responses consistently highlighted the key characteristic as adaptability: "we are flexible in that we will ask people on the group that we take at the moment, what are you interested in? What would you like us to talk about? We have got a series of topics that we think you should get information on, but if you have particular components, let us know." Leaders commonly spoke of the need to be sensitive to the different ways and environment in which learning occurred: "the experience of good teaching is to be mindful of what people are bringing to the classroom and to make sure that in the discourse we have some are not being alienated by only talking to others."

The importance of observing the variety of learning styles and levels in a tour group was noted by one female academic leader: "several of them will be taking notes. And with some of them they will also come up to you later and ask for clarification of certain of the points that you've made." The opportunity to pose questions with the leader was highlighted by many leaders as a common feature of participant learning. One brochure, for example, quoted a participant: "I found the lectures on culture & history excellent & informative. Good to have opportunities to ask questions." This suggests that beyond the formal delivery of lectures, an important aspect of client learning takes place in informal settings. These may be places where the participants felt comfortable and supported, unafraid to ask questions, to verify their learning or to reflect upon the sites visited and their meanings.

In addition to the challenge of clients' differing levels of subject familiarity, learning styles, and abilities, catering to different degrees of interest in learning was a critical feature for most leaders. One described his method for responding to different learning styles and degrees of prior knowledge: "while we do start up with a generalised kind of thing, you know that not everyone will perhaps want to walk down that path of more detailed or more specific knowledge that's what those before departure or before evening meal sessions are for... equally of course as a tour leader you're available for discussions whenever people want. ... what I will do is walk on the bus and talk and then sit with people." Another described his approach as follows: I prepare comprehensive notes for myself which I take and then you really play it by ear... If they're particularly interested sometimes we will have a meeting in the evening. If they initialise it. I don't organise that. If they say, "We'd like to learn more about this." I say, "Okay let's get together after dinner." As these examples suggest, tour leaders' skills include not just knowledge expertise but also critical social skills in detecting levels of engagement and responding appropriately to them.

Being "on site" was seen for many to provide distinct pedagogical insights, both for clients and for academic scholars as well. The delivery required and the value of being in place was articulated by one academic tour leader: "there is a different dynamic and you can draw on that shared experience without having to spell it out". Another observed that it was unlike classroom lectures because of the immediacy of the content: "depending on what we've seen that day, they may be more focused perhaps on what they've just seen. For instance ... you know what XYZ looked like, you've just been down it, therefore you can visualise it. So there's a difference." A number highlighted overlap between their work in the institution and beyond. One academic observed that "A lot of what I do is taken straight out of what I do in lectures. And then a lot goes back in to the lectures afterwards." The variety of the teaching environments on a tour was a feature that attracted some leaders, as one academic explained: " always intriguing, trying to teach in different places, in different contexts, in different ways. I think teaching in universities is... well, it's the same, rather repetitive."

The influence that being in place has on the production of new knowledge cannot be underestimated, according to tour leaders. As one academic observed: "the impact of it there in person – stays in your memory very much better. You can see it in context, explain better how something got there, which really can't happen on a page in a book." A female tour leader reflected: "you take them to the monuments, then you go around the monuments with them, they can actually see it... They've got it in all it's glory so to speak and they can walk about. The significance of the "real" over visuals, as well as the ability to move through the spaces, to be active in them, not just passive." One academic explained: "doing it in situ, absolutely there are things that you can teach only when you are there. It's partly indescribable, just the sense of place... that you can't convey in the classroom. There's also an intensity to the teaching".

Academics were able to advance their own learning and research through tour locations: the company "can gain access – because of their contacts and reputation to sites that you wouldn't be able to see yourself." Another academic reflected that "they've given me access to opportunities I never would have had".

Beyond "being in place" however, academics observed important learning which clients experienced outside of site visits. "Most of the time you are there on the site and then in the evening there is a discussion, sometimes, over dinner. If someone wants to know something I'm happy to explain it to them". Others however utilised such informal times to promote reflection, much like a tutorial or workshop. One academic tour leader articulated his technique: everybody on that tour is going to have a different story, from just from the day's journey. And so over dinner at night I'd go round the table. I mean, I'd still run a constructed sort of workshop, if you like. ... And then that becomes quite interesting because we've all seen the same things and yet they've all had different experiences of the same things. That's what leads to the creative discourse.

A tour leader for one company used these sessions as an opportunity to extend learning and cater to those of different learning interests and levels: what I will do every second morning or every second evening is get our guide and say, "whoever wants to join me for half an hour straight after breakfast or half an hour before dinner will come and we'll talk through the progress of what we've doing. We'll talk through what we've seen, where we've been and where we're going, and that will enable me to cater to a more advanced interest if that's the requirement.

In such contexts, the leader acts as a facilitator of client learning, using the relationships built over the length of the tour. This also distinguished the role of the leader and of local guide who might deliver a one off lecture. Most leaders described their experiences and practices in ways which suggested a strong emphasis on tutorial type teaching, rather than as formal lectures.

The idea of creating a tour learning community is suggested through phrasing such as "sharing experiences with like minded travellers" which is commonly found in provider literature. A learning community can be defined as a group of people who share some values and beliefs, and are actively engaged in learning together from each other. Learning communities include concepts of membership ("belonging"), shared experiences and emotional connections. Much of the work on learning communities has focused on alternative teaching strategies for students, or professional.

Three assumptions underlie the support for learning communities: that they will a) create a group that will work together b) increase intellectual interaction and c) enhance learning. More recently, the rise of the internet has seen the emergence of "virtual" learning communities. Whilst research has been conducted on learning communities using tourism to further their goals, educational tourism itself as a learning community appears to have been somewhat overlooked. In survey responses for this project, leaders and clients both identified the group experience as a valuable learning resource and rated group learning/travel experiences higher than individual experiences. A tour leader for one educational tour company described the advantages of the group learning environment: "that person is sharing all their excitement and enthusiasm and knowledge for what they're looking at. They're also sharing that experience with like minded enquirers".

One male academic who ran tours for independent groups of travellers, friends and companies explained his motivation: "I enjoy the interaction with other people and it's really good when you have a group of people who share the same interests. You can sit around the hotel at drinks times and discuss what we've seen". Academics, as well as clients, have found the sense of learning together an enriching feature of their work in this domain. One female academic leader explained: I enjoy meeting the people and I certainly enjoy imparting the knowledge that I have to those people. And some of them are extremely interested, they will come up with questions, no doubt about it, so I enjoy that aspect of it... on the whole I enjoy it, I thoroughly enjoy it, I enjoy meeting them, being with them.

Another male scholar, experienced in tour leading, reflected on distinctions between the insights gained on tours with mature learners and his undergraduate classroom teaching experiences: I think from my point of view that the more people you talk to about this you get lots of different perspectives from them and you learn. I think we learn from talking to them because we can go into a student classroom here, particularly if it's first or second level, you don't get any feedback. A female academic leader commented: "It's not only looking at the monuments yet again, seeing perhaps new monuments. That would help, but no, interaction with the people on the tour would enhance my understanding of my research."

Authors

Beyond participating as tour leaders, the project research has highlighted a range of other opportunities for academic input. Many do not require scholars to travel on, or lead, tours. Organising travel itineraries; identifying seminal historical moments, architectural features, geographic regions; writing travel literature; speaking at information sessions are also all educational tourism opportunities for engagement of the expertise of the academy. A significant facet of academic engagement with educational tourism occurs off tour, writing preparatory materials and designing tours. Tourist information has been shown to have an important influence on the choice of vacation destinations by travellers. Despite the advent of new technologies such as the internet, great quantities of money are still being assigned to the publication of more traditional texts, such as guidebooks (ibid).

There has been much scholarly research on the role of such publications in the decision making process of potential travellers. Robinson and Anderson (2002) explore the ways in which authors and their books can influence people's choice of destination and how they perceive them. However, research is scant concerning the role guidebooks play in education.

Werry does however refer to travel literature as a "de facto teacher" of tourism's knowledges and ways of knowing. Botterill and Crompton (1996) have noted that how the tourist "vacates" their normal space and creates an understanding of the new, holidaying space is an area where intermediaries, such as tour guides and travel writers, can be important in enabling the traveller. This research is mirrored in our project's findings. Responses investigating educational aids highlighted the fact that the educational tourism experience was not confined to the actual travel component, but extended to encompass learning opportunities either side of the tour. There were significant opportunities for scholarly interactions in off site educational tour opportunities.

Clients were asked to rank in importance a series of statements regarding preparation for tours. The results indicated that prior information (such as handouts, books, other educational aids) was highly valued. Female clients showed a much stronger preference for preparing their learning. Survey participants were also asked to consider what types of educational aids they would find useful for learning on an educational tour, and the point at which they would be most useful (i.e. before, during or after the tour). Almost unanimously, maps were considered to be the most valuable educational aid, consistently ranking highly at all stages of the educational travel experience. Handbooks were almost as highly valued as maps pre and during tour. One leader reflected on how his group used their textual resources on tour: if we're walking around we have these available to us, people can jot notes down in that sort of way or above all when we meet in the evening we've got this shared resource to actually work with. So these take the place fairly obviously of visuals, overheads, things like that which we would use in the teaching classroom setting. So it does enable people to, I think, have a fairly good and comprehensive aid memoir for what's going on, a bit of resource which can actually be used in the field, in the hotel to enhance their knowledge.

Participant feedback was often used in company marketing to highlight the quality of materials provided to clients: I have just received ... preparatory material, and wish to convey my pleasure at receiving such a beautifully presented package, full of clear, detailed and fascinating material. This package would have to rank as one of the best ever. Superb!

The inclusion of such a comment demonstrates that the educational tourism experience extends beyond the time of the tour itself. Within such materials, a participant might find more identifiable "Objectives of the Program" although these were noticeably broader and measured against one's own personal starting point in comparison to most university units: "At the conclusion of our program.... we will have developed: "a greater understanding" "an appreciation", "a sense of wonder", "a greater knowledge".

Apart from introductory information and details about the sites to be visited, such course handbooks often included a suggested reading list that may contain novels as well as scholarly textbooks. A manager at one educational tour company described the documentation prepared by their company:

The preparatory material is quite a large document which can be anything up to sort of 33 pages, and gives details on where they're going to be going to, it gives them the history of the places they're going to, and it gives them more detail on the places that they're going to visit....we also offer a reading and reference list and that's given to them as soon as they deposit on a program so that they can begin to read about the program... We encourage them in their welcome letter to go the library, use the resources at the library. A tour leader for one educational tour company described the materials he prepared for participants of his tours as: Good solid introductions to daily visits that we're doing in that way. Extensive bibliography which everyone gets of course a month or so before. But I think perhaps more importantly and as a very important teaching aid what all these books contain are maps which can be used as historical discussions points... Or they might include individual plans of buildings.

How such material is used was highly variable, as one male academic leader observed from his experience: "the people that come on these tours don't want to go overseas for three weeks and study in the way that we would think it. They don't really want to do much reading in the evening. They... a few of them will prepare themselves, the majority will not."

Another academic took a different (and unusual) approach to providing literature for the clients to use on tour however: "At the beginning we took the decision that the city was the text, and the handbook just accompanied that... but the internet has changed everything. There's just so much more that they can access now, wherever they are." Interestingly, the web appeared to play little part in post tour reflection according to respondents, although at least one academic interviewed had extended the educational experience both before and beyond the on site engagement with his group: "on my website I keep the reports from the tours and I've given detailed notes beforehand and I keep them on the site as well, so I think it makes a huge difference."

A number of academic scholars interviewed had been asked to compose the content for tour handbooks. One academic described his motivation for writing such texts: "I thought it would be interesting, to see if I could... I came to the realisation not only that I could do it, but that it was quite interesting to write for a general audience." Asked what is involved in pitching to this audience, one academic responded: "I think you do have a duty to be interesting and to write reasonably clearly." How this has impacted academics' other scholarly writing was also explored.

As one male academic put it: I found it quite interesting. It made realise that this was something that I could do and that it's quite enjoyable doing it ... The point is: everything you do is a dialogue with an audience that is either there, or is a potential audience. And so many times the dialogue comes back to you unexpectedly, without you planning or even knowing it. You don't know who you're writing for, you never know who you're writing for. And I find that extraordinarily interesting, that you can get something out of the blue... So you're always learning new stuff out of the blue. And of course it feeds into your teaching.

Conclusions

Academic engagement with educational tourism has occurred in a variety of roles, both on and off site.

- The educational roles of a tour leader are distinct from those of local lecturers and guides.
- Social skills, as well as knowledge expertise, are vital in tour leaders because these enable leaders to identify levels and degrees of capacity and engagement in the clientele and to respond accordingly.
- Most leaders act as learning facilitators, teaching in a variety of formal and informal contexts on tours.
- Preparatory and post tour phases are important complementary opportunities for enhancing learning in educational tourism.

Generating Educational Tourism Narratives

Heritage/cultural tourism, ecotourism, agritourism, and other types of information-centric tourism have been of increasing importance in recent years, both to the tourist and to the tourism industry. However, these types of tourism have not yet fully taken advantage of the dramatic increase in available data that has been a hallmark of the Information Age, particularly with respect to the adoption of mobile technologies.

One aspect of tourism that is particularly in need of better mobile device applications is that of educational tourism. Most mobile technologies aimed at the tourism market are either (1) tourist tools can do nothing more than inform users of optimal or nearby tourist facilities or attractions and thus can do little educating or (2) educational devices that are limited in scope due to the amount of required custom content development. With Minotour, we attempt to fill this vacuum, and our central methodology is the employment of intelligent narrative technology, particularly data mining techniques informed by narrative theory. Why use narrative?

Much research has concluded that humans have an inherent predilection towards narrative approaches. In addition, aside from the innateness of narratives to the human experience, narrative has been shown to play a particularly important role within the two constituent fields of our educational tourism test platform-education and tourism-as well as in the combined platform itself. Wells (1986), Mott et. all (1999), and many others have identified the myriad benefits of narrative to education and Gretzel and Fesenmaier (2002) have done the same for tourism. In the educational tourism context, Lanegran (2005) concluded that a high-quality educational tour is one in which a cohesive story is woven while travelling through the landscape. A similar assumption is made in.

Minotour utilizes Wikipedia as its primary data source, thus eliminating the need for *any* knowledge base development, which, as noted above, is a rarity in the world of automated tour guides with an educational focus. Wikipedia is an online, user-contributed encyclopedia that is available in more than 100 languages and has more than 1.7 million articles in its English version and over 500,000 in its German version, the two languages our implementation supports. Through the use of the Wikipedia corpora, Minotour inherits all of Wikipedia's user-friendly advantages, such as democratized and free information that is global in scope. We also utilize several other unique properties of Wikipedia, as described in section three. However, the text of Minotour's generated narratives -- derived directly from Wikipedia – obviously also exhibits Wikipedia's well-publicized disadvantages, most notably with regard to concerns about accuracy, motives, uncertain expertise, volatility, coverage, and sources.

In its current implementation, Minotour operates on a simple premise: with a mobile device, the user selects a destination and a narrative tour from the user's current location to that destination is provided. The user's position is determined via GPS and the tour is generated on a server and delivered back to the client. These tours are designed to be experienced *while* the user moves to the destination (in our prototype, this is done via text display; we are also exploring other options, including audio). An example tour with Berlin's Brandenburg Gate as the start feature (feature *a*) and Unter den Linden as the end feature (feature *b*) is provide. In this paper, we will walk through the theory and methods that are used to generate these tours. The second section provides a quick summary of related work in narrative intelligence. In the third section, we discuss the Wikipedia context of the project and the operation of the narrative generation algorithm. In the fourth section, we outline our understanding of narrative theory and the two key narrative cues, unity and progression, that underlie our conceptualization of the ideal narrative function, the function on which the narrative generation algorithm is based. In the fifth section, we detail the implementation of the project. Finally, we close with concluding thoughts and a description of our plans for future work.

Related Work in Narrative Intelligence

In the narrative intelligence framework laid out by Mateas and Sengers (1999) and Mateas and Sengers (2003), the Minotour narrative generation system draws most heavily from the then-state-of-the-art (1999) body of work designed to support human narrative intelligence. Indeed, the key presumption in Minotour is that there is inherent value-increased cohesion, improved recall and comprehension, the ability to overcome certain cognitive obstacles, increased synergy with how tourism is experienced, closer alignment with geography education, etc.-in providing information to users in a form that is easier to interpret as a narrative than in the dominant manner in which Internet information is accessed. In the context in the 2003 version of Mateas and Sengers' framework, this trait of Minotour places it in the Narrative Interfaces category, as Minotour essentially provides a narrative-based interface to Wikipedia, albeit a unique and highly spatial one.

In order to provide narrative support, however, we make a concrete assumption as to the definition of narrative, at least in the context of our system. This definition, outlined in section 4, is used to generate stories, thus placing our work also well within Mateas and Sengers' Storytelling Systems category of work, and within the story-centric sub-category.

While Minotour's feature base lies firmly in narrative support and Storytelling Systems, Mateas and Sengers' Interactive Fiction and Drama category also applies to Minotour. Users interact with Minotour in both spatial and non-spatial ways: they are only allowed to obtain tours beginning in their present spatial location and end destinations are chosen via the medium of the mobile device. In addition, because Wikipedia is editable by any user, a measure of interactivity pervades all aspects of the tours. This feature of Wikipedia, along with our system's ability to bring out emergent features of the link structure and raw text of the encyclopedia, allows any user to influence the narrative that she and all other users experience.

The Narrative Generation Algorithm

In order to understand Minotour's narrative generation algorithm-the computational methodology we use to generate tours such as that is necessary to first highlight some properties. In their review of narrative intelligence research, Mateas and Sengers (2003) note that, with narrative being such a rich and complex concept, it is critical for narrative intelligence scholars to be explicit about their approach. As an interdisciplinary team bridging the sciences, engineering and the humanities, our approach to narrative is based in narratology, a field of narrative theory developed from the analysis of literature, film and other media.

Much work that is adopted from this field draws from structuralist authors and their rigorous interpretation of underlying narrative structures. Structuralist approaches translate these underlying structures into sets of variables, codes, and functions that reside in the text. One of the earliest examples of this approach is Vladimir Propp's *Morphology of the Folktale* (1928), which delineated 8 basic character types and a series of possible functions that each character could enact. Structuralist theories assume that one can define narrative as a text that aligns to a certain set of rules, such as the depiction of characters, plot, and cause-effect relationships. The problem with adopting this model in narrative intelligence research is that these approaches often sidestep the psychological and spatial conditions that influence narrative experience.

We draw our narrative approach, rather, from recent research in narratology that is influenced by cognitive science, including the narrative theories of David Bordwell and Edward Branigan.

These theories are grounded in the same rigorous interpretation of structures as Structuralism, but rather than defining "narrative" as the sum of these structures, they locate narrative as a perceptual activity.

Edward Branigan writes that narrative is a "perceptual activity that organizes data into a special pattern which represents and explains experience". It is this understanding of narrative that we use to develop our ideal narrative function. Rather than trying to model a text out of Wikipedia, which possesses a certain set of traits (such as characters who have goals), our narrative algorithm shapes a disparate text corpus according to characteristics of a desired narrative experience. According to Bordwell, a precondition for understanding a fiction film as narrative is the unity of the text as a formal system. He writes that, in the most formally unified films, "every element present has a specific set of functions, similarities and differences are determinable, the form develops logically, and no element is superfluous. In turn, the film's overall unity gives our experience a sense of completeness and fulfilment". Thus, for a reader or viewer to understand the narrative as unified, they must perceive the individual elements as interrelating and nothing must seem "out of place." As is also noted in this passage, a sense of development is also key to a sense of unity. Bordwell defines formal development as a progression moving from beginning through middle to end.

Simply including unity and development, also termed "progression," will not designate a given text as a narrative. However, they are two of the most common narrative cues that elicit a narrative mode of organization. Bordwell delineates this narrative comprehension process as follows: cues are organized "to encourage the spectator to execute story construction activities. The film presents cues, patterns and gaps that shape the viewer's application of schemata and the testing of hypothesis". We hypothesize that incorporating these narrative cues of unity and progression into a representation of Wikipedia will encourage the reader to execute story construction activities and to utilize narrative schema in making sense of the individual snippets.

Unity in the Ideal Narrative Function

Taken as a whole, a disparate collection of facts (and some opinions) with no inter-article coherence. However, as noted above, unity is a critical narrative cue. As such, unity must be an important characteristic of the ideal narrative function, the function against which all possible narratives between two 3D articles are evaluated. Of course, the most obvious way that we provide unity is by linking 3D article *a* to 3D article *b* through a series of other articles. Before the user reads the narrative, these articles were likely perceived as distinct entities; afterwards, they are inherently connected. But this form of unity is weak and only informs our ideal narrative function in the most basic way.

More significantly, we provide unity by highlighting the themes in the user's space. This approach to unity is informed by our educational tourism focus. A critical element of geography education is the highlighting of themes embedded in the geography of a region. In fact, a key element of regionalization – a backbone of the United States National Geography Standards – is being able to reduce the complexity of a diverse area through the construction of thematic regions.

While it might seem that incorporating a number of themes might disconnect the narrative, the presence of multiple themes can unify the narrative experience as a whole. Each theme serves to draw a conceptual link between two or more snippets. For example, in our sample narrative, issues about German freedom, unification, and community are directly referenced in the snippets about the "Brandenburg Gate," "Hans Modrow," "Strausbourg," and "Humbolt University of Berlin." The themes of German freedom, unity, and community thread together these snippets. On the other hand, the intersection of the academic institution with political and religious forces is present in the snippets from "Strausbourg," "Martin Luther," and "Humbolt University of Berlin."

The need to quantify the thematic requirement is the reason we chose in-links as the defining variable in the ideal narrative function. In the context of Wikipedia, in-links are a highly accurate proxy for generality. When an author working on one entry links to another entry, that author is essentially saying "this entry is important to my entry". Articles that are more important to more entries are more general articles.

For instance, in the German, the article for "Poker" has far more in-links than the article for the "1990 World Series of Poker". We make the assumption-proven to be mostly true experimentally-

that more general articles have more thematic content. Given the in-links/generality/theme relationship and the ideal narrative function's focus on high in-links articles, the reason for the appearance of themes in our ideal narrative function becomes clear. It is important to note that we include in the narrative function a maximum number of in links that is less than the actual maximum number of in links. We found through experiments that articles with extremely high in-link totals are too broad to carry much interesting thematic significance. The most common example of excessive in-links are the articles about days of the year, i.e. the "October 5" article. In the English Wikipedia, this article has thousands of in-links, but has little to no thematic content.

Development in the Ideal Narrative Function

If we were just focused on theme, it would be ideal to find a set of articles with a high number of in-links (but not too high) and present these to the user. However, it is critical to the narrative foundation of our tours that the reader understands the snippets of the text as developing in a certain direction.

As was the case with unity, there is an obvious answer to the question of how our ideal narrative function incorporates development: each snippet is linked to the next snippet. However, just as with unity, the function also includes conceptually deeper models of development. We accomplish this by incorporating a *small* positive slope in the first two-thirds or so of the function. In this part of the function, each snippet becomes only slightly more general than the next.

As such, the reader gains a sense of movement toward generality. She can then question and form hypotheses about the broader themes of her space and how they will connect her start to her destination. This activity mirrors the experience of the traditional narrative reader. In the traditional narrative text, conflict builds to a climax, followed by a resolution. In the context of our ideal narrative function, this conflict is manifested in the question "What does this snippet from this thematic article have to do with the specific space in which I am moving"? As such, before the user is returned from wiki-space to a 3D article, the broadest theme of that space – the climax – is revealed. Then, the movement from the broadest theme back to the concluding 3D article – the resolution – provides a sense of completeness and closure to the experience.

In the case of our sample narrative, the climax occurs at the Martin Luther snippet. At this point, we expect that the user is maximally wondering what a highly broad article like "Martin Luther" has to do with the specific space in between the Brandenburg Gate and Unter den Linden. This curiosity is quickly satisfied in a mere two hops through the Wikipedia graph, as the user learns of the connection through Humboldt University.

Since Minotour's generated texts are designed to be delivered as the user travels from feature *a* to feature *b*, they are accompanied by the plotline the user is experiencing by moving through the space. The progression of this two-trajectory context in which the stories diverge at the beginning (at *a*) and rejoin at the end (at *b*), is one that the user is used to perceiving within a narrative, and thus aids development. Thousands of examples of this context exist in pop culture media. For instance, nearly all Seinfeld episodes begin with one narrative that splits into two (or more) at the beginning and intersects at the end.

Implementation

We have taken a basic client/server approach to our implementation, an approach that maximizes the individual flexibility of the client and the server. All of the narrative generation work takes place on the server, while all of the narrative delivery is done by the client. When a narrative is desired, the client, sends the article id number of 3D articles *a* and *b* to the server, and the server returns the optimal narrative between these two features.

The server operates on information provided by a My SQL database of Wikipedia data parsed by a custom Wikipedia processor designed to operate on the semi-regular Wikipedia dumps provided by the Wikimedia Foundation, the operator of Wikipedia. In addition to extracting links, snippets, and other critical data, this parser is responsible for identifying the existing geo-information in Wikipedia, as well as doing the rudimentary georeferencing and tagging of purely temporal articles. We have written the parser to support any of the hundreds of languages for which a Wikipedia version exists, but so far, only the English Wikipedia and the German Wikipedia have been tested. The client side of this project is the lesser-developed side, and we are exploring delivery platforms other than hand-held devices. That said, our current hand-held software, developed in C# and the Windows

Mobile Native C++ API, is effectively a mini-geographic information system (GIS) with GPS capabilities, customized for the various features and desired user experience of Minotour. Because no suitable open-source code could be located, it was necessary to write this software from scratch. A screen shot of a software-emulated version of the application can be found.

Conclusion and Future Work

In this paper, we have presented a novel, narrative theory-informed approach to data mining from a Wikipedia corpus within the context of educational tour generation. While we have completed a proof-of-concept system, we have many more research avenues to explore. First and foremost, we intend to rigorously investigate both theoretical and artistic methods for increasing the narrative pleasure of our generated narratives. One idea currently in the works is eliminating spatially-referenced articles (in addition to temporally-referenced articles) from the body of the narratives. Spatially-referenced articles play a critical role as the start and the end points of our narratives.

However, we have found that when they have snippets that appear in the body, these snippets suffer from the same semantic weakness problems as purely-temporally referenced articles. For instance, the implicit "lies on" relationship between Humboldt University and Unter den Linden is a rather uninteresting and non-educational one, and one that would be obvious to any user who looked at the map on their mobile device client. Other possible avenues for increased narrative pleasure include providing theme-based tours and using Wikipedia's link structure to include more articles in the narratives that are closely tied to the space in which the user is travelling.

Secondly, we are exploring different narrative theoretical constructs with which to examine and improve our generated narratives. We aim to develop further research in the area of cognitive science-based narrative theory with the goal of proposing better strategies for the interdisciplinary adoption of contemporary narratology.

We are also excited about the possibilities for client-side development. Raw text presentation is not the best delivery format for our narratives. We are exploring many possibilities for ways to utilize the presentation as a means to aid narrative interpretation, either through the increase of unity and development, or via other theoretical constructs. One idea on the table includes audio. We are also looking into turning the faceless narrator of our stories into a more explicit character, perhaps even similar to that in or. We have many ideas for using the properties of Wikipedia to enact Person's suggestion to closely integrate character behaviour and presented content. This might include placing greater emphasis on the real life Wikipedia users who input content, as well as considering article conflict statistics.

Following, we are taking steps towards designing an appropriate evaluation for Minotour. We will determine the average user's reliance on narrative schema for the comprehension of a random series of linked snippets (our baseline) as opposed to Minotour generated narratives. Finally, we also plan on implementing spatial feature contribution functionality. Ideally, users should be able to enter information about a spatial feature on which Wikipedia has no information and, immediately afterwards, receive a tour with that feature as the start or end destination. This would add a whole new level of interactivity to our current system.

Minotour is currently heavily customized towards its educational tour narrative generation test platform. However, the ideas behind the implementation can be utilized in other areas and with different goals. Most apparently, the concept can be applied to generating narratives, spatial or not. In initial tests, the authors learned a lot from narratives generated between biographies and even between two mathematical concepts. More broadly, we are considering how this idea could be employed on the Internet as a whole. While we have not explored the narratology implications of such non-spatial and/or non-Wikipedia applications, these are vital further research directions.

5

Prospects of Employment in Hospitality Sector

Introduction

The hospitality sector includes all businesses that provide food, beverages, and/or accommodation services, and convention centres. It includes hotels, restaurants, pubs, bars and clubs, contract catering, etc. This industry has grown at a considerable pace in the last few years. However, at present, it is one of the badly hit industries due to the economic recession. The global energy efficiency market in the hospitality sector includes all the revenues generated by implementation of energy efficient equipment and consultation services provided for the hotels and restaurants, worldwide. Hospitality is the relationship between a guest and a host, or the act or practice of being hospitable, that is, the reception and entertainment of guests, visitors, or strangers, with liberality and goodwill. Hospitality frequently refers to the hospitality industry jobs for hotels, restaurants, casinos, catering, resorts, clubs and any other service position that deals with tourists.

Hospitality is also known as the act of generously providing care and kindness to whoever is in need.

Meaning of Hospitality

The word hospitality derives from the Latin *hospes,* which is formed from *hostis,* which originally meant a 'stranger' and came to take on the meaning of the enemy or 'hostile stranger' (cristal-hostilis) + pets (polis, poles, potentia) to have power. The meaning of "host" can be literally read as "lord of strangers." Furthermore, the word *hostire* means equilize/compensate.

In the Homeric ages, hospitality was under the protection of Zeus, the chief deity of the Greek pantheon. Zeus was also attributed with the title 'Xenios Zeus' ('xenos' means stranger), emphasizing the fact that hospitality was of the utmost importance. A stranger passing outside a Greek house could be invited inside the house by the family. The host washed the stranger's feet, offered him/her food and wine, and only after he/she was comfortable could be asked to tell his/her name.

The Greek concept of sacred hospitality is illustrated in the story of Telemachus and Nestor. When I Telemachus arrived to visit Nestor, was unaware that his guest was the son of his old comrade Odysseus. Nonetheless, Nestor welcomes Telemachus and his party lavishly, thus demonstrating the relationship between *hostis*, "stranger," and *hostire*, "equalize," and how the two combine in the concept of hospitality.

Later, one of Nestor's sons slept on a bed close by Telemachus to take care that he should not suffer any harm. Nestor also put a chariot and horses at Telemachus' disposal so that he could travel the land route from Pylos to Sparta rapidly, and set his son Pisistratus as the charioteer. These illustrate the two other elements of ancient Greek hospitality, protection and guidance.

Based on the story above and its current meaning, hospitality is about compensating/equalizing a stranger to the host, making him feel protected and taken care of, and at the end of his hosting, guiding him to his next destination.

Contemporary Usage

In the contemporary West, hospitality is rarely a matter of protection and survival, and is more associated with etiquette and entertainment. However, it still involves showing respect for one's guests, providing for their needs, and treating them as equals. Cultures and subcultures vary in the extent to which one is expected to show hospitality to strangers, as opposed to personal friends or members of one's in-group.

The hospitality service industry includes hotels, casinos, and resorts, which offer comfort and guidance to strangers, but only as part of a business relationship. The terms hospital, hospice, and hostel also derive from "hospitality," and these institutions preserve more of the connotation of personal care.

Hospitality ethics is a discipline that studies this usage of hospitality.

In the western context, with its dynamic tension between Athens and Jerusalem, two phases can be distinguished with a very progressive transition: a hospitality based on an individually felt sense of duty, and one based on "official" institutions for organized but anonymous social services: special places for particular types of "strangers" such as the poor, orphan(s), ill, alien, criminal, etc. Perhaps this progressive institutionalization can be aligned to the transition between Middle Ages and Renaissance.

Hospitality Around the World

Biblical and Middle Eastern

In Middle Eastern Culture, it was considered a cultural norm to take care of the strangers and foreigners living among you. These norms are reflected in many Biblical commands and examples. Perhaps the most extreme example is provided in Genesis. Lot provides hospitality to a group of angels (who he thinks are only men); when a mob tries to rape them, Lot goes so far as to offer his own daughters as a substitute, saying "Don't do anything to these men, for they have come under the protection of my roof.".

The obligations of both host and guest are stern. The bond is formed by eating salt under the roof, and is so strict that an Arab story tells of a thief who tasted something to see if it was sugar, and on realizing it was salt, put back all that he had taken and left.

Hospitality in Celtic Cultures

Celtic societies also valued the concept of hospitality, especially in terms of protection. A host who granted a person's request for refuge was expected not only to provide food and shelter to his/her guest, but to make sure they did not come to harm while under their care.

A real-life example of this is rooted in the history of the Scottish Clan MacGregor, from the early seventeenth century. The chief of Clan Lamont arrived at the home of the MacGregor chief in Glenstrae, told him that he was fleeing from foes and requested refuge. The MacGregor welcomed his brother chief with no questions asked. Later that night, members of the MacGregor clan came looking for the Lamont chief, informing their chief that the Lamont had in fact killed his son and heir in a quarrel. Holding to the sacred law of hospitality, the MacGregor not only refused to hand over the Lamont to his clansmen, but the next morning escorted him to his ancestral lands. This act would later be repaid when, during the time that the MacGregors were outlawed, the Lamonts gave safe haven to many of their number.

Hospitality in India

India is one of the oldest civilizations on earth, and like every culture has its own favourite stories including quite a few on hospitality. That of a simpleton readily sharing his meager morsels with an uninvited guest, only to discover that the guest is a God in disguise, who rewards his generosity with abundance. That of a woman who lovingly cooks up all the Khichdi she can afford, for everyone who is hungry... till one day when she runs out of food for the last hungry person to whom she offers her own share, and is rewarded by the god in disguise with a never ending pot of Khichdi. Most Indian adults having grown up listening to these stories as children, believe in the philosophy of "Atithi Devo Bhava", meaning the guest is God. From this stems the Indian approach of graciousness towards guests at home, and in all social situations.

Cultural Value or Norm

Hospitality as a cultural norm or value is an established sociological phenomenon that people study and write papers about. Some regions have become stereotyped as exhibiting a particular style of hospitality. Examples include:

- Minnesota nice
- Southern hospitality

Hospitality Ethics

The term "Hospitality Ethics" is used to refer to two different, yet related, areas of study:

1. The philosophical study of the moral obligations that hold in hospitality relationships and practices.
2. The branch of business ethics that focuses on ethics in commercial hospitality and tourism industries.

Whereas Ethics goes beyond describing what is done, in order to prescribe what *should* be done; Hospitality Ethics prescribes what should be done in matters related to hospitality. Hospitality theories and norms are derived through a critical analysis of hospitality practices, processes, and relationships; in various cultures and traditions; and throughout history. Ultimately, hospitality theories are applied, and put to practice in commercial and non-commercial settings.

As a standard of conduct, hospitality has been variously considered throughout history as a law, an ethic, a principle, a code, a duty, a virtue, etc. These prescriptions were created for negotiating ambiguous relationships between guests, hosts, citizens, and strangers. Despite its ancient origins and ubiquity amongst human cultures, the concept of hospitality has received relatively little attention from moral philosophers, who have tended to focus their attention on other ethical concepts, e.g. good, evil, right, and wrong.

Yet hospitality as a moral imperative, or ethical perspective, preceded many other prescriptions for ethical behaviour: In ancient Middle Eastern, Greek and Roman cultures, the Ethic of Hospitality was a code that demanded specific kinds of conduct from both guests and hosts. One example: Chivalry required men of station to offer food and lodging to any men of station that requested it.

In many ways, these standards of behaviour have survived into the present day in the commercial hospitality industry, where descendents of the ancient ideas continue to inform current standards and practices.

Hospitality Ethics in Practice

Ethics in commercial hospitality settings. Applied ethics is the branch of Ethics which investigates the application of our ethical theories and judgments. There are many branches of Applied Ethics: Business ethics, professional ethics, medical ethics, educational ethics, environmental ethics, and more.

Hospitality Ethics is a branch of Applied Ethics. In practice, it combines concerns of other branches of Applied Ethics, such as business ethics, environmental ethics, professional ethics, and more. For instance, when a local hospitality industry flourishes, potential ethical dilemmas abound: What effect do industry practices have on the environment? On the host community? On the local economy? On citizens' attitudes about their local community; about outsiders, tourists, and guests? These are the kinds of questions that Hospitality Ethics, as a version of Applied Ethics, might ask.

Since Hospitality and tourism combine to create one of the largest service industries in the world, there are many opportunities for both good and bad behaviour, and right and wrong actions by hospitality and tourism practitioners. Ethics in these industries can be guided by codes of conduct, employee manuals, industry standards (whether implicit or explicit), and more. Though the World Tourism Organization has proposed an industry-wide code of ethics, there is presently no universal code for the hospitality industry. Various textbooks regarding ethics in commercial hospitality settings have been published recently, and are currently used in hospitality education courses.

The concept of Hospitality Exchange, also known as "accommodation sharing", "hospitality services" (short "hospex"), and "home stay networks", refers to centrally organized social networks of individuals, generally travellers, who offer or seek accommodation without monetary exchange.

History

In 1949, Bob Luitweiler founded the first hospitality service called Servas Open Doors as a cross national, non-profit, volunteer run organization advocating interracial and international peace. In 1965, John Wilcock set up the Traveller's Directory as a listing of his friends willing to host each other when travelling. In 1988, Joy Lily rescued the organization from imminent shutdown, forming Hospitality Exchange. In 2000, Veit Kuhne founded Hospitality Club, the first Internet-based service. In 2004, Casey Fenton started CouchSurfing, now the largest hospitality exchange organization.

How they Work

Generally, after registering, members have the option of providing very detailed information and pictures of themselves and of the sleeping accommodation being offered, if any. The more information provided by a member improves the chances that someone will find the member trustworthy enough to be their host or guest. Names and addresses may be verified by volunteers.

Members looking for accommodation can search for hosts using several parameters such as age, location, sex, and activity level.

Home stays are entirely consensual between the host and guest, and the duration, nature, and terms of the guest's stay are generally worked out in advance to the convenience of both parties. No monetary exchange takes place except under certain circumstances (e.g. the guest may compensate the host for food).

After using the service, members can leave a noticeable reference about their host or guest. Instead of or in addition to accommodation, members also offer to provide guide services or travel-related advice. The websites of the networks also provide editable travel guides and forums where members may seek travel partners or advice. Many such organizations are also focused on "social networking" and members organize activities such as camping trips, bar crawls, meetings, and sporting events.

Some networks cater to specific niche markets such as students, activists, religious pilgrims, and even occupational groups like police officers.

Benefits

Monetary Savings

As these networks provide accommodation at no charge, monetary savings can be significant.

Local Contact

Hospitality exchange gives travellers the chance to experience what life is like for people living in other places. In addition, making interpersonal connections and fostering understanding of different cultures may in the long run also be important to international relations. During hospitality exchanges, hosts may show off their local knowledge and exciting places "off the tourist map". Not only may travellers get a distinct experience, but they will also get a feel for the everyday lives of local residents.

Reciprocity

These systems foster richer and more convenient travel experiences not so much on the premise of altruism, but on the basis of social exchange theory. Implicit in the agreement to host travellers is the ability to ask to be hosted by them in the future.

If one enjoys having interesting guests in their home, this works out well for both parties. It works comparatively better if you are visited by travellers from a locale you find particularly attractive. Thus, hosting someone from New York City in Gainesville, Florida seems to be an unbelievable opportunity. Moreover, if you are a Westerner visiting someone in a developing country, your stay might be the only way that this individual or family could afford a trip to a rich nation. This may mean more than just a relaxing vacation for such disadvantaged parties.

Ecological Sustainability

Accommodation sharing reduces the demand for hotels, which, depending on the location can be detrimental for the environment.

Drawbacks: Lack of Guarantee

There is no contractual agreement between users in these systems. Reservations are made, but if they are for some reason broken, there is no higher authority to which one could plead for a refund or other compensation. The only repercussion will be the poor rating you give that user and your only consolation will be that your warning will deter others from visiting or hosting them. For those who feel insecure unless their travel arrangements are written in stone before departure, this system will not be comforting.

Potential Interpersonal Conflict or Awkwardness

There is a chance that guest and host will not get along. Perhaps there will be scheduling or ideological conflicts. Maybe you will find that hosts or visitors have misrepresented themselves. Perhaps the experience will not live up to your expectations. Intense interpersonal communications in advance and a flexibility once you have arrived is your best bet. These experiences require additional planning and courtesy towards the demands of your host. Thus, your living conditions, length of stay, and overall experience will be circumscribed by the living conditions you enter into.

Digital divide and demographic segregation

As use of these services generally requires access to the internet and knowledge of the English language, the sample population found in searches of these databases is really much less diverse than a geographical representation of worldwide users might suggest.

Security

Staying in someone's house, or inviting people into your house leaves open the possibility of being taken advantage of.

The Structure of the Accommodation Sector

The Nature of Demand for Accommodation Facilities

The tourism industry for the economy of Jordan is significant. Tourism is the largest export sector and second largest private sector employer and producer of foreign exchange. Moreover, it contributes to more than US$800 million to the national economy and accounts for approximately 10% of the country's gross domestic product. Jordan's prime destinations: Petra, Wadi Rum and the Dead Sea are directly dependent on the rich natural and cultural resources in the area. However, Jordan has been subject to environmental pressure from tourism due to unsatisfactory performance in protecting the environment. It is therefore crucial for the sustainability of the country to protect and preserve these natural sites. In light of this, the present study focused on three main objectives for the Jordanian Tourism Industry: to assess the current situation, to assess the environmental impacts caused and to develop methods to encourage the improvement of the environmental performance of the tourist accommodation sector.

The Distribution of Accommodation

Environmental Issues

'Environmental' issues have emerged as hot subjects in economic discussions since the early 1970. So far, the term has usually been used to the analysis of exhaustible and productive resources. Lately, it is being also applied to amenity use of natural resources and in investigating the economic role of the environment and the associated causes and effects of its degradation and over-use, pollution etc.

The basic lesson that we have learnt from the environmental economics is that the environment can not be perceived as separate from other resources. Most human activities affect it and in turn changes in its state have economic repercussions. It is therefore important that economic decisions take into account the welfare of the future generation. Accordingly, greater awareness of interdependence of the environment, economic activity and quality of life raises political, social and scientific issues in addition to those that are directly economic.

Tourism is almost wholly dependent on the environment. Natural resources and man made resources (historic cities, heritage buildings and sites, monuments etc) constitute the primary source of tourism. Any degradation of the primary sources is likely to lead to a decline of tourism. Therefore, their analysis within economics is particularly relevant to tourism.

Key Environmental Issues

International business and holiday tourism travel, according to the World Trade Organization (WTO, 2006) has grown at the rate of 5,4 percent and total 826 million arrivals. The domestic tourism is estimated to be ten times bigger. Major economic, environmental and social impacts follow this mass movement. In addition to the primary sources, tourists require the secondary supportive sources such as accommodation, transport facilities, shops, restaurants and other facilities which entail physical changes and expansion in general economic activity.

Like other economic activities, tourism consumes resources. Today, tourism is one of the major economic activities in the world. It contributes roughly 6 per cent of the world income. Naturally, it has a marked impact on the demand for exhaustible and renewable resources. It generates significant wastes and thus disposal problems. The operation of tourism firms reflects the market driven characteristics of other economic sectors. Extended tourism expansion or concentration in certain destinations has neglected the long term dependence of the industry on environment and led over exploitation of natural resource base and the generation of non-priced effects.

The environmental effects, widely defined, include cultural and social elements, and are probably the biggest problem of tourism. Areas where overcrowding and overdevelopment occur are often relatively small and possess fragile environments. At peak season visitors can outnumber the resident population. Hosts, tourism firms are seldom aware of the unintentional damage being caused to monuments, paintings, ecosystem. Other effects are more deliberate, e.g. off-road use of vehicles. Excess numbers also increases the demand for secondary resources, water, energy which might be scarce at certain destinations. Loss of flora and fauna occurs due to tourism expansion. The influx of tourists with a different life-style, large financial resources, and non-indigenous services can not only disturb existing economic life but also can destroy the cultures.

These problems have been recognized by many involved in tourism and have become issues of concern. The attainment of sustainable tourism has been seen as the urgent need. It would imply balanced commercialization, resource conservation, waste disposal management, pollution control, etc. Attention has to be diverted on 'ecotourism'.

Environmental impact of tourism is most visible in tourist destinations. But effects are also visible at points of origin and transit. For example, the output of aircrafts, ferries, buses, cars equipment and promotional material consumes productive and energy resources and generates waste in origin areas while travel creates pollution in the atmosphere and adversely effects the environment of areas traversed. These problems have come to be increasingly addressed in the 1990s, but serious efforts to mitigate them have lacked. This in part is reflection on the government's failure to seriously commit to pursue the environmental policies and in part lack of comprehension by the business companies of the environmental issues and objectives.

Economic analysis of resource use and their costs has been expressed in terms of opportunity cost, i.e. the benefits lost by not using them for an alternative use. The guiding principle has been the benefits must outweigh the costs. Given the nature of environmental issues, economists have used cost-benefit analysis (CBA) as a suitable framework for the assessment of monetary and non-monetary costs and benefits, as well as large capital outlays, over a long period over which costs and benefits accrue. Another method used method is the planning balance sheet analysis (PBSA). The method was devised in the 1950s to overcome the fact that many cost benefits are not easily measured in money terms. Using the ranks according to criteria thought to be the 'best' multi-criteria analysis (MCA) has also been developed. Mathematical approach in decision making between alternatives is the analytic hierarchy process developed and used by Saaty (1987).

Issues in Tourism

Very often mentioned and discussed issues in tourism generally refer to:

- Sustainable development
- Sustainable tourism
- Maximum sustainable income
- Resources conservation
- Recycling
- Market failures

Sustainable Development

Sustainability of economic development has become the catchword since Brundtland Commission Report was published in 1987 and Rio Declaration in 1992 defined a set of principles that define actions and agreements in which biodiversity, climate change, forest management and conservation were accorded prominence along with a priority to be given to the poorest sections of population. The essence of sustainable development is to manage world economies in such a way that the present needs should be met without impairing the capacity to meet the future needs. The implication of such a strategy is that the growth rates will have to be moderated. Moreover, it has been stressed that quality of life, that can not be measured in monetary terms, should be taken into account. Reductions in adverse externalities such as chemical pollution, noise levels, air and water quality etc. should be taken as measures. Further, the cost of production should be inclusive of social and environmental costs.

The main issue associated with sustainable development is how to reconcile economic development and growth with open access public good and nature of the natural environment which consequently suffers from detrimental externalities. We feel that in a sense sustainable development, although initially partial only, can be achieved through various types of sustainability, e.g. sustainable agriculture, sustainable cities, sustainable ecological systems and sustainable tourism.

Sustainable Tourism

Sustainability should be the cornerstone of the development of tourism since the natural environment constitutes most of its primary resource base. Moreover, with growing awareness of both tourists and residents, firms and governments are under increased pressure to take concrete action to attain sustainability. In tourism sector experts as well as governments are trying to enforce the concept of 'viable tourism' as sustainability in the commercial sense that business is profitable and will survive.

So far, the concrete measures taken by firms confine to the conservation of energy and materials and minimization of wastes as a means of cutting their costs and thus increase revenues and profits. Firms have also taken the concern of tourists and residents alike that tourism should be environmentally responsible. In order to achieve such effect firms need to comply with environmental regulations and standards. However, there is no coherent strategy on sustainability because the past incentives have generated tourism expansion only. Because of a largely fragmented structure of tourism the issue remains complex and only the public sector has the potential to resolve.

Tourist Transport

Tourism and Air Transport industry are complement each other. Tourism depends on transportation to bring visitors, while the transportation industry depends on tourism to generate demand for its services. The growth in tourism industry directly reflects onto the air transportation. Over the last 25 years, the number of international tourists has more than doubled. The expansion of international tourism has a large impact on the discipline of transport geography.

Transport is the cause and the effect of the growth of tourism. To start with, the improved facilities have stimulated tourism, and the expansion of tourism has stimulated transport. Accessibility is the main function behind the basics of tourism transport. In order to access the areas that are mainly aimed, tourists will use any transportation mode. However, air transport is the main mode for international tourism. Air transport plays a dominant role in inter-regional movements of tourists, which normally entails travel over long-distance. Growth rates of international air traffic are pegged with growth rates of international tourism. Attractive package tours, competitive airfare attract more and more tourist day by days, therefore both the industry is expanding rapidly.

Transport policies and decisions of governments can make a big difference in the destinations available to tourists, for instance the Suvarnabhumi airport Bangkok, Thailand. Air transport is far advance than the transport mode. Air transport has revolutionized the geographical aspect of distances; the most remote areas can now be attained, any journey around the world can be measured in terms of hours of travelling. With jet that, can reach up to 1950 km/hrs, international tourism is no longer an on going adventure.

About 6.7 million jobs worldwide are in tourism industry directly supported by the spending of foreign visitors arriving by air. Taking into account both the overseas visors and work force employed it can be said that the Industry is giant in shape "The worlds largest industry of Travel and Tourism". How big the airline industry and its market share are an example will give you a clear image-in a statistics it shown that, American Airlines saves US$40,000 in a year by eliminating one olive from each salad served in first class only.

In the modern world, travelling is more centred to the annual holidays and can be fairly well predicted. The demand in international and even national transport infrastructures implies a very large number of people who wants to move in an efficient, fast and inexpensive manner. It requires heavy investments and complex organization. Well-organized terminals and intelligently planned schedules are essential in promoting effective transportation facilities for tourists, notably since the industry is growing at a fast rate.

Tourism dominantly takes place in Europe and North America. Travelling has always been an important feature of society. First the explorers travelled the world to learn more about geographical regions, potential markets and to exploit resources. As time moved on as transportation became more reliable definitely the air transportation, travelling became a mundane activity taking place in an organized environment, tourism. The importance of tourism as an economic activity has increased dramatically in recent years.

The travel and tourism industry employs 72 million people worldwide. Global tourism expenditure is estimated to be nearly

US$ 3 trillion. Tourism accounts directly for 3.8% of worlds GDP. Tourism is expected to maintain its growth by 2014, the World Travel and Tourism Council expects the torsion industry to employ more than 84 million people globally.

Tourism as an Up coming Industry

The World Tourism Organization (UNWTO) forecasts that international tourism will continue growing at the average annual rate of 4 %. By 2020 Europe will remain the most popular destination, but its share will drop from 60 % in 1995 to 46 %. Long haul will grow slightly faster than intraregional travel and by 2020 its share will increase from 18 % in 1995 to 24 %. With the advent of e-commerce, tourism products have become one of the most traded items on the Internet. Tourism products and services have been made available through intermediaries, although tourism providers (hotels, airlines, etc.) can sell their services directly. This has put pressure on intermediaries from both on-line and traditional shops. It has been suggested there is a strong correlation between Tourism expenditure per capita and the degree to which countries play in the global context. Not only as a result of the important economic contribution of the tourism industry, but also as an indicator of the degree of confidence with which global citizens leverage the resources of the globe for the benefit of their local economies. Space tourism is expected to "take off" in the first quarter of the 21st century, although compared with traditional destinations the number of tourists in orbit will remain low until technologies such as a space elevator make space travel cheap. Technological improvement is likely to make possible air-ship hotels, based either on solar-powered airplanes or large dirigibles. Underwater hotels, such as Hydropolis, expected to open in Dubai in 2009. On the ocean tourists will be welcomed by ever larger cruise ships and perhaps floating cities.

Some futurists expect that movable hotel "pods" will be created that could be temporarily erected anywhere on the planet, where building a permanent resort would be unacceptable politically, economically or environmentally.

International Travel Tips

1. Check the latest travel advice for your destination and subscribe to receive free e-mail notification each time the travel advice for your destination is updated.

2. Take out appropriate travel insurance to cover hospital treatment, medical evacuation and any activities, including adventure sports, in which you plan to participate.
3. Before travelling overseas register your travel and contact details online or at the local Australian embassy, high commission or consulate once you arrive, so we can contact you in an emergency.
4. Obey the law Consular assistance cannot override local laws, even where local laws appear harsh or unjust by Australian standards.
5. Check if you require visas for the country or countries you are visiting or transiting. Be aware that a visa does not guarantee entry.
6. Make copies of your passport details, insurance policy, traveller checks, visas and credit card numbers. Carry one copy in a separate place to the originals and leave a copy with someone at home.
7. Check with health professionals for information on recommended vaccinations or other precautions and find out about overseas laws on travelling with medicines.
8. Make sure your passport has at least six months validity and carry additional copies of your passport photo with you in case you need a replacement passport while overseas.
9. Leave a copy of your travel itinerary with someone at home and keep in regular contact with friends and relatives while overseas.

High Fliers

* To beat jetlag, book an overnight flight or one that arrives in the evening when travelling east so you can either catch your sleep on the flight or as soon as you get in to your destination.
* To prevent the swelling of feet as is wont to happen on long flights, walk in the aisle at intervals and try not to take off your shoes.
* Refrain from OD-ing on the free booze when on a flight, as too much alcohol causes dehydration. Tank up instead on aqua-pura.

* When making flight reservation, remember to request for special meals if you have any food restrictions.
* After September 11, airlines follow very strict security procedures. So make sure you reach the airport for check in well before departure time. Its best to check with the airline regarding how much in advance you should be at the airport.
* If your baggage does not arrive on the same flight as you, fill out a Property Irregularity Report (PIR), with a description of the baggage, a list of contents and address to which it should be forwarded. If your baggage does not arrive at all, place a claim with the airline within 21 days.
* Overbooking is a fact of life in the airline industry. If you are not in a particular hurry to get to your destination then volunteer to give your seat up and take the next flight. The airline will provide you a hotel room and other frills, so you can end up having an extended vacation at the airlines expense!
* Do not accept any package from a stranger.
* For a smooth ride on a plane, choose the seats located near the wings as if the plane hits an air pocket, this is where you will get the least amount of bumps.
* If you are planning to watch the in flight movie, choose the fourth or fifth row from the screen to avoid getting a neck cramp.
* If you are prone to motion sickness, take an anti sickness pill before the flight. The pill won't help much, if you have it after you have started feeling sick!
* Abide by the list of items prohibited on board and carry most items like skis/cues/walking canes/sticks/Swiss knives in checked in baggage-this smoothens the check-in process plus avoids the risk of confiscation and unnecessary delays.
* Last and this is equally important-report any unattended items in the airport or aircraft to the nearest airport or airline personnel.
* Keep track of the weather at your destination and be prepared, especially if you are going to a hurricane prone area.

Heartbreak Hotel

* Make your hotel reservations in advance, especially if you are visiting a place in peak season. You don't want to be caught without a roof over your head!
* Negotiating room tariffs over the phone? Call the hotel twice to confirm the rates. Note down the name of the person you have talked to and request a written/faxed confirmation. This way you can be sure that you will not be wrongly billed by the hotel.
* Don't depend solely on the hotel's alarm service. Carry your own little alarm clock to catch an early morning flight or that pre-dawn sightseeing trip.
* When you check into your hotel, ask the reception to give you a card with the hotel's name address and telephone number. This will come in handy if you get lost or forget the name of your hotel.
* Check whether your hotel has a hair-dryer, iron, coffee percolator, etc, to avoid carrying these gadgets and also making it easy to skip the 110/220 conversion problem when travelling to foreign countries.

Most hotels frown on guests doing their own laundry in the bathrooms, but if you do need to wash some smalls, carry a length of nylon twine to improvise a clothesline.

The Airlaine Business

An airline provides air transport services for passengers or freight, generally with a recognized operating certificate or license. Airlines lease or own their aircraft with which to supply these services and may form partnerships or alliances with other airlines for mutual benefit.

Airlines vary from those with a single airplane carrying mail or cargo, through full-service international airlines operating hundreds of airplanes. Airline services can be categorized as being intercontinental, intra continental, domestic, or international and may be operated as scheduled services or charters.

Delag, *Deutsche Luftschiffahrts-Aktiengesellschaft* was the world's first airline. It was founded on November 16, 1909 with government assistance, and operated airships manufactured by

The Zeppelin Corporation. Its headquarters were in Frankfurt. The five oldest non-dirigible airlines that still exist are Australia's Qantas, Netherlands' KLM, Colombia's Avianca, Czech Republic's Czech Airlines and Mexico's Mexicana. KLM first flew in May 1920 while Qantas (for the Queensland and Northern Territory Aerial Services Limited) was founded in Queensland, Australia in late 1920.

The DC-3, often regarded as one of the most influential aircraft in the history of commercial aviation, revolutionized the aviation industry.

Tony Jannus conducted the United States' scheduled commercial airline flight on 1 January 1914 for the Saint Petersburg-routes, Braniff Airways, American Airlines, Delta Air Lines, United Airlines (originally a division of Boeing), Trans World Airlines, Northwest Airlines, and Eastern Air Lines, to name a few. Service during the early 1920s was sporadic: most airlines at the time were focused on carrying bags of mail. In 1925, however, the Ford Motor Company bought out the Stout Aircraft Company and began construction of the all-metal Ford Trimotor, which became the first successful American airliner. With a 12-passenger capacity, the Trimotor made passenger service potentially profitable. Air service was seen as a supplement to rail service in the American transportation network. At the same time, Juan Trippe began a crusade to create an air network that would link America to the world, and he achieved this goal through his airline, Pan American World Airways, with a fleet of flying boats that linked Los Angeles to Shanghai and Boston to London. Pan Am and Northwest Airways were the only U.S. airlines to go international before the 1940s. With the introduction of the Boeing 247 and Douglas DC-3 in the 1930s, the U.S. airline industry was generally profitable, even during the Great Depression. This trend continued until the beginning of World War II.

Development Since 1945

In October 1945, the American Export Airlines became the first airline to offer regular commercial flights between North America and Europe. Shown here is Am Ex Boeing 377 *Stratocruiser* in 1949.

As governments met to set the standards and scope for an emergent civil air industry toward the end of the war, the U.S. took a position of maximum operating freedom; U.S. airline companies were not as hard-hit as European and the few Asian ones had been. This preference for "open skies" operating regimes continues, within limitations, to this day.

World War II, like World War I, brought new life to the airline industry. Many airlines in the Allied countries were flush from lease contracts to the military, and foresaw a future explosive demand for civil air transport, for both passengers and cargo. They were eager to invest in the newly emerging flagships of air travel such as the Boeing Stratocruiser, Lockheed Constellation, and Douglas DC-6. Most of these new aircraft were based on American bombers such as the B-29, which had spearheaded research into new technologies such as pressurization. Most offered increased efficiency from both added speed and greater payload.

In the 1950s, the De Havilland Comet, Boeing 707, Douglas DC-8, and Sud Aviation Caravelle became the first flagships of the Jet Age in the West, while the Soviet Union bloc had Tupolev Tu-104 and Tupolev Tu-124 in the fleets of state-owned carriers such as Czechoslovak ESA, Soviet Aeroflot and East-German Interflug. The Vickers Viscount and Lockheed L-188 Electra inaugurated turboprop transport.

The next big boost for the airlines would come in the 1970s, when the Boeing 747, McDonnell Douglas DC-10, and Lockheed L-1011 inaugurated widebody ("jumbo jet") service, which is still the standard in international travel. The Tupolev Tu-144 and its Western counterpart, Concorde, made supersonic travel a reality. Concorde first flew in 1969 and operated through 2003. In 1972, Airbus began producing Europe's most commercially successful line of airliners to date. The added efficiencies for these aircraft were often not in speed, but in passenger capacity, payload, and range. Airbus also features modern electronic cockpits that were common across their aircraft to enable pilots to fly multiple models with minimal cross-training.

The deregulation of the American airline industry increased the financial troubles of the iconic airline which ultimately filed for bankruptcy in December 1991.

1978's U.S. airline industry deregulation lowered barriers for new airlines just as a downturn occurred. New start-ups entered during the downturn, during which time they found aircraft and funding, contracted hangar and maintenance services, trained new employees, and recruited laid off staff from other airlines.

As the business cycle returned to normalcy, major airlines dominated their routes through aggressive pricing and additional capacity offerings, often swamping new startups. Only America West Airlines (which has since merged with US Airways) remained a significant survivor from this new entrant era, as dozens, even hundreds, have gone under.

In many ways, the biggest winner in the deregulated environment was the air passenger. Indeed, the U.S. witnessed an explosive growth in demand for air travel, as many millions who had never or rarely flown before became regular fliers, even joining frequent flyer loyalty programs and receiving free flights and other benefits from their flying. New services and higher frequencies meant that business fliers could fly to another city, do business, and return the same day, for almost any point in the country. Air travel's advantages put intercity bus lines under pressure, and most have withered away.

By the 1980s, almost half of the total flying in the world took place in the U.S., and today the domestic industry operates over 10,000 daily departures nationwide. Toward the end of the century, a new style of low cost airline emerged, offering a no-frills product at a lower price. Southwest Airlines, JetBlue, AirTran Airways, Skybus Airlines and other low-cost carriers began to represent a serious challenge to the so-called "legacy airlines", as did their low-cost counterparts in many other countries. Their commercial viability represented a serious competitive threat to the legacy carriers. However, of these, ATA and Skybus have since ceased operations.

Thus the last 50 years of the airline industry have varied from reasonably profitable, to devastatingly depressed. As the first major market to deregulate the industry in 1978, U.S. airlines have experienced more turbulence than almost any other country or region. Today, American Airlines is the only U.S. legacy carrier to survive bankruptcy-free.

The Airline "Bailout"

Congress passed the Air Transportation Safety and System Stabilization Act (P.L. 107-42) in response to a severe liquidity crisis facing the industry in the aftermath of the September 11th terrorist attacks. Congress sought to compensate carriers for both the cost of the four-day federal shutdown of the airlines and the incremental losses incurred through December 31, 2001 as a result of the terrorist attacks. Congress expressly sought to preserve a viable, safe, and efficient air transportation system. In recognition of the essential national economic role of a healthy aviation system, Congress authorized partial compensation of up to $5 billion in cash subject to review by the Department of Transportation and up to $10 billion in loan guarantees subject to review by a newly created Air Transportation Stabilization Board (ATSB). The applications to DOT for reimbursements were subjected to rigorous multi-year reviews not only by DOT program personnel but also by the Government Accountability Office and the DOT Inspector General.

Ultimately, the federal government provided $4.6 billion in one-time, subject-to-income-tax cash reimbursements to 427 U.S. air carriers, including numerous charter and cargo carriers. (Passenger carriers operating scheduled service received approximately $4 billion, subject to tax.) In addition, the ATSB approved loan guarantees to six airlines totaling approximately $1.6 billion. Data from the Treasury Department show that taxpayers eventually recouped the $1.6 billion and a profit of $339 million from the fees, interest and stock associated with loan guarantees.

European Airline Industry

The Imperial Airways Empire Terminal, Victoria, London. Trains ran from here to flying boats in Southampton, and to Croydon Airport. The first countries in Europe to embrace air transport were Finland, France, Germany, the Netherlands and the United Kingdom. KLM, the oldest carrier still operating under its original name, was founded in 1919. The first flight (operated on behalf of KLM by Aircraft Transport and Travel) transported two English passengers to Schiphol, Amsterdam from London in 1920. Like other major European airlines of the time, KLM's early growth depended heavily on the needs to service links with far-flung colonial possessions (Dutch Indies). It is only after the loss of the Dutch Empire that KLM found itself based at a small country with few potential passengers, depending heavily on transfer traffic, and was one of the first to introduce the hub-system to facilitate easy connections.

France began an air mail service to Morocco in 1919 that was bought out in 1927, renamed Aeropostale, and injected with capital to become a major international carrier. In 1933, Aeropostale went bankrupt, was nationalized and merged with several other airlines into what became Air France.

In Finland, the charter establishing Aero O/Y (now Finnair, one of the oldest still-operating airlines in the world) was signed in the city of Helsinki on September 12, 1923. Junkers F 13 D-335 became the first aircraft of the company, when Aero took delivery of it on March 14, 1924. The first flight was between Helsinki and Tallinn, capital of Estonia, and it took place on March 20, 1924, one week later.

Germany's Lufthansa began in 1926. Lufthansa, unlike most other airlines at the time, became a major investor in airlines outside of Europe, providing capital to Varig and Avianca. German airliners built by Junkers, Dornier, and Fokker were the most advanced in the world at the time. The peak of German air travel came in the mid-1930s, when Nazi propaganda ministers approved the start of commercial zeppelin service: the big airships were a symbol of industrial might, but the fact that they used flammable hydrogen gas raised safety concerns that culminated with the Hindenburg disaster of 1937. The reason they used hydrogen instead of the not-flammable helium gas was because the United States was the only source of helium and at the time the Americans refused to deliver helium to Germany.

The British company Aircraft Transport and Travel commenced a London to Paris service on August 25, 1919, this was the world's first regular international flight. The United Kingdom's flag carrier during this period was Imperial Airways, which became BOAC (British Overseas Airways Co.) in 1939. Imperial Airways used huge Handley-Page biplanes for routes between London, the Middle East, and India: images of Imperial aircraft in the middle of the Rub'al Khali, being maintained by Bedouins, are among the most famous pictures from the heyday of the British Empire.

In Soviet Union the Chief Administration of the Civil Air Fleet was established in 1921. One of its first acts was to help found

Deutsch-Russische Luftverkehrs A.G. (Deruluft), a German-Russian joint venture to provide air transport from Russia to the West. Domestic air service began around the same time, when Dobrolyot started operations on 15 July 1923 between Moscow and Nizhni Novgorod. Since 1932 all operations had been carried under the name Aeroflot. By the end of the 1930s Aeroflot had become the world's largest airline, employing more than 4,000 pilots and 60,000 other service personnel and operating around 3,000 aircraft (of which 75% were considered obsolete by its own standards). During the Soviet era Aeroflot was synonymous with Russian civil aviation, as it was the only air carrier. It became the first airline in the world to operate sustained regular jet services on 15 September 1956 with the Tupolev Tu-104.

Deregulation

Deregulation of the European Union airspace in the early 1990s has had substantial effect on structure of the industry there. The shift towards 'budget' airlines on shorter routes has been significant. Airlines such as EasyJet and Ryanair have grown at the expense of the traditional national airlines.

There has also been a trend for these national airlines themselves to be privatised such as has occurred for Aer Lingus (Ireland) and British Airways. Other national airlines, including Italy's Alitalia, have suffered-particularly with the rapid increase of oil prices in early 2008.

Asian Airline Industry

India was one of the first countries to embrace civil aviation. One of the first Asian airline companies was Air India, which had its beginning as Tata Airlines in 1932, a division of Tata Sons Ltd. (now Tata Group). The airline was founded by India's leading industrialist, JRD Tata. On October 15, 1932, J. R. D. Tata himself flew a single engined De Havilland Puss Moth carrying air mail (postal mail of Imperial Airways) from Karachi to Bombay via Ahmedabad. The aircraft continued to Madras via Bellary piloted by Royal Air Force pilot Nevill Vincent. Tata Airlines was also one of the world's first major airlines which began its operations without any support from the Government.

Philippine Airlines was founded on February 26, 1941, making it one of Asia's oldest carriers and also the oldest operating under its current name. The airline was started by a group of businessmen led by Andres Soriano, hailed as one of the Philippines' leading industrialists at the time. The airline's first flight was made on March 15, 1941 with a single Beech Model 18 NPC-54 aircraft, which started its daily services between Manila (from Nielson Field) and Baguio, later to expand with larger aircraft such as the DC-3 and Vickers Viscount.

With the outbreak of World War II, the airline presence in Asia came to a relative halt, with many new flag carriers donating their aircraft for military aid and other uses. Following the end of the war in 1945, regular commercial service was restored in India and Tata Airlines became a public limited company on July 29, 1946 under the name Air India. After the independence of India, 49% of the airline was acquired by the Government of India. In return, the airline was granted status to operate international services from India as the designated flag carrier under the name Air India International.

On July 31, 1946, a chartered Philippine Airlines (PAL) DC-4 ferried 40 American servicemen to Oakland, California from Nielson Airport in Makati City with stops in Guam, Wake Island, Johnston Atoll and Honolulu, Hawaii, making PAL the first Asian airline to cross the Pacific Ocean. A regular service between Manila and San Francisco was started in December. It was during this year that the airline was designated as the flag carrier of Philippines. During the era of decolonization, newly-born Asian countries started to embrace air transport. Among the first Asian carriers during the era were Cathay Pacific (founded in September 1946), Orient Airways (later Pakistan International Airlines; founded in October 1946), Malayan Airlines (later Singapore and Malaysian Airlines; founded in 1947), Garuda Indonesia in 1949, Japan Airlines in 1951, and Korean Air in 1962.

Latin American Airline Industry

TAM Airlines is the largest airline in Latin America in terms of number of annual passengers flown.

Along the first countries to have regular airlines in Latin America were Colombia with Avianca, Chile with LAN Chile (today LAN Airlines), Dominican Republic with Air Dominicana, Mexico with Mexicana de Aviacion, Brazil with Varig, and TACA as a brand of several airlines of Central American countries

(Honduras, El Salvador, Costa Rica, Guatemala and Nicaragua). All the previous airlines started regular operations before World War II.

The air travel market has evolved rapidly over recent years in Latin America. Some industry estimations over 2000 new aircraft will begin service over the next five years in this region.

These airlines serve domestic flights within their countries, as well as connections within Latin America and also overseas flights to North America, Europe, Australia, Africa and Asia. Just one airline, LAN (Latin American Networks) has international subsidiaries: Chile as the central operation along with Peru, Ecuador, Argentina and some operations in the Dominican Republic.

The main hubs in Latin America are Sao Paulo and Rio de Janeiro in Brazil, Bogòta in Colombia, Caracas in Venezuela, Guayaquil in Ecuador, Lima in Peru, Mexico City in Mexico, Buenos Aires in Argentina, Santiago in Chile and Santo Domingo in the Dominican Republic.

Regulatory Considerations

National

Pakistan International Airlines Boeing 747-300. The Government of Pakistan is the majority stake-holder in the country's flag carrier.

Many countries have national airlines that the government owns and operates. Fully private airlines are subject to a great deal of government regulation for economic, political, and safety concerns. For instance, the government often intervenes to halt airline labour actions in order to protect the free flow of people, communications, and goods between different regions without compromising safety.

The United States, Australia, and to a lesser extent Brazil, Mexico, the United Kingdom and Japan have "deregulated" their airlines. In the past, these governments dictated airfares, route networks, and other operational requirements for each airline. Since deregulation, airlines have been largely free to negotiate their own operating arrangements with different airports, enter and exit routes easily, and to levy airfares and supply flights according to market demand.

The entry barriers for new airlines are lower in a deregulated market, and so the U.S. has seen hundreds of airlines start up (sometimes for only a brief operating period). This has produced far greater competition than before deregulation in most markets, and average fares tend to drop 20% or more. The added competition, together with pricing freedom, means that new entrants often take market share with highly reduced rates that, to a limited degree, full service airlines must match. This is a major constraint on profitability for established carriers, which tend to have a higher cost base. As a result, profitability in a deregulated market is uneven for most airlines. These forces have caused some major airlines to go out of business, in addition to most of the poorly established new entrants.

International

Singapore Airlines Airbus A380 lands at Changi Airport. The Singapore Airlines was the first international airline to operate the A380, the world's largest passenger airliner.

Groups such as the International Civil Aviation Organization establish worldwide standards for safety and other vital concerns. Most international air traffic is regulated by bilateral agreements between countries, which designate specific carriers to operate on specific routes.

The model of such an agreement was the Bermuda Agreement between the US and UK following World War II, which designated airports to be used for transatlantic flights and gave each government the authority to nominate carriers to operate routes.

Bilateral agreements are based on the "freedoms of the air," a group of generalized traffic rights ranging from the freedom to overfly a country to the freedom to provide domestic flights within a country (a very rarely granted right known as cabotage). Most agreements permit airlines to fly from their home country to designated airports in the other country: some also extend the freedom to provide continuing service to a third country, or to another destination in the other country while carrying passengers from overseas.

In the 1990s, "open skies" agreements became more common. These agreements take many of these regulatory powers from state governments and open up international routes to further competition. Open skies agreements have met some criticism, particularly within the European Union, whose airlines would be at a comparative disadvantage with the United States' because of cabotage restrictions.

Economic Considerations

Juan Trippe, the founder of Pan American World Airways, surveying his globe. The collapse of Pan Am, an airline often credited for shaping the international airline industry, in December 1991 highlighted the financial complexities faced by major airline companies.

Historically, air travel has survived largely through state support, whether in the form of equity or subsidies. The airline industry as a whole has made a cumulative loss during its 120-year history, once the costs include subsidies for aircraft development and airport construction.

One argument is that positive externalities, such as higher growth due to global mobility, outweigh the microeconomic losses and justify continuing government intervention. A historically high level of government intervention in the airline industry can be seen as part of a wider political consensus on strategic forms of transport, such as highways and railways, both of which receive public funding in most parts of the world. Profitability is likely to improve in the future as privatization continues and more competitive low-cost carriers proliferate.

Although many countries continue to operate state-owned or parastatal airlines, many large airlines today are privately owned and are therefore governed by microeconomic principles in order to maximize shareholder profit.

Ticket Revenue

Airlines assign prices to their services in an attempt to maximize profitability. The pricing of airline tickets has become increasingly complicated over the years and is now largely determined by computerized yield management systems.

Because of the complications in scheduling flights and maintaining profitability, airlines have many loopholes that can be used by the knowledgeable traveller. Many of these airfare secrets are becoming more and more known to the general public, so airlines are forced to make constant adjustments.

Most airlines use differentiated pricing, a form of price discrimination, in order to sell air services at varying prices simultaneously to different segments. Factors influencing the price include the days remaining until departure, the booked load factor, the forecast of total demand by price point, competitive pricing in force, and variations by day of week of departure and by time of day. Carriers often accomplish this by dividing each cabin of the aircraft (first, business and economy) into a number of travel classes for pricing purposes.

A complicating factor is that of origin-destination control ("O&D control"). Someone purchasing a ticket from Melbourne to Sydney (as an example) for AU$200 is competing with someone else who wants to fly Melbourne to Los Angeles through Sydney on the same flight, and who is willing to pay AU$1400.

Should the airline prefer the $1400 passenger, or the $200 passenger plus a possible Sydney-Los Angeles passenger willing to pay $1300? Airlines have to make hundreds of thousands of similar pricing decisions daily.

The advent of advanced computerized reservations systems in the late 1970s, most notably Sabre, allowed airlines to easily perform cost-benefit analyses on different pricing structures, leading to almost perfect price discrimination in some cases (that is, filling each seat on an aircraft at the highest price that can be charged without driving the consumer elsewhere).

The intense nature of airfare pricing has led to the term "fare war" to describe efforts by airlines to undercut other airlines on competitive routes. Through computers, new airfares can be published quickly and efficiently to the airlines' sales channels. For this purpose the airlines use the Airline Tariff Publishing Company (ATPCO), who distribute latest fares for more than 500 airlines to Computer Reservation Systems across the world.

The extent of these pricing phenomena is strongest in "legacy" carriers. In contrast, low fare carriers usually offer preannounced and simplified price structure, and sometimes quote prices for each leg of a trip separately.

Computers also allow airlines to predict, with some accuracy, how many passengers will actually fly after making a reservation to fly. This allows airlines to overbook their flights enough to fill the aircraft while accounting for "no-shows," but not enough (in most cases) to force paying passengers off the aircraft for lack of seats.

Since an average of S! of all seats are flown empty, stimulative pricing for low demand flights coupled with overbooking on high demand flights can help reduce this figure. This is especially crucial during tough economic times as airlines undertake massive cuts to ticket prices in order to retain demand.

Operating Costs

Full-service airlines have a high level of fixed and operating costs in order to establish and maintain air services: labour, fuel, airplanes, engines, spares and parts, IT services and networks, airport equipment, airport handling services, sales distribution, catering, training, aviation insurance and other costs. Thus all but a small percentage of the income from ticket sales is paid out to a wide variety of external providers or internal cost centres. Moreover, the industry is structured so that airlines often act as tax collectors. Airline fuel is untaxed because of a series of treaties existing between countries. Ticket prices include a number of fees, taxes and surcharges beyond the control of airlines. Airlines are also responsible for enforcing government regulations. If airlines carry passengers without proper documentation on an international flight, they are responsible for returning them back to the original country.

Analysis of the 1992–1996 period shows that every player in the air transport chain is far more profitable than the airlines, who collect and pass through fees and revenues to them from ticket sales. While airlines as a whole earned 6% return on capital employed (2-3.5% less than the cost of capital), airports earned 10%, catering companies 10-13%, handling companies 11-14%, aircraft lessors 15%, aircraft manufacturers 16%, and global distribution companies more than 30%. (Source: Spinetta, 2000, quoted in Doganis, 2002)

In contrast, Southwest Airlines has been the most profitable of airline companies since 1973.

The widespread entrance of a new breed of low cost airlines beginning at the turn of the century has accelerated the demand that full service carriers control costs. Many of these low cost companies emulate Southwest Airlines in various respects, and like Southwest, they are able to eke out a consistent profit throughout all phases of the business cycle.

As a result, a shakeout of airlines is occurring in the U.S. and elsewhere. United Airlines, Continental Airlines (twice), US Airways (twice), Delta Air Lines, and Northwest Airlines have all declared. Some argue that it would be far better for the industry as a whole if a wave of actual closures were to reduce the number of "undead" airlines competing with healthy airlines while being artificially protected from creditors via bankruptcy law. On the other hand, some have pointed out that the reduction in capacity would be short lived given that there would be large quantities of relatively new aircraft that bankruptcies would want to get rid of and would re-enter the market either as increased fleets for the survivors or the basis of cheap planes for new startups.

Where an airline has established an engineering base at an airport then there may be considerable economic advantages in using that same airport as a preferred focus (or "hub") for its scheduled flights.

Assets and Financing

Airline financing is quite complex, since airlines are highly leveraged operations. Not only must they purchase (or lease) new airliner bodies and engines regularly, they must make major long-term fleet decisions with the goal of meeting the demands of their markets while producing a fleet that is relatively economical to operate and maintain. Compare Southwest Airlines and their reliance on a single airplane type (the Boeing 737 and derivatives), with the now defunct Eastern Air Lines which operated 17 different aircraft types, each with varying pilot, engine, maintenance, and support needs.

A second financial issue is that of hedging oil and fuel purchases, which are usually second only to labour in its relative cost to the company. However, with the current high fuel prices it has become the largest cost to an airline. While hedging instruments can be expensive, they can easily pay for themselves many times over in periods of increasing fuel costs, such as in the 2000–2005 period.

In view of the congestion apparent at many international orts, the ownership of slots at certain airports (the right to take-off or land an aircraft at a particular time of day or night) has become a significant tradable asset for many airlines. Clearly take-off slots at popular times of the day can be critical in attracting the more profitable business traveller to a given airline's flight and in establishing a competitive advantage against a competing airline. If a particular city has two or more airports, market forces will tend to attract the less profitable routes, or those on which competition is weakest, to the less congested airport, where slots are likely to be more available and therefore cheaper. Other factors, such as surface transport facilities and onward connections, will also affect the relative appeal of different airports and some long distance flights may need to operate from the one with the longest runway.

Airline Partnerships

A Japan Airlines Boeing 777-300 with special Oneworld livery. Oneworld is the third largest airline alliance after Star Alliance and SkyTeam.

Code sharing is the most common type of airline partnership; it involves one airline selling tickets for another airline's flights under its own airline code. An early example of this was Japan Airlines' code sharing partnership with Aeroflot in the 1960s on flights from Tokyo to Moscow: Aeroflot operated the flights using Aeroflot aircraft, but JAL sold tickets for the flights as if they were JAL flights. This practice allows airlines to expand their operations, at least on paper, into parts of the world where they cannot afford to establish bases or purchase aircraft. Another example was the Austrian-Sabena partnership on the Vienna-Brussels-New York JFK route during the late '60s, using a Sabena Boeing 707 with Austrian colours.

Since airline reservation requests are often made by city-pair (such as "show me flights from Chicago to Düsseldorf"), an airline who is able to code share with another airline for a variety of routes might be able to be listed as indeed offering a Chicago-Düsseldorf flight. The passenger is advised however, that Airline 1 operates the flight from say Chicago to Amsterdam, and Airline 2 operates the continuing flight (on a different airplane, sometimes from another terminal) to Düsseldorf. Thus the primary rationale for code sharing is to expand one's service offerings in city-pair terms so as to increase sales.

A more recent development is the airline alliance, which became prevalent in the 1990s. These alliances can act as virtual mergers to get around government restrictions. Groups of airlines such as the Star Alliance, Oneworld, and SkyTeam coordinate their passenger service programs (such as lounges and frequent flyer programs), offer special interline tickets, and often engage in extensive codesharing (sometimes systemwide). These are increasingly integrated business combinations—sometimes including cross-equity arrangements—in which products, service standards, schedules, and airport facilities are standardized and combined for higher efficiency. One of the first airlines to start an alliance with another airline was KLM, who partnered with Northwest Airlines. Both airlines later entered the SkyTeam alliance after the fusion of KLM and Air France in 2004.

Often the companies combine IT operations, buy fuel, or purchase airplanes as a bloc in order to achieve higher bargaining power. However, the alliances have been most successful at purchasing invisible supplies and services, such as fuel. Airlines usually prefer to purchase items visible to their passengers to differentiate themselves from local competitors. If an airline's main domestic competitor flies Boeing airliners, then the airline may prefer to use Airbus aircraft regardless of what the rest of the alliance chooses.

Environmental Impacts

MODIS tracking of contrails generated by air traffic over the southeastern United States on January 29, 2004.

Aircraft engines emit noise pollution, gases and particulate emissions, and contribute to global warming and global dimming, even though it is one of the least-polluting forms of travel in the world.

Modern turbofan and turboprop engines are considerably more fuel-efficient and less polluting than earlier models. However, despite this, the rapid growth of air travel in recent years contributes to an increase in total pollution attributable to aviation, offsetting some of the reductions achieved by automobiles. In the EU greenhouse gas emissions from aviation increased by 87% between 1990 and 2006.

CO2 emissions from the jet fuel burned per passenger on an average 3200 kilometres (1992 miles) airline flight is about 353 kilograms (776 pounds). Loss of natural habitat potential associated with the jet fuel burned per passenger on a 3200 kilometres (1992 miles) airline flight is estimated to be 250 square meters (2700 square feet).

In the context of climate change and peak oil, there is a debate about possible taxation of air travel and the inclusion of aviation in an emissions trading scheme, with a view to ensuring that the total external costs of aviation are taken into account. The airline industry is responsible for about 11 percent of greenhouse gases emitted by the U.S. transportation sector. Boeing estimates that biofuels could reduce flight-related greenhouse-gas emissions by 60 to 80 percent. The solution would be blending algae fuels with existing jet fuel:

- Boeing and Air New Zealand are collaborating with leading Brazilian biofuels maker Tecbio and Aquaflow Bionomic of New Zealand and other jet biofuel developers around the world.
- Virgin Atlantic and Virgin Green Fund are looking into the technology as part of a biofuels initiative.

Call Signs

Each operator of a scheduled or charter flight uses an airline call sign when communicating with airports or air traffic control centres. Most of these call-signs are derived from the airline's trade name, but for reasons of history, marketing, or the need to reduce ambiguity in spoken English (so that pilots do not mistakenly make navigational decisions based on instructions issued to a different aircraft), some airlines and air forces use call-signs less obviously connected with their trading name. For example, British Airways uses a *Speedbird* call-sign, named after the logo of its predecessor, BOAC, while SkyEurope used *Relax*.

Airline Personnel

The various types of airline personnel include: Flight operations personnel including flight safety personnel.

- Flight crews, responsible for the operation of the aircraft. Flight crew members include:
  - o Pilots (Captain and First Officer: some older aircraft also required a Flight Engineer and or a Navigator)
  - o Flight attendants, (led by a purser on larger aircraft)

  - in-flight security personnel on some airlines (most notably El Al)
- Groundcrew, responsible for operations at airports. Ground crew members include:
  - Aerospace and avionics engineers responsible for certifying the aircraft for flight and management of aircraft maintenance
    - Aerospace engineers, responsible for airframe, powerplant and electrical systems maintenance
    - Avionics engineers responsible for avionics and instruments maintenance
  - Airframe and powerplant technicians
  - Electric System technicians, responsible for maintenance of electrical systems
  - Avionics technicians, responsible for maintenance of avionics
  - Flight dispatchers
  - Baggage handlers
  - Ramp Agents
  - Gate agents
  - Ticket agents
  - Passenger service agents (such as airline lounge employees)
- Reservation agents, usually (but not always) at facilities outside the airport.

Airlines follow a corporate structure where each broad area of operations (such as maintenance, flight operations(including flight safety), and passenger service) is supervised by a vice president. Larger airlines often appoint vice presidents to oversee each of the airline's hubs as well. Airlines employ lawyers to deal with regulatory procedures and other administrative tasks.

Industry Trends

The pattern of ownership has gone from government owned or supported to independent, for-profit public companies. This occurs as regulators permit greater freedom and non-government ownership, in steps that are usually decades apart. This pattern is not seen for all airlines in all regions. The overall trend of demand has been consistently increasing. In the 1950s and 1960s, annual growth rates of 15% or more were common. Annual growth of 5-6% persisted through the 1980s and 1990s. Growth rates are not consistent in all regions, but countries with a de-regulated airline industry have more competition and greater pricing freedom. This results in lower fares and sometimes dramatic spurts in traffic growth. The U.S., Australia, Canada, Japan, Brazil, Mexico, India and other markets exhibit this trend. The industry has been observed to be cyclical in its financial performance. Four or five years of poor earnings precede five or six years of improvement. But profitability even in the good years is generally low, in the range of 2-3% net profit after interest and tax.

In times of profit, airlines lease new generations of airplanes and upgrade services in response to higher demand. Since 1980, the industry has not earned back the cost of capital during the best of times. Conversely, in bad times losses can be dramatically worse. Warren Buffett once said that despite all the money that has been invested in all airlines, the net profit is less than zero. He believes it is one of the hardest businesses to manage.

As in many mature industries, consolidation is a trend. Airline groupings may consist of limited bilateral partnerships, long-term, multi-faceted alliances between carriers, equity arrangements, mergers, or takeovers. Since governments often restrict ownership and merger between companies in different countries, most consolidation takes place within a country. In the U.S., over 200 airlines have merged, been taken over, or gone out of business since deregulation in 1978. Many international airline managers are lobbying their governments to permit greater consolidation to achieve higher economy and efficiency.

The International Air Transport Association (IATA) is an international industry trade group of airlines headquartered in Montreal, Quebec, Canada, where the International Civil Aviation Organization is also headquartered. IATA's mission is to represent, lead and serve the airline industry. IATA represents some 230 airlines comprising 93% of scheduled international air traffic. The Director General and Chief Executive Officer is Giovanni Bisignani. Currently, IATA is present in over 150 cou History

IATA was formed in April 1945, in Havana, Cuba. It is the successor to the International Air Traffic Association, founded in

The Hague in 1919, the year of the world's first international scheduled services. At its founding, IATA had 57 members from 31 nations, mostly in Europe and North America. Today it has about 230 members from more than 140 nations in every part of the world.

Mission

IATA's stated mission is to represent, lead and serve the airline industry.

Price Setting

One of its core functions is to act as a price setting body for international airfare. In an arrangement going back to 1944, international fare prices have been set through bilateral governmental agreements rather through market mechanisms. Airlines have been granted a special exemption by each of the main regulatory authorities in the world to consult prices with each other through this body.

Originally both domestic and international aviation were highly regulated by IATA. Since 1978 in US and later in Europe, domestic deregulation highlighted the benefits of open markets to consumers in terms of lower fares and companies in terms of more efficient networks. This led to the formation of bilateral "open skies" agreements that weakened IATA's price fixing role. Negotiations are underway since 2003 to create a completely deregulated aviation market covering European and US airspace.

In recent years the organisation has been accused of acting as a cartel, and many low cost carriers are not full IATA members. The European Union's competition authorities are currently investigating the IATA. In 2005, Neelie Kroes, the European Commissioner for Competition, made a proposal to lift the exception to consult prices. In July 2006, the United States Department of Transportation also proposed to withdraw antitrust immunity. IATA teamed with SITA for an electronic ticketing solution.

For fare calculations IATA has divided the world in three regions:

1. South, Central and North America.

2. Europe, Middle East and Africa. IATA Europe includes the geographical Europe and Turkey, Israel, Morocco, Algeria and Tunisia.
3. Asia, Australia, New Zealand and the islands of the Pacific Ocean.

Other Activities

IATA assigns 3-letter IATA Airport Codes and 2-letter IATA airline designators, which are commonly used worldwide. ICAO also assigns airport and airline codes. For Rail&Fly systems, IATA also assigns IATA train station codes. For delay codes, IATA assigns IATA Delay Codes.

IATA is pivotal in the worldwide accreditation of travel agents with exception of the U.S., where this is done by the Airlines Reporting Corporation. Permission to sell airline tickets from the participating carriers is achieved through national member organisations. Over 80% of airlines' sales come from IATA accredited agents. IATA administrates worldwide the Billing and Settlement Plan (BSP) and Cargo Accounts Settlement Systems (CASS) that serve as a facilitator of the sales, reporting and remittance of accredited travel and cargo agencies. Both settlement programmes are ruled by standards and resolutions.

IATA regulates the shipping of dangerous goods and publishes the IATA Dangerous Goods Regulations manual, a globally accepted field source reference for airlines' shipping of hazardous materials.

IATA coordinates the Scheduling process which govern the allocation and exchange of slots at congested airports worldwide, applying fair, transparent and non-discriminatory principles. In consultation with the airline and airport coordinator communities, IATA manages and publishes the industry standards in the Worldwide Scheduling Guidelines (WSG) intended to provide guidance on managing the allocation of slots at airports.

IATA maintains the Timatic database containing cross border passenger documentation requirements. It is used by airlines to determine whether a passenger can be carried, as well as by airlines and travel agents to provide this information to travellers at the time of booking.

IATA publishes standards for use in the airline industry. The Bar Coded Boarding Pass (BCBP) standard defines the 2-

Dimensional (2D) bar code printed on paper boarding passes or sent to mobiles phones for electronic boarding passes.

IATA publishes the IATA Rates of Exchange (IROE) four times per year, used with the Neutral Unit of Construction (NUC) fare currency-neutral construction system that superseded the older Fare Construction Unit (FCU) system in 1989.

In 2004, IATA launched Simplifying the Business-a set of five initiatives which it says will save the industry US$6.5 billion every year. These projects are BCBP, IATA e-freight, CUSS (common use self-service), Baggage Improvement Programme (BIP) and the Fast Travel Programme. In 2003, the IATA Safety Operational Audit (IOSA) was launched with the aim to serve as a standard and worldwide recognized certification of airlines' operational management. The IOSA certification has now become an mandatory requisite for all IATA member airlines.

IATA is member of the Air Transport Action Group (ATAG).

Countries covered through 101 offices around the globe.

International Civil Aviation Organization

The International Civil Aviation Organization (ICAO), a major agency of the United Nations, codifies the principles and techniques of international air navigation and fosters the planning and development of international air transport to ensure safe and orderly growth. Its headquarters are located in the *Quartier International* of Montreal, Canada.

The ICAO Council adopts standards and recommended practices concerning air navigation, its infrastructure, Flight inspection, prevention of unlawful interference, and facilitation of border-crossing procedures for international civil aviation. In addition, the ICAO defines the protocols for air accident investigation followed by transport safety authorities in countries signatory to the Convention on International Civil Aviation, commonly known as the *Chicago Convention.*

The ICAO should not be confused with the International Air Transport Association (IATA), a trade organization for airlines also headquartered in Montreal, or with the Civil Air Navigation Services Organisation (CANSO), an organization for Air Navigation Service Providers (ANSP's) with its headquarters at Amsterdam Airport Schiphol in the Netherlands.

Statute

The 9th edition of the Convention on International Civil Aviation includes modifications from 1948 up to year 2006. The ICAO refers to its current edition of the Convention as the *statute*, and designates it as ICAO Doc 7300/9. The Convention has 18 Annexes. These Annexes are listed by title in the article Convention on International Civil Aviation.

Standards

The ICAO also standardizes certain functions for use in the airline industry, such as the Aeronautical Message Handling System AMHS; this probably makes it a standards organization.

The ICAO defines an International Standard Atmosphere (also known as ICAO Standard Atmosphere), a model of the standard variation of pressure, temperature, density, and viscosity with altitude in the Earth's atmosphere. This is useful in calibrating instruments and designing aircraft.

The ICAO standardizes machine-readable passports worldwide. Such passports have an area where some of the information otherwise written in textual form is written as strings of alphanumeric characters, printed in a manner suitable for optical character recognition. This enables border controllers and other law enforcement agents to process such passports quickly, without having to input the information manually into a computer. ICAO publishes Doc 9303, Machine Readable Travel Documents, the technical standard for machine-readable passports.

A more recent standard is for biometric passports. These contain biometrics to authenticate the identity of travellers. The passport's critical information is stored on a tiny RFID computer chip, much like information stored on smartcards. Like some smartcards, the passport book design calls for an embedded contactless chip that is able to hold digital signature data to ensure the integrity of the passport and the biometric data.

Codes Registered with ICAO

Both ICAO and IATA have their own airport and airline code systems. ICAO uses 4-letter airport codes and 3-letter airline codes. In the continental United States, the ICAO codes are usually the same as the IATA code, with a prefix of "K" — LAX is KLAX. Canada follows a similar pattern, where a prefix of "C" is usually added to an IATA code to find the ICAO code — YEG is CYEG. In the rest of the world, the codes are unrelated, as the IATA code is phonic and the ICAO code is location-based; for example, Charles de Gaulle Airport has an ICAO code of LFPG, and an IATA code of CDG.

ICAO is also responsible for issuing alphanumeric aircraft type codes that contain 2-4 characters. These codes provide the identification that is typically used in flight plans. An example of this is the Boeing 747 that would use (depending on the variant) B741, B742, B743, etc. ICAO provides telephony designators to aircraft operators worldwide. These consist of the three-letter airline identifier and a one-or two-word designator. They are usually, but not always, similar to the aircraft operator name. For example, the identifier for Aer Lingus is EIN and the designator is Shamrock, while Japan Airlines International is JAL and Japan Air. Thus, a flight by Aer Lingus numbered 111 would be written as "EIN111" and pronounced "Shamrock One Eleven" on the radio, while a similarly numbered Japan Airlines flight would be written as "JAL111" and pronounced "Japan Air One Eleven".

ICAO maintains the standards for aircraft registration ("tail numbers"), including the alphanumeric codes that identify the country of registration.

Regions and Regional Offices

ICAO World Headquarters, Montreal, Canada

The ICAO has seven regional offices serving nine regions:

1. Asia and Pacific, Bangkok, Thailand
2. Middle East, Cairo, Egypt
3. Western and Central Africa, Dakar, Senegal
4. South America, Lima, Peru
5. North America, Central America and Caribbean, Mexico City, Mexico
6. Eastern and Southern Africa, Nairobi, Kenya
7. Europe and North Atlantic, Paris, France

Leadership

List of Secretaries General

- Albert Roper (France) (1944-1951)

- Carl Ljungberg (Sweden) (1952-1959)
- Ronald MacAllister Macdonnell (Canada) (1959-1964)
- Bernardus Tielman Twigt (Netherlands) (1964-1970)
- Assad Kotaite (Lebanon) (1970-1976)
- Yves Lambert (France) (1976-1988)
- Shivinder Singh Sidhu (India) (1988-1991)
- Philippe Rochat (Switzerland) (1991-1997)
- Renato Claudio Costa Pereira (Brazil) (1997-2003)
- Taieb Cherif (Algeria) (2003-2009)
- Raymond Benjamin (France) (2009-present)

List of Council Presidents

- Edward Pearson Warner (United States) (1947-1957)
- Walter Binaghi (Argentina)(1957-1976),
- Assad Kotaite (Lebanon) (1976-2006)
- Roberto Kobeh Gonzalez (Mexico) (2006-Present)

Emissions from international aviation are specifically excluded from the targets agreed under the Kyoto Protocol. Instead, the Protocol invites developed countries to pursue the limitation or reduction of emissions through the International Civil Aviation Organisation (ICAO). ICAO's environmental committee continues to consider the potential for using market-based measures such as trading and charging, but this work is unlikely to lead to global action. It is currently developing guidance for states who wish to include aviation in an emissions trading scheme (ETS) to meet their Kyoto commitments, and for airlines who wish to participate voluntarily in a trading scheme.

Emissions from domestic aviation are included within the Kyoto targets agreed by countries. This has led to some national policies such as fuel and emission taxes for domestic air travel in the Netherlands and Norway respectively. Although some countries tax the fuel used by domestic aviation, there is no duty on kerosene used on international flights. ICAO is currently against the inclusion of aviation in the European Union Emissions Trading Scheme (EU ETS). However, the EU is pressing ahead with its plans to include aviation from 2011.

Investigations of Air Disasters

ICAO has conducted just two investigations involving air disasters. Both incidents involved passenger airliners shot down while in international flight over hostile territory. The first incident occurred on February 21, 1973, during a period of tension which would lead to the Israeli-Arab "October war", when a Libyan Arab Airlines Flight 114 was shot down by Israeli F-4 jets over the Sinai Peninsula. The second incident occurred on Sept. 1, 1983, during a period of heightened Cold War tension, when a Soviet Su-15 interceptor shot down a straying Korean Air Lines Flight 007 just west of Sakhalin Island. KAL 007 was carrying 269 people..

Air Transport Regulation

Introduction to the Model Civil Aviation Safety Act and Model Regulations

[STATE] is a Signatory to the Convention on International Civil Aviation (Chicago Convention, signed at Chicago on 7 December 1944). Under Article 12 of the Convention, [STATE], as a Contracting State, is obligated to adopt measures to insure safety through conformity with international standards in its safety oversight obligations. The fundamental elements of national safety oversight are legislation establishing and empowering a civil aviation authority in [STATE], and the promulgation of specific operating regulations for civil aviation.

The Model Civil Aviation Safety Act and the Model Regulations are published to assist the government of [STATE] in carrying out its aviation safety oversight responsibilities. The Model Civil Aviation Safety Act and the Model Regulations provide primary information sufficient to allow [STATE] to meet its overall safety oversight responsibilities and to emphasize [State]'s commitment to aviation safety. Under Articles 37 and 38 of the Chicago Convention, [STATE] has agreed to conform to the standards and recommended practices (SARP) presented by the International Civil Aviation Organization (ICAO) in a series of ICAO Annexes addressing subjects ranging from the licensing of airmen to the shipment of dangerous goods by air.

Each ICAO Annex sets forth ICAO standards, which are the minimum standards required for operation in international aviation by aircraft registered in a Contracting State. Recommended practices set forth in each ICAO Annex, while not mandatory, provide information about what standards should be adhered to in order to insure aviation safety.

Model Civil Aviation Safety Act

The Model Aviation Safety Act (Act) provides a legal basis for the establishment of a Civil Aviation Authority, or CAA in [STATE], referred to in the Model Statute and the Model Regulations as the "Authority." The Act establishes the Authority under the Director of Civil Aviation, and defines both the duties and the authority granted the Director under the law of [STATE]. Subchapters I through IV address the organization, administration, general powers, and duties of the Authority.

Subchapter V requires the registration of aircraft in [STATE] and makes the maintenance of a system of recordation of such registration a matter of law. Subchapter VI sets forth the statutory bases for safety regulation by the Authority, including the certification of aviation personnel and entities, the duties required of aviation operators and airmen, the power of inspection granted the Authority and prohibitions applicable to all citizens of [STATE] respecting aviation. Subchapter VII sets forth the civil and criminal penalties that may be imposed by the Authority for violations of the law or the regulations, and Subchapter VIII establishes the procedure that is to be followed by the Authority in enforcement action.

Statutory authority for the economic regulation of air operators is also necessary, but due to the variation in national systems, no such language is provided in this Model Civil Aviation Safety Act. It is recognized that most Signatories to the Chicago Convention may already have a civil aviation law. The purpose of the Model Civil Aviation Safety Act is to provide the basis for review and modification of existing law, where such review and modification is deemed necessary by [STATE].

Model Regulations

The Model Regulations present ICAO standards as regulatory requirements for aircraft expected to operate internationally from and into [STATE]. Where applicable, ICAO recommended standards are included for completeness. Each model regulation presents the standards and recommended practices in the appropriate ICAO Annex supplemented by sections from the United States Federal Aviation Regulations (14 CFR) and/or the European Joint Aviation Requirements (JAR). Supplementation by 14 CFR or JAR allows efficient implementation of the basic ICAO standards and recommended practices, based upon the experience gained by the FAA and the JAA.

In some instances, modern regulatory practice in aviation either exceeds the ICAO Annex requirements or regulates in areas not yet addressed by the ICAO. Where Model Regulations exceed the requirements of a specific ICAO Annex, or address an area not covered by the ICAO Annex, those model regulations will be based upon the appropriate provisions of 14 CFR and the JAR.

Modern aviation practice presents complex situations to an Authority. These model regulations attempt to address the present situation faced by most countries, with aircraft operating both within the country and in international aviation. One of the assumptions underlying the Model Regulations is that most aircraft registered in [STATE] will have the range to operate in both local and international aviation. Simplicity in the regulation of civil aviation under such circumstances supports the consistent application of ICAO rules throughout the aviation community within [STATE].

In most cases, a modern Authority must account for a number of different situations while regulating its aviation community. The key to satisfactory assurance of safety and accountability is the use of efficient and effective means of communication and data transfer. The Model Regulations assume that the following situations will be present in [STATE], and in most Contracting States:

- there are aircraft registered in [STATE] that were designed and manufactured in another Contracting State;
- there are aircraft registered in [STATE] that were designed in one Contracting State and manufactured in another Contracting State;
- [STATE] may have Air Operator Certificate (AOC) holders who operate aircraft registered in another Contracting State, which may have different states of design and manufacture;

- [STATE] may have AOC holders who are part of a regional consortium, with operations and maintenance facilities in a neighbouring country;
- [STATE] international air carriers may operate in countries requiring pilot's licenses with terms and conditions additional to those required by ICAO Annex 1, and which differ from one country or region to another;
- [STATE] may host air operators and/or aviation repair facilities that are required to follow the regulations of another country or region in addition to those of [STATE];

The Model Regulations are presented in eleven Parts. Part 1, *General Policies, Procedures and Definitions,* sets forth the basic rules of construction and application of the regulations, definitions applicable to more than one Part, and the rules governing the administration of licenses and certifications. Of special interest are the Implementing Standards that accompany each Part. These Implementing Standards provide detailed requirements that support the intent of a regulation presented in a Part, but gain the force and effect of the governing regulations only if specifically referred to in the governing regulation. Implementing Standards are used in the Model Regulations to allow an Authority the flexibility to incorporate new practices or procedures as they become available without the procedures required for promulgation of legally binding regulations.

Part 2 addresses the licensing of personnel. Article 32 of the Chicago Convention requires [STATE] to issue certificates of competency and licenses or validate such certificates or licenses issued by other Contracting States to the pilot of every aircraft and to other members of the operating crew of every aircraft engaged in international navigation. The basis of this obligation is the goal of promoting and conducting safe and regular aircraft operations through the development and implementation of internationally acceptable certification and licensing processes. If the same process is extended to domestic operations, [STATE] can ensure the overall safety of aircraft operation through unification of licensing requirements. ICAO Annex 1, Personnel Licensing, presents the broad international specifications for personnel licensing agreed upon by Contracting States. Most of the specifications in ICAO Annex 1 are not given in enough detail to satisfy the day-to-day management of a country's personnel licensing activities. Part 2 of the Model Regulations presents detailed requirements for the general rules of licensing and detailed requirements for the certification of airmen, pilots, non-pilot flight crewmembers, and airmen, such as mechanics, who are not flight crew. Part 2 also presents medical standards for the granting of licenses and certification, and for the administration of medical examinations. The licensing and medical standards are based upon ICAO Annex 1, as well as both 14 CFR and the JAR.

Part 3 of the Model Regulations addresses the certification and administration of Aviation Training Organizations (ATO). No ICAO Annex presently covers international standards for an ATO. Consequently, Part 3 relies heavily upon regulations presented in 14 CFR and the JAR. The use of an ATO for the training and qualification of airmen is common in modern aviation, most particularly as operators upgrade their aircraft inventory and airmen transition to new aircraft.

The interrelation between ATO requirements under Part 3 and the licensing and certification requirements of Part 2 is plain. Even if [STATE] does not have an ATO located in the country, the requirements for ATO operation do apply to the standards required for adequate training for qualification for a [STATE] certification. Thus, [STATE] citizens who receive training from a foreign ATO should be trained by an ATO meeting [STATE] standards. This situation will be encountered when a [STATE] holder of an Air Operator Certificate (AOC), such as a national airline, is part of a regional consortium with AOC holders from other Contracting States in the region, and the consortium has established an ATO in only one of the regional Contracting States. The regulations set forth in Part 3 allow for this situation.

Part 4 of the Model Regulations set forth the requirements for registration of aircraft in [STATE], and governs the application of nationality and registration marks. This Part is derived from ICAO Annex 7.

Part 5 of the Model Regulations presents regulatory requirements for the airworthiness of aircraft expected to operate in [STATE] using the standards and recommended practices in ICAO Annexes 6 and 8 supplemented by sections from 14 CFR and the JAR. Part 5 is designed to address the complex situation faced by most countries today respecting the airworthiness of aircraft operating within the country and in international aviation. In most such cases, there are aircraft registered in [STATE] that were designed and manufactured in another Contracting State, and aircraft registered in [STATE] that were designed in one Contracting State and manufactured in another Contracting State.

In addition, [STATE] may have AOC holders who operate aircraft registered in another Contracting State, with different states of design and manufacture. Additionally, [STATE] may have AOC holders who are part of a regional consortium, with maintenance facilities in a neighbouring country. Proper airworthiness of aircraft registered in [STATE] is the result of communication. The Model Regulations require all persons operating [STATE] registered aircraft to notify the Authority when certain events occur. The Authority is required to open lines of communication with the State of Design and/or the State of Manufacture, so that the Authority can receive all safety bulletins and airworthiness directives for each type of aircraft operating in [STATE]. Maintenance requirements are set forth in Part 5 for persons who are neither employees of an Approved Maintenance Organization (AMO) nor work for an Air Operator.

Part 6 of the Model Regulations provides regulations for the registration and monitoring of Approved Maintenance Organizations (AMO) in [STATE]. The proper maintenance of aircraft is fundamental to aviation safety, and requires meticulous record-keeping. Modern practice among Contracting States varies. In the United States, persons may be individually licensed, or may be granted maintenance authority as a member of an AMO. Similarly, a United States AOC holder may use an AMO, or may employ a maintenance organization using licensed personnel.

In JAA practice, the maintenance organization of an AOC holder must qualify as an AMO in its own right. Whether or not [STATE] adopts the FAA or JAA approach with their AOC holders, there will be a need for oversight and regulation of AMO's. Maintenance requirements for AOC holders with integral maintenance organizations with no AMO certificate are addressed in Part 9. Many regional airline consortia use common maintenance facilities in one Contracting State. This practice does not relieve [STATE] from approving the AMO that its AOC holders use.

Knowledge of the other Contracting State's AMO licensing and regulating practices will allow the Authority both to communicate with the Authority overseeing the AMO certificate, and to weigh the AMO requirements of the other Contracting State for satisfaction of [STATE]'s own regulations.

Part 7 of the Model Regulations presents regulatory requirements for instruments and equipment on aircraft expected to operate in [STATE]. The requirements in Part 7 address three categories of aircraft operations. The sections of Part 7 applicable to all aircraft address minimum requirements, and are noted by the key [AAC] preceding the particular section. It is important to note that the AAC designation applies to all aircraft in the Commercial Air Transport [CAT] and AOC Holder [AOC] categories unless other, more specific regulations supplant the [AAC] requirement. In some instances, certain items such as Mach meters or sea anchors apply only to aircraft with performance characteristics requiring such items. Some [AAC] requirements apply to passenger-carrying aircraft.

In such instances, the requirement addresses the operation of any passenger-carrying aircraft, most particularly corporate aircraft, that may have performance and range capabilities matching the type of aircraft operated by commercial air transport entities or AOC holders. Similarly, some equipment specified for [CAT] or [AOC] aircraft have sections keyed as [AAC]. In such instances, if a non-[CAT] or [AOC] aircraft is fitted with such equipment, the equipment characteristics must comply with the applicable sections designated [AAC].

The key [CAT] addresses those aircraft operated commercially, that is, for compensation or hire, within [STATE] or into or from [STATE]. [CAT] requirements will apply to [AOC] aircraft unless a section designated as [AOC] supplies a more specific requirement. The key [AOC] applies to AOC holders operating in [STATE], whether on domestic or international flights. Certain sections, such as those addressing MNPS airspace, may not address airspace contiguous to [STATE], but anticipate that [STATE] AOC holder's aircraft may operate through such airspace in the course of commerce. Such requirements are intended to facilitate the integration of [STATE] AOC holders into such operations. As in other Parts of these Model Regulations, operators of aircraft operated in [STATE] but registered in another Contracting State must notify the Authority in [STATE] when alterations, major repairs or major alterations are made to the aircraft. [STATE] may have unique territorial or geographic features that may affect the operation of aircraft, and must be kept informed of the condition of aircraft operated within its borders. Part 7 includes survival equipment requirements that may apply to [STATE]. The Authority is encouraged to review geographic areas within [STATE], and designate those areas requiring specific types of survival equipment.

Part 8 of the Model Regulations presents regulatory requirements for the operation of aircraft in [STATE], based upon the requirements of ICAO Annexes 6 and 8. Part 8 prescribes the requirements for operations conducted by airmen certificated in [STATE] while operating aircraft registered in [STATE], as well as operations of foreign registered aircraft by [STATE] AOC holders, and operations of aircraft within [STATE] by airman or AOC holders of a foreign State. Part 8 applies to operations outside of [STATE] by all [STATE] pilots and operators unless compliance would result in a violation of the laws of the foreign State in which the operation is conducted. The regulations apply to all aircraft, except where superseded by the more stringent requirements put upon entities engaged on commercial air transport and upon AOC holders.

Part 9 of the Model Regulations sets forth the requirements for persons or entities to be granted an AOC certification from [STATE]. Part 9 includes regulations concerning the AOC certificate, flight operations management, maintenance requirements, security management, and dangerous goods management. Note that the requirements for an AOC-operated maintenance organization are contained in this part, and shall apply where the AOC does not use the services of an AMO, or does not gain an AMO certification for its maintenance organization.

Part 10 of the Model Regulations prescribes requirements applicable to foreign air carriers. Commercial air transport by a foreign air carrier is the operation of any civil aircraft or helicopter for the purpose of commercial air transportation operations by any air carrier whose Air Operator Certificate is issued and controlled by a civil aviation authority other than [STATE]. Part

10 does not apply to aircraft and helicopters when used by military, customs, and police services, unless those flights are made for compensation or hire. Part 10 sets forth the requirements for operations specifications, documents to be carried aboard the aircraft, and security and dangerous goods requirements placed upon a foreign air carrier operating into or out of [STATE].

Part 11 of the Model Regulations sets forth the requirements for aerial work operations, including agricultural aviation, helicopter external load carrying, glider and banner towing, TV and movie operations, sight-seeing flights, fish spotting and traffic reporting. Although the requirements of Part 11 appear to address operations internal to [STATE], in some instances, aircraft registered in [STATE] will be able to perform aerial work in contiguous states. If such operations can be carried out outside the boundaries of [STATE], the aircraft must be operated and maintained in accordance with ICAO standards set forth in other Parts of these Model Regulations.

Regional Coordination

The Authority of [STATE] should consider the benefit of correlating their civil aviation laws and regulations with those of other Contracting States in the region. Correlation of regulations can lead to greater unity of air safety efforts by [STATE] and its neighbours. This approach can facilitate the safety regulation of commercial consortia operating in a region that includes [STATE]. The Model Civil Aviation Safety Act and the Model Regulations provide a basis for such correlation.

Deregulation of Air Transport

Deregulation: Deregulation is, in its most simplistic terms, when the government removes certain regulations on businesses, to encourage the industry. The premise behind deregulation is that with fewer regulations impeding operations, businesses will become more competitive. This increased competition will then result in higher productivity levels, increased efficiencies, and lower prices for consumers. There have been some failures in attempts to deregulate certain industries. Most notably, the deregulation of the Savings and Loan industry in the 1980s was perceived as a failure and was subjected to re-regulation in order to balance out the industry.

The Savings and Loan scenario is a perfect example of why regulation or deregulation must be handled responsibly and intelligently, taking into account and utilizing sophisticated economic theories to help predict the future results. The Airline Deregulation Act was signed into law on October 28, 1978. The Act was created to remove governmental control and open up the passenger air transport industry to free market forces. As noted above, the desire was to increased efficiencies within the industry by promoting competition, which would hopefully le Deregulation:

Deregulation is, in its most simplistic terms, when the government removes certain regulations on businesses, to encourage the industry. The premise behind deregulation is that with fewer regulations impeding operations, businesses will become more competitive. This increased competition will then result in higher productivity levels, increased efficiencies, and lower prices for consumers. There have been some failures in attempts to deregulate certain industries. Most notably, the deregulation of the Savings and Loan industry in the 1980s was perceived as a failure and was subjected to re-regulation in order to balance out the industry.

The Savings and Loan scenario is a perfect example of why regulation or deregulation must be handled responsibly and intelligently, taking into account and utilizing sophisticated economic theories to help predict the future results. The Airline Deregulation Act was signed into law on October 28, 1978. The Act was created to remove governmental control and open up the passenger air transport industry to free market forces. As noted above, the desire was to increased efficiencies within the industry by promoting competition, which would hopefully lead to reduced airfares for consumers.

Given the last three decades of outburst and turbulence in the world economy, there are tremendous and irreversible changes in the structure of production, institutional characteristics, and geographical boundaries of markets and industries around the globe. These changes include the transnationalization of capital and emergence of institutions and networks that are able to carry out the task of production and the distribution of goods and serves beyond the confining borders of nation-states in the complete and connected circuit of *social capital* worldwide. As a result, there has been a remarkable disintegration and re-integration in the structure of firms, industries and markets through the spread of transnational activities. At the present stage of global integration, the centerpieces of global accumulation include, among others, the unifying control over the global labour process, universal and unified access to technology, and the expansion of networks of information, cost-and-revenue-sharing, globalization of product design, and transnationalization of finance capital.

Another side of this epochal transformation pertains to the fast-paced, hyper-competitive, and highly volatile character of economic production and exchange that, in turn, measure the magnitude of global successes and/or failures of capitalism in the contemporary world economy. For our limited purpose here, we shall focus on global alliances in the Air Transport Industry to illustrate attempts at cost-and-revenue-sharing within networks of information sharing and the turbulent impact of hypercompetition. The present globalization, therefore, is the process of continuous integration, disintegration, and re-integration of the world economy in terms of hypercompetition, and fast-paced technological and organizational change beyond the confinement of the nation-states.

Deregulation, introduced in the United States in 1978, has led to dramatic changes in the Air Transport industry. Prior to 1978, The Civil Aeronautics Board (CAB) set airline passenger fares, and entry into the industry and route structures were tightly controlled. Most airlines were party to a multilateral agreement that required they honour tickets issued by other participants. Carriers were mutually reliant upon each other to supply one another feeder traffic. The result was that route licenses by CAB ensured a stability, interdependence of carriers, and reinforced linear route structures. Indeed, before deregulation, fully one-fourth of U.S. domestic passengers were "interlining", or transferring from one carrier to another at major airports to get to their destinations. Upon relaxation of CAB's controls, the strategic vulnerability of the linear route systems operated by the major airlines became clear. New entrants such as People Express, Air Florida, and Midway quickly targeted the profitable high-density city-pair markets.

By 1980, 22 entrants challenged incumbents with low fares, and all but two of the major carriers lost money (HBS, 1995). To compete against lower-cost new entrants, major airlines needed a new source of competitive advantage. One advantage emerged when the major airlines realized that, given their recently acquired choice to enter new markets, there was no benefit in having passengers "interline" if they were able to carry them on their own airplanes for an entire journey. Accordingly, they began to establish nationwide networks. As a result, interlining fell from 25% of passenger traffic prior to deregulation to below less than 10% in 1984.

In building nation-wide networks, the most efficient mechanism to overcome the production indivisibilities inherent in the use of large aircraft was to redesign route systems into the now familiar hub and spoke configuration in which routes radiate from a central hub airport to a number of outer spoke airports. According to Hanlon (1996) the main advantage of this system is due to its enhanced number of available city pairs in comparison with direct linking of airports. The value of any hub is directly related to the size of the network it serves. A larger network allows a hub airline to offer a wide range of flights and, by consolidating long-distance travellers from many markets at one sight, integrates what were separate consumer markets into a single captive customer base.

In addition, hub creation allowed carriers to increase their local market power and also lower costs from reduced overhead expenses in ground operations. The economic advantages are powerful: hub systems quickly came to dominate the U.S. route system. Prior to deregulation, only five airports served as major traffic hubs. By 1987, there were 30 airports nationwide fulfilling this role.

While the major carriers realized the strategic importance of a nation-wide service network, most did not initially have a presence in smaller regional markets. Drawing feeder traffic to their hubs from these regional routes became a strategic imperative. As the hub system evolved, almost all the hub airlines formed alliances with commuter and regional carriers to increase traffic feed. Regional airlines were happy to oblige: they also benefited from an ever-increasing number of city pairs they could offer their customers. Oum, Park and Zhang (2000) note that a similar pattern of hub building occurred in Canada and the European Union following the deregulation of their markets.

Hub airlines coordinated and managed the commuter's flight schedules, provided reservation services, and shared airport and ground handling facilities. Notwithstanding these efforts vis-a-vis independent regional carriers, alliances would often fracture as the regionals played one competitor against another. To solidify their relationship with the regional airlines, American, Continental, Air Canada and others purchased majority stakes in their feeder airlines.

One indication of the increasing importance of the domestic "network" in the industry is the relative rise of regional airlines in the last twenty years. A passengers enplaned from regional airlines has increased by more than five-fold during the 1981-2001 period. Revenue passenger miles have increased by more than twelve fold in the same period. Available-seat-miles increased by more than 100% from 1993 to 2001. The evolution of the role of the regional airline is also underscored by changes in the range of markets they serve and their fleet composition. The length of an average trip on a regional airline more than doubled in the 1981-2001 period, as has the seating capacity of the regional fleet. These trends are a sharp departure from the industry as a whole.

It also became apparent to national carriers that a true national network required more than one hub. Hub set-up required enormous financial investments ($100-$150 million) and time (up to 10 years) to build the terminals and acquire strategically located gates (HBS, 1995). A far quicker way to achieve multiple hub airports was to acquire a competitor's hub. Indeed, the merger wave that occurred in the industry in the mid-1980s is mostly explicable by strategic efforts to realize the full potential of the new route structure: via the acquisition of either feeder airlines or strategic hubs. These acquisitions. The steady increase in ownership concentration in the industry over the period is also the result of this business strategy. By the end of the 1980s, consolidations led to 8 airlines controlling 92% of U.S. air traffic (HBS, 1995)

Parallel to these changes in the route structure and ownership concentration there emerged the change in the composition of the capital stock—aircraft—in the industry. The development of hub systems resulted in the addition of flights to small cities around the major hubs. This, in turn, increased the demand for small-and medium-sized aircraft. One case in point is the changing product-mix ordered from Boeing, among the world's largest aircraft manufacturers.

In orders for Boeing's aircraft, is divided into five product categories: single-aisle short-range (SASR), single-aisle mid-range (SAMR), twin-aisle mid-range (TAMR), twin-aisle long-range, and twin-aisle, twin-deck long-range (TDLR). The increasing importance of the single aisle mid-range aircraft. The trend is clearer when the additional seating capacity of the ordered aircrafts are considered. As presented, the majority of planned additional seating capacity is on SAMR aircraft. These versatile machines, including some models of the Boeing 737 and the Boeing 757, are to economically serve smaller cities and the regional hubs of the hub route structure. Yet, having a range of 5000-10,000 kilometres, and a seating capacity of 125 to 250, they provided needed flexibility and were assigned to all but the longest point-to-point routes.

Not captured in the Boeing data is the sharp increase in the number of jets in the U.S. regional fleet. Regional jets, introduced in the late 1980's, are small planes that fly shorter distances and have fewer seats than their counterparts: large mainline jets. Being the industry leaders, however, the jets manufactured by Canada's Bombardier and Brazil's Embrear, have a range up to 1300 miles and seating capacity of 50 to 70. The turboprop aircrafts they are replacing usually are confined to flights of up to 350 miles, with seating capacity for only 20 to 40 passengers. By the end of 2001, some 800 regional jets were in operation in the U.S., as opposed to only 137 in 1997, while the number of regional aircraft remained roughly constant at 2300 level.

Similar changes are also occurring in Europe. In particular, the advantage of building hub systems was clear to European airlines as well, although limits on international ownership meant consolidation within one's own national borders. During the 1980's, acquisition of British Caledonia by British Airways is one example. Some large European carriers also purchased minority stakes in smaller European airlines in order to solidify their positions at certain hub airports. Lufthansa purchased a minority position in Interflug—the (formerly) East German airline. Swissair purchased a share of the Zurich based Crossair. British Airways took control of 40% of Brymon Airlines, a commuter carrier. KLM purchased two Dutch commuter airlines (Cityhopper, Netherlines) and took a minority stakes in a British commuter (Air UK). And Air France was aggressive in acquiring or taking minority stakes in French commuter airlines (UTA, Air Inter).

The elaborate hub system, and the route structure that goes with it, played as a unifying framework that allowed a continuous access to arrival and departure points by both the major airlines and their regional affiliates and thus provided a ready platform to lunch a multiplied line of service by all involved. This indeed constitutes as a *de facto* or "social" (collective) capital for a particular alliance and, perhaps, a potential platform for future alliances. However, provision of such a structure embodies the double-edged sword of competition. Given the fierce competitive environment within the industry, having access to such an extensive hub system by already low-cost regional airlines, has led to a further competitive struggle between major U.S. carriers and the smaller airlines within the same alliances. This has given the regional airlines an intra-alliance competitive advantage, in addition to the inter-alliance competition, a norm in the industry. One indication of this is the relatively rapid increase in the revenue passenger miles generated by the regional airlines, when compared with their major airlines counterparts, as discussed above.

Global Alliances

As hub systems came to dominate domestic markets in the U.S. and Europe, the airlines began to rely heavily on inter-continental alliances to expand their networks, increase customer service, and generally to increase the value of their domestic hubs. This pattern is occurring globally. For U.S.-based airlines, international enplanements climbed 112% between 1986 and 1999, more than twice the growth in domestic travel.

In 2000, international travel was 8.5% of total enplanements, compared to 6% in 1986.

The underlying economic advantages of the hub system operate in international as well as domestic markets. Because of the advantages of network size, carriers have sought to expand their operations geographically and thereby gained significant competitive advantage. Strategically, exploiting the hub system internationally required carriers to plan on a global basis. Most international routes, however, remain governed by bilateral Air Service Agreements (ASAs) between governments. These agreements designate such matters as the types of applicable fares, the authorized carriers on certain routes, and the type of plane and allowable flight frequency. As such, they provide a protected source of economic profits for those carriers with rights to the routes. For example, more than half of the business of large European carriers is in longer-haul international routes covered by bilateral agreements, yet more than two-thirds of the revenue of U.S. carriers is derived from the competitive, domestic arena accounting, in part, for European airlines ability to weather the recent downturn in the global industry.

Recently, the U.S. has been proposing new ASAs called "Open Sky Agreements". These imply no limits on the number of airlines that may be designated by country, unrestricted capacity, frequency of flights, unlimited ability to change aircraft type, and, finally, full pricing freedom unless both governments object. Since the first open skies pact was reached between the U.S. and the Netherlands in 1992, 57 agreements have emerged.

The Open Sky Agreements and deregulation introduced around the globe have, to varying degrees, opened previously protected national and regional markets to penetration by new competitors. Some airlines, notably Northwest and KLM, and United and Luthhansa were given anti-trust immunity and took advantage of "Open Skies" to engage in unprecedented cooperation. Never the less, no nation has to date opened its markets to carriers from all countries. This limitation has carriers ally with, rather than purchase or attempt to directly challenge foreign carriers in their own hubs.

Alliances offer a form of consolidation without having to seek authority for the full cross-national mergers that most governments have refused to allow. As Pekar, Jr. (2001) points out, alliances fall between "transactional conventional sourcing and servicing arrangements at one extreme to acquisitions and mergers at the other." Importantly, they allow a firm to acquire (or capture) core capabilities from a foreign firm that directly advance its competitive position—gate access, route network, customer base, etc.—without having to invest in new airport facilities and aircraft or acquiring other assets that are unnecessary from a strategic point of view. It is important to point out that these advantages accrue to both parties within the alliance. Indeed, we believe that alliances are ultimately undermining the position of major carriers and portend realignment of the industry.

Despite all this, alliance growth in recent years has been notable. Air Florida and British Island formed the first international alliance in 1986. As firms learned of the success of the initiative, it was quickly emulated throughout the industry. The most recent figures available number 579 alliances involving 220 major international airlines. Most international alliances have initially been formed between European and North American airlines.

In the early 1990s, however, Asia Pacific airlines began to join the alliances. From Europe, North America, and Asia-Pacific, alliances have recently extended into new regions in Africa and Latin America. The gradual expansion of what would become the Star Alliance, the worlds largest, suggests the Alliance's rapid development of its global reach.

6

Development of Rural Tourism as Employment Opportunities

Rural Tourism Development: Constraints and Possibilities with a Special Reference to Agri Tourism

The Indian Agriculture and Tourism Industry Scenario

India is known as "Land of villages". More than 77 crore farmers live in 5.5 lakhs of village (2001).

Agriculture contributed about 18.5% of the national income (2006-07) as compared to a high 50% in 1950.

85% of population of India still depends on Agriculture hence Agriculture is not mere business, but is still the "True Culture of India".

Indian Agriculture Scenario

Today the Indian Agriculture has to face tremendous competition because of the driven global trends. To add to this the agriculture crop growth is also weakened due to the uncertain climatic conditions. There is no minimum support price guarantee also. These changes have altered the form and practices of farming operation. Farmers are looking beyond traditional farming to generate income via various forms of direct on farm marketing and farm based non-agriculture business.

Indian Tourism Industry

The Indian Tourism sector contributes 5.3 percent of India's GDP 2006-07. The tourism industry shows that India had 367 million domestic tourists and 3.92 million international tourists.

The Forex earnings from the tourism industry were 25,000 crores. The tourism industry created 38.8 million direct and indirect jobs. The tourism trend shows as per the 10th five year plan Indian government is willing to spend over Rs.2900 crores in the next five years to boost the growth in this sector. It is also seen that domestic tourism has displayed greater buoyancy and resilience. The centre has committed to contribute 765 crores for the state tourism development.

Domestic Tourism Growth

India has achieved great prosperity in tourism as a product. India being the home to many leading religions of the world has many important pilgrim sites of different religions scattered throughout the country. Besides the average Indian is also an avid sightseer. As per the study report of FICCI A.F. Ferguson and Co. 2004, every additional Rs.10 lakhs invested can create 47.5 direct jobs and each direct job can create 11 indirect jobs. It also stated that every 30 million additional tourist translate into Rs.4300 crores in revenue. It also stated that farm tourism if developed along unique indigenous lines could have a multiplier effect and high revenue capital ratio.

Within last 15 years, domestic tourism has grown by more than 304 million from 63 million in 1990 to 367 million in 2005 registering a growth of 20% p.a.

The World Travel and Tourism Council has Rated India as one of the Five Fastest Growing Tourism Economies in the World

Tourism Potential in Maharashtra

Maharashtra is the third largest state of India, both in area and population. It is located on the West Coast of India with a 720 km long coastline along the lush green Konkan region of Maharashtra, with its dense forests is home to several wild life sanctuaries and nature parks.

Maharashtra abounds in numerous tourist attractions ranging from ancient cave, temples, unspoiled beaches, ancient forts and monuments, forest and wild life unique hill stations, pilgrimage centres, a rich tradition of festivals, art and culture. The tourism market in Maharashtra is estimated to be around 250 million domestic tourists in 2005.

Objectives of the Study

With the growing importance of Agri-tourism and the thrust given by the government to promote tourism:

1) examines the key issues involved in the development of Agri-tourism in India
2) the challenges faced by Agri-tourism industry
3) suggest recommendations for the success of this industry.

The Agri-tourism industry being a very vast subject and also considering the several diversities of the Indian sub-continent, it was physically not possible to study the Agri-tourism market for the whole country.

Consequently, a study was conducted in Malegaon, Baramati district of Maharashtra.

Status of Agri-Tourism Internationally with Specific Focus on Europe

Most of the European countries pay lots of attention to rural tourism. The growth of rural tourism is difficult to quantify because few countries collect statistics in a way, which separates purely rural from other forms of tourism. The concept of Agri-Tourism developed in 80's in Europe, the participating farms have doubled in countries like Italy, the United Kingdom, and France. The number of agri-tourism accommodation units exceeds 600.00.

In the middle of the 90s, 12 European countries (Belgium, Denmark, Greece, Netherlands, Portugal, Spain, Ireland, Great Britain, Italy, Austria, France and Germany had more than 100.00 farm enterprises involve with different tourism activities. It is obvious that most of the European countries have positive attitude towards rural tourism development because of the advantages this strategy has on rural areas and their overall development. Agritourism in India: Innovative Income generating activity for Enterprising Farmers

Agriculture is backbone of Indian economy. This sector's contribution towards GDP is decreasing and farmers are finding it difficult to carry the agricultural activities without an additional income. Whereas tourism is termed as an instrument for employment generation, poverty alleviation and development,

Agri-Tourism brings in together the declining and booming sector.

Advantages of Agri-Tourism:

1. It brings major primary sector Agriculture closer to major service sector tourism expected to create win-win situation for both the sectors.
2. Tourism sector has the potential to enlarge.
3. Agriculture sector has the capacity to absorb expansion in Tourism sector.

Scope of Agri-Tourism

1. An inexpensive gateway: The cost of food, accommodation, recreation and travel and tourism is low, widening the scope of tourism.
2. Curiosity for the urban about farming industry and life style: Agri-tourism, which involves villages and agriculture, has the capacity to satisfy the curiosity of the urban segment by providing scope for re-discovering the rural life, which is rich in diversity.
3. Strong family oriented recreational activities: through rural games, festivals, food, dress.
4. Finding solace with nature friendly life style: Peace and tranquility are in-built in Agri-tourism.
5. Nostalgia for their roots on the farm: For tourists it is like returning back to their roots.
6. Educational value of Agri-Tourism spreading knowledge about Agriculture science where urban students are moving with the pace of technology.

Basic Principles of Agri-Tourism

1. Have something for visitors to see: Animals, birds, farms, culture of the village, dress and festivals.
2. Have something for visitors to do: Participating in agricultural operations, riding camel, buffalo, cooking and participating in the rural games i.e. gillidanda, gotti (marble etc.).
3. Have something for visitors to buy: Rural crafts, dress materials, farm gate fresh processed food are few items.

Detailed discussions with various knowledgeable persons indicated the following three factors:

1. Farmer: Majority cases farmer is less educated, less exposed and innocent for him outsider as guest is (like god) is treated wholeheartedly without any commercial motive. He entertains the guest while entertaining himself in the process he fills all the service gaps . This makes him a natural businessman.
2. Village: Village being located far from the city lacks urban facilities but is rich in natural resources. The investment is the natural resources itself.
3. Agriculture field: Each field is unique which adds to the attraction of the urban population. This is the incentive wealth of the rural people.

Facts 40 years back

- Only 22 villages in the tehsil received water from Neera river left bank canal, and few more villages were fed water from Karha River which presents a picture of prosperity and happiness.
- In glaring contrast to this, there were 43 villages which were at the mercy of fate and famine with neither any hope of river nor any water resource around.

Year 1967

- Group of farmers came together to do some concrete rural development work in the Baramati tehsil.
- Their development work was construction of percolation tanks, providing loans for digging wells, blasting units, supply of seeds and fertilizers of improved variety and also agricultural equipments.
- Baramati receives on an average, just 16 – 18" of rainfall for the whole year. Further the entire water is lost due to poor storage/ reservoir facilities.
- Farmers were restless, they started exploring the ways and solutions and thus the idea of "percolation tanks" came up.
- Drought sufferers came forward to share the dream of self-sufficiency.

Year 1968

Tandulwadi village: 1st percolation tanks were constructed providing irrigation to thousand areas of agricultural land. 250 percolation tanks were executive and computed. To give an impetus to the work accomplish by these group of former, the trust was formed on June 22.

1971 (Agriculture Development Trust)

The objective of the Agriculture Development Trust was :-

- To popularize and spread the actual demonstration and cultivation of new varieties of crops.
- To test and spread the use of improved seed varieties.
- To improve methods of crop cultivation.
- To develop vocations supplementary to Agriculture.
- To undertake various projects of water supply.
- To train the farmers for the vocational projects.
- To undertake afforestation in barren and fallow land.
- To spread the use of cross bred cows.
- To educate and provide facilities to poor, promising and deserving women for earning their livelihood.
- Agricultural research laboratory to guide farmers to built library providing books to update farmers knowledge.
- To organize seminars, workshop related to agricultural activities.

Year 1970: The year 1970 was a landmark for Malegaon, Baramati it came with the Model Demonstration Farm.

The trust did not rest on its laurels, to prove that an uncultivable rocky land of 110 across was converted into a fertile track of cultivable land on which grows various crops, fruits, fodder for cattle. This was initiated by Dr. Appasaheb Pawar and is now followed by Mr. Rajendra Pawar who is the present President of the trust.

Today the Model Demonstration farm encloses:

- Horticulture Unit.
- Dairy Division.

- Sericulture unit.
- Bee Hive Unit.
- Alternative Energy Unit.
- Krishi Vigyan Kendra.
- Analytical Laboratory – Provides farmers about weather, forecast, velocity of wind, and maximum and minimum temperature and undertakes analysis of soil, water, fertilizers animal.

As years passed by Agriculture as a business was becoming more and more expensive that many farmers were not able to afford it. To add to this there was gradual loss of fertility of land giving the farmers to brainstorm to meet the expense by retaining the farm and opening a supplementary business unit.

Formation of Agri-Tourism Development Corporation

ATDC's mission is "To promote agriculture tourism to achieve income, employment and economic stability in rural communities in India. To help boosting a range of activities, services and amenities provided by farmers and rural people to attract urban tourists to their area. Thus providing opportunity to urban people to get back to the rural roots".

ATDC's Role in Agri-Tourism

- Prepare Agri Tourism project report and business plan for each applicant agriculture farm.
- Help to facilitate the financial support from Nationalize banks, institutes and government agencies to built agri and rural tourism facilities and infrastructure like accommodation, sanitation, approach road etc.
- Conduct Agri Tourism Business Training Program.
- Conduct Seminars and conferences on agri-tourism business.
- Provide sales and marketing support.
- Co-ordinate tours from urban areas to the farms.

The trust decided to experiment Agri-Tourism concept on a pilot scale on its own 110 acres model farm, Malegaon, Baramati.

Prior to setting up the successful Pilot Agri and Rural Tourism Project in Maharashtra, Malegaon, Baramati

Taluka, Dist. Pune in October, 2005 a market survey was conducted by ATDC with sample size of 2,440.

The analysis of the survey was:

- 35% do not have relatives in village.
- 43% never stayed or visited village.
- 57% never visited dairy farm.

This survey promoted to experiment Agri-Tourism in the 110 acre model farm of the agriculture development trust.

The Agri Tourism Destination Malegaon village, Taluka Baramati, Dist. Pune, Maharashtra, India (Pilot Project)

This Agri Tourism destination belongs to "Agricultural Development Trust Malegaon". The detailed study has helped in bringing to light the following facts about the model project at Malegaon, Baramati.

Attractions

Agri Tourism activities include farm tours; tractor and bullock cart rides; grapes, mangoes, and other horticulture farms and by-product farms; birds and animal farms; There are lot of things the visitors or guests can enjoy in this agri tourism unit/farm.

Total area under cultivation here is of 110 acres, primarily use for agricultural purposes, out of which 65 acres is used for Horticultural plantations and cultivation, consisting of various seasonal fruits farms.

The added attractions here are the poultry farm; dairy farm; goat farm; and most visited point silk processing unit.

The visitors here can also visit the gram panchayat village office and school; village fairs and markets, near by Jaggery making unit; Emu bird Farm; Sugar factory; Taluka Milk Collection Centres and some of the oldest religious temples and also Museum.

Accomodation

The over night stay arrangement is at the farm itself, there are 12 rooms and 1 big hall.

The occupancy is quadruple sharing every room having 4 single beds. One Room is allotted to each Family. The accommodation facilities are basic but very hygienic neat and clean. Two toilets (one western style) (and one bathroom attached to block of every three rooms, this arrangement is purposely kept to experience the joint family atmosphere.

The Solar Water heaters at the rooftop are fitted to provide the running hot water for bathing in the morning. There is also the facility of dormitory hall, wherein more than 250 people can easily accommodate.

Outdoor Recreational Activities

The outdoor recreational activities for children and adults during daytime are farm tours and agricultural education programs, how to grow sugarcane, grapes, pomegranate, guava, watermelon, other fruits and what are the food values of each fruits, how to take care of the cattle, nature education programs, domestic animals and emu bird farms visits and education of the different trees, demonstrations such as goat and cow milking, honey making, silk making, jaggery making, rural games that they can play as gotya; bovhra; surparanbhya; vittidandu; Buffalo ride; bullock cart ride; tractor rides; watching domestic animals; clay molding; painting the nature scenery; tree climbing or simply run with the cycle tree.

Entertainment Programs

The Evenings are generally fun filled, star gazing activity and the rural Maharashtra folk dances and folk song programs is organized. Bonfire/campfire during winter seasons, family games, children games, and lots of fun filled programs.

Meals for Tourists

The food served is pure vegetarian Maharashtrian style, for breakfast Poha, Upma, or Shira, for the lunch usually jawar or bajra bhakri, chapattis, rice, varan, pickle, papad, kurdaya, bhaji, thecha, wangeche bharit, jhunka/pitla, any fresh green vegetable sabji, matki/ chawli usual shabji, etc.

Safety & Security Aspects

The Agri Tourism unit at Malegaon is very safe and secure for all the guests and visitors, there is only one main entrance gate, during daytime almost 400 people work in the farm, plus the entire area of 110 acres is barbed wire fenced and over and above there is adequate 24 hours security persons at the main entrance gate and for the entire area.

Medical Facilities

This Agri Tourism unit is just 1 km from the Malegaon village. Apart from the onsite medical doctor there are specialist doctors available 24 hours on call.

Risk And Liability in Case of Accidents

ATDC has examined the risks associated with some of the activities of agri-tourism. For example: one may decide to ride the bullock cart ride or tractor tailor ride which is not risk free, since there is always a possibility that a guest will fall off the bullock cart or the tractor tailor, however ATDC has established rules and regulations that protects the guests from potential risks.

Sometimes accidents cannot be avoided during agri tourism visits at the farms, However, ATDC makes sure that the operations and the farm activity and the sight seeing tours at the farm and outside the farms to sugar factory, jaggery making unit is safe as possible and they have taken appropriate safety precautions.

Health and Medical Tourism

Medical tourism (also called medical travel, health tourism or global healthcare) is a term initially coined by travel agencies and the mass media to describe the rapidly-growing practice of travelling across international borders to obtain health care. It also refers pejoratively to the practice of healthcare providers travelling internationally to deliver healthcare.

Services typically sought by travellers include elective procedures as well as complex specialized surgeries such as joint replacement, cardiac surgery, dental surgery, and cosmetic surgeries. However, virtually every type of health care, including psychiatry, alternative treatments, convalescent care and even burial services are available. As a practical matter, providers and customers commonly use informal channels of communication-connection-contract, and in such cases this tends to mean less regulatory or legal oversight to assure quality and less formal recourse to reimbursement or redress, if needed.

Over 50 countries have identified medical tourism as a national industry. However, accreditation and other measures of quality vary widely across the globe, and there are risks and ethical issues that make this method of accessing medical care controversial. Also, some destinations may become hazardous or even dangerous for medical tourists to contemplate.

In the context of global health, "medical tourism" is a pejorative because during such trips health care providers often practice outside of their areas of expertise or hold different (i.e., lower) standards of care. Greater numbers than ever before of student volunteers, health professions trainees, and researchers from resource-rich countries are working temporarily and anticipating future work in resource-starved areas. This emphasizes the importance of understanding this other definition.

History

The concept of medical tourism is not a new one. The first recorded instance of medical tourism dates back thousands of years to when Greek pilgrims traveled from all over the Mediterranean to the small territory in the Saronic Gulf called Epidauria. This territory was the sanctuary of the healing god Asklepios. Epidauria became the original travel destination for medical tourism.

Spa towns and sanitariums may be considered an early form of medical tourism. In eighteenth century England, for example, patients visited spas because they were places with supposedly health-giving mineral waters, treating diseases from gout to liver disorders and bronchitis.

Description

Factors that have led to the increasing popularity of medical travel include the high cost of health care, long wait times for certain procedures, the ease and affordability of international travel, and improvements in both technology and standards of care in many countries.

Medical tourists can come from anywhere in the First World, including Europe, the Middle East, Japan, the United States, and Canada. This is because of their large populations, comparatively high wealth, the high expense of health care or lack of health care options locally, and increasingly high expectations of their populations with respect to health care. An authority at the Harvard Business School recently stated that "medical tourism is promoted much more heavily in the United Kingdom than in the United States".

A forecast by Deloitte Consulting published in August 2008 projected that medical tourism originating in the US could jump by a factor of ten over the next decade. An estimated 750,000 Americans went abroad for health care in 2007, and the report estimated that a million and a half would seek health care outside the US in 2008. The growth in medical tourism has the potential to cost US health care providers billions of dollars in lost revenue.

A large draw to medical travel is convenience and speed. Countries that operate public health-care systems are often so taxed that it can take considerable time to get non-urgent medical care. Using Canada as an example, an estimated 782,936 Canadians spent time on medical waiting lists in 2005, waiting an average of 9.4 weeks. Canada has set waiting-time benchmarks, e.g. 26 weeks for a hip replacement and 16 weeks for cataract surgery, for non-urgent medical procedures.

Additionally, patients are finding that insurance either does not cover orthopedic surgery (such as knee/hip replacement) or imposes unreasonable restrictions on the choice of the facility, surgeon, or prosthetics to be used. Medical tourism for knee/hip replacements has emerged as one of the more widely accepted procedures because of the lower cost and minimal difficulties associated with the travelling to/from the surgery. Colombia provides a knee replacement for about $5,000 USD, including all associated fees, such as FDA-approved prosthetics and hospital stay-over expenses. However, many clinics quote prices that are not all inclusive and include only the surgeon fees associated with the procedure.

According to an article by the University of Delaware publication, Daily:

"The cost of surgery in India, Thailand or South Africa can be one-tenth of what it is in the United States or Western Europe, and sometimes even less. A heart-valve replacement that would cost $200,000 or more in the US, for example, goes for $10,000 in India—and that includes round-trip airfare and a brief vacation package. Similarly, a metal-free dental bridge worth $5,500 in the US costs $500 in India, a knee replacement in Thailand with six days of physical therapy costs about one-fifth of what it would in the States, and Lasik eye surgery worth $3,700 in the US is available in many other countries for only $730. Cosmetic surgery savings are even greater: A full facelift that would cost $20,000 in the US runs about $1,250 in South Africa."

Popular medical travel worldwide destinations include: Argentina, Brunei, Cuba, Colombia, Costa Rica, Hong Kong, Hungary, India, Jordan, Lithuania, Malaysia, The Philippines, Singapore, South Africa, Thailand, and recently, Saudi Arabia, UAE, South Korea, Tunisia and New Zealand. Popular cosmetic surgery travel destinations include: Argentina, Bolivia, Brazil, Colombia, Costa Rica, Cuba, Mexico and Turkey. In South America, countries such as Argentina, Bolivia, Brazil and Colombia lead on plastic surgery medical skills relying on their experienced plastic surgeons. In Bolivia and Colombia, plastic surgery has also become quite common. According to the "Sociedad Boliviana de Cirugia Plastica y Reconstructiva", more than 70% of middle and upper class women in the country have had some form of plastic surgery. Colombia also provides advanced care in cardiovascular and transplant surgery.

In Europe Belgium, Poland and Slovakia are also breaking into the business. South Africa is taking the term "medical tourism" very literally by promoting their "medical safaris".

A specialized subset of medical tourism is reproductive tourism and reproductive outsourcing, which is the practice of travelling abroad to undergo in-vitro fertilization, surrogate pregnancy and other assisted reproductive technology treatments including freezing embryos for retro-production.

However, perceptions of medical tourism are not always positive. In places like the US, which has high standards of quality, medical tourism is viewed as risky. In some parts of the world, wider political issues can influence where medical tourists will choose to seek out health care.

Health tourism providers have developed as intermediaries to unite potential medical tourists with provider hospitals and other organisations. Companies are beginning to offer global health care options that will enable North American and European patients to access world health care at a fraction of the cost of domestic care. Companies that focus on medical value travel typically provide nurse case managers to assist patients with pre- and post-travel medical issues. They also help provide resources for follow-up care upon the patient's return.

Process

The typical process is as follows: the person seeking medical treatment abroad contacts a medical tourism provider. The provider usually requires the patient to provide a medical report, including the nature of ailment, local doctor's opinion, medical history, and diagnosis, and may request additional information. Certified medical doctors or consultants then advise on the medical treatment. The approximate expenditure, choice of hospitals and tourist destinations, and duration of stay, etc., is discussed. After signing consent bonds and agreements, the patient is given recommendation letters for a medical visa, to be procured from the concerned embassy. The patient travels to the destination country, where the medical tourism provider assigns a case executive, who takes care of the patient's accommodation, treatment and any other form of care. Once the treatment is done, the patient can remain in the tourist destination or return home.

International Healthcare Accreditation

Because standards are important when it comes to health care, there are parallel issues around medical tourism, international healthcare accreditation, evidence-based medicine and quality assurance.

The oldest international accrediting body is Accreditation Canada, formerly known as the Canadian Council on Health Services Accreditation, which accredited the Bermuda Hospital Board as soon as 1968. Since then, it has accredited hospitals and health service organizations in ten other countries.

In the United States, the best known accreditation group is the Joint Commission International (JCI). They have been inspecting and accrediting health care facilities and hospitals outside of the United States since 1999. Many international hospitals today see obtaining international accreditation as a way to attract American patients.

Joint Commission International is a relative of the Joint Commission in the United States. Both are independent private sector not-for-profit organizations that develop nationally and internationally recognized procedures and standards to help improve patient care and safety. They work with hospitals to help them meet Joint Commission standards for patient care and then accredit those hospitals meeting the standards.

In the UK and Hong Kong, the Trent International Accreditation Scheme is a key player. The different international healthcare accreditation schemes vary in quality, size, cost, intent and the skill and intensity of their marketing. They also vary in terms of cost to hospitals and healthcare institutions making use of them. A forecast by Deloitte Consulting regarding medical tourism published in August 2008 noted the value of accreditation in ensuring quality of healthcare and specifically mentioned JCI, ISQUA and Trent.

Increasingly, some hospitals are looking towards dual international accreditation, perhaps having both JCI to cover potential US clientele, Trent for potential British and European clientele and Accreditation Canada. As a result of competition between clinics for American medical tourists, there have been initiatives to rank hospitals based on patient-reported metrics.

Other organizations providing contributions to quality practices include:

- The Society for International Healthcare Accreditation, a free-to-join group providing a forum for discussion and for the sharing of ideas and good practice by providers of international healthcare accreditation and users of the same. The primary role of this organisation is to promote a safe hospital environment for patients.
- Medical Tourism Association (MTA), the second non-profit trade association for medical tourism (after the International Medical Travel Association), is made up of the top international hospitals, healthcare providers, medical travel facilitators, insurance companies, and other affiliated companies and members with the common goal of promoting the highest level of quality of healthcare to patients in a global environment. The Association promotes the interests of its healthcare provider and medical travel facilitator members. The MTA claims three tenets: Transparency, Communication and Education. These tenets were recently called into question in a Reuters article during the time of one if its conferences. Further questions about the legitimacy of the organization were discussed in an International Medical Travel Journal piece on a legal dispute involving the MTA.

- The United Kingdom Accreditation Forum (UKAF) is an established network of accreditation organisations with the intention of sharing experience good practice and new ideas around the methodology for accreditation programmes, covering issues such as developing healthcare quality standards, implementation of standards within healthcare organisations, assessment by peer review and exploration of the peer review techniques to include the recruitment, training, monitoring and evaluation of peer reviewers and the mechanisms for awards of accredited status to organisations.

Risks

Medical tourism carries some risks that locally-provided medical care does not. Some countries, such as India, Malaysia, or Thailand have very different infectious disease-related epidemiology to Europe and North America. Exposure to diseases without having built up natural immunity can be a hazard for weakened individuals, specifically with respect to gastrointestinal diseases (e.g. Hepatitis A, amoebic dysentery, paratyphoid) which could weaken progress, mosquito-transmitted diseases, influenza, and tuberculosis. However, because in poor tropical nations diseases run the gamut, doctors seem to be more open to the possibility of considering any infectious disease, including HIV, TB, and typhoid, while there are cases in the West where patients were consistently misdiagnosed for years because such diseases are perceived to be "rare" in the West.

The quality of post-operative care can also vary dramatically, depending on the hospital and country, and may be different from US or European standards. However, JCI and Trent fulfill the role of accreditation by assessing the standards in the healthcare in the countries like India, China and Thailand.

Also, travelling long distances soon after surgery can increase the risk of complications. Long flights and decreased mobility in a cramped airline cabin are a known risk factor for developing blood clots in the legs such as venous thrombosis or pulmonary embolus economy class syndrome. Other vacation activities can be problematic as well — for example, scars may become darker and more noticeable if they sunburn while healing. To minimise these problems, medical tourism patients often combine their medical trips with vacation time set aside for rest and recovery in the destination country.

Also, health facilities treating medical tourists may lack an adequate complaints policy to deal appropriately and fairly with complaints made by dissatisfied patients.

Differences in healthcare provider standards around the world have been recognised by the World Health Organization, and in 2004 it launched the World Alliance for Patient Safety. This body assists hospitals and government around the world in setting patient safety policy and practices that can become particularly relevant when providing medical tourism services.

Legal Issues

Receiving medical care abroad may subject medical tourists to unfamiliar legal issues. The limited nature of litigation in various countries is one reason for the lower cost of care overseas. While some countries currently presenting themselves as attractive medical tourism destinations provide some form of legal remedies for medical malpractice, these legal avenues may be unappealing to the medical tourist. Should problems arise, patients might not be covered by adequate personal insurance or might be unable to seek compensation via malpractice lawsuits. Hospitals and/or doctors in some countries may be unable to pay the financial damages awarded by a court to a patient who has sued them, owing to the hospital and/or the doctor not possessing appropriate insurance cover and/or medical indemnity.

Ethical Issues

There can be major ethical issues around medical tourism. For example, the illegal purchase of organs and tissues for transplantation has been alleged in countries such as India and China prior to 2007.

Medical tourism may raise broader ethical issues for the countries in which it is promoted. For example in India, some argue that a "policy of 'medical tourism for the classes and health missions for the masses' will lead to a deepening of the inequities" already embedded in the health care system. In Thailand, in 2008 it was stated that, "Doctors in Thailand have become so busy with foreigners that Thai patients are having trouble getting care". Medical tourism centred on new technologies, such as stem cell treatments, is often criticized on grounds of fraud, blatant lack of scientific rationale and patient safety. However, when pioneering advanced technologies, such as providing 'unproven' therapies to patients outside of regular clinical trials, it is often challenging to differentiate between acceptable medical innovation and unacceptable patient exploitation.

Employer-sponsored Health Care in the US

Some US employers have begun exploring medical travel programs as a way to cut employee health care costs.

Such proposals have raised stormy debates between employers and trade unions representing workers, with one union stating that it deplored the "shocking new approach" of offering employees overseas treatment in return for a share of the company's savings. The unions also raise the issues of legal liability should something go wrong, and potential job losses in the US health care industry if treatment is outsourced.

Employers may offer incentives such as paying for air travel and waiving out-of-pocket expenses for care outside of the US. For example, in January 2008, Hannaford Bros., a supermarket chain based in Maine, began paying the entire medical bill for employees to travel to Singapore for hip and knee replacements, including travel for the patient and companion. Medical travel packages can integrate with all types of health insurance, including limited benefit plans, preferred provider organizations and high deductible health plans.

In 2000 Blue Shield of California began the United States' first cross border health plan. Patients in California could travel to one of the three certified hospitals in Mexico for treatment under California Blue Shield. In 2007, a subsidiary of BlueCross BlueShield of South Carolina, Companion Global Healthcare, teamed up with hospitals in Thailand, Singapore, Turkey, Ireland, Costa Rica and India. A 2008 article in *Fast Company* discusses the globalization of healthcare and describes how various players in the US healthcare market have begun to explore it.

Dental

Dental tourism involves individuals seeking dental care outside of their local healthcare systems.

Fertility

Fertility tourism is the practice of travelling to another country for fertility treatments. The main reasons for fertility tourism are legal regulation of the sought procedure in the home country, or lower price. In-vitro fertilization, donor insemination and surrogacy are major procedures involved.

Destinations

Africa and Middle East

Countries in this region involved in medical tourism include Saudi Arabia, South Africa, and Tunisia.

Israel

Israel is emerging as a popular destination for medical tourists. In 2006, 15,000 foreigners travelled to the country for medical procedures, bringing in $40 million of revenue.

Medical tourists choose Israel for several reasons. Some come from European nations such as Romania where certain procedures are not available. Others come to Israel, perhaps most commonly from the US, because they can receive quality health care at a fraction of the cost it would be at home, for both surgeries and in-vitro fertilization treatments.

Other medical tourists come to Israel to visit the Dead Sea, a world-famous therapeutic resort. The Israel Ministry of Tourism and several professional medical services providers have set out to generate awareness of Israel's medical capabilities.

Jordan

Jordan is an emerging medical tourism destination, with related revenues exceeding one billion dollars in 2007. More than 250,000 patients from other countries sought treatment in Jordan that year. This included an estimated 45,000 Iraqis and approximately 25,000 patients each from Palestine and Sudan. An estimated 1,800 US citizens, 1,200 UK citizens, and 400 Canadians also sought treatment in Jordan that year.

Treatment costs can be as low as 25 percent of costs in the US. The kingdom was rated as number one in the region and fifth in the world as a medical tourism hub in a study by the World Bank.

UAE

Hospitals in Dubai and other emirates have expressed an intent to develop in medical tourism. Some have American-sourced international healthcare accreditation, while others are looking towards the UK, Australia and Canada for accreditation services.

The Americas

Countries in the Americas that are treating foreign patients include Argentina, Bolivia, Brazil, Colombia, Costa Rica, Cuba, Dominican Republic, Guatemala, Mexico, Panama, Peru and Uruguay.

Brazil

Brazil has long been known as a destination for cosmetic surgery. For non-cosmetic procedures, Brazil is only now entering the global market. However, Albert Einstein Jewish Hospital in Sao Paulo was the first JCI-accredited facility outside of the US, and more than a dozen Brazilian medical facilities have since been similarly accredited. Brazil requires visas for US citizens based on a reciprocal arrangement since Brazilians are required to obtain a visa to visit the US.

Canada

Canada has entered the medical tourism field. In comparison to US health costs, medical tourism patients can save 30 to 60 percent on health costs in Canada.

Cuba

Cuba has been a popular medical tourism destination for more than 40 years. Thousands of patients travel to Cuba, particularly from Latin America and Europe, attracted by the "fine reputation of Cuban doctors, the low prices and nearby beaches on which to recuperate." In 2006, Cuba attracted nearly 20,000 health tourists.

Medical treatments included joint replacement, cancer treatment, eye surgery, cosmetic surgery and addictions rehabilitation. Costs are about 60 to 80 percent less than US costs.

Cuba has hospitals for Cuban residents and others that focus on serving foreigners and diplomats. In the 2007 American documentary film, *Sicko*, which criticizes the US healthcare system, producer Michael Moore leads a group of uninsured American patients to Cuba to obtain more affordable medical treatment. *Sicko* has greatly increased foreigners' interest in Cuban healthcare. A recent Miami Herald story focused on the high quality of health care that Canadian and American medical tourism patients receive in Cuba.

The Cuban government has developed Cuban medical tourism to generate income for the country. Residents of Canada, the UK and most other countries can travel to Cuba without any difficulty a tourist visa is generally required. For Americans, however, because of the US trade policy towards Cuba, travellers must either obtain US government approval, or, more frequently, travel to Cuba from Canada, Mexico, the Bahamas, Jamaica or the Dominican Republic. Cuban immigration authorities do not stamp the passports of US visitors so that Americans can keep their travels a private matter.

Mexico

Americans, particularly those living near the Mexican border, now routinely cross to Mexico for medical care. Popular specialties include dentistry and plastic surgery. Mexican dentists often charge one-fifth to one-fourth of US prices, while other procedures typically cost a third what they would in the US.

This trend has alarmed American healthcare providers who, fearing a loss of business, warn patients away from Mexico. "The phenomenon has unsettled US-based dentists who tell horror stories of rampant infections, undetected cases of oral cancer and shoddy work south of the border", claims hotly disputed by Mexican dentists.

"In Texas, legislators explored the possibility of allowing health maintenance organizations to operate on both sides of the border. However, physicians in south Texas lobbied against the changes, arguing that local doctors could not compete with the lower costs in Mexico". US doctors point out that the Mexican legal system makes it almost impossible to sue Mexican doctors for malpractice.

However, many who travel to Mexico for care report that they are satisfied. According to a report commissioned by Families U.S.A., a Washington advocacy group for health-care issues, "About

90 percent [feel] the care they had received in Mexico had been good or excellent. About 80 percent rated the care they had received in the United States as good or excellent".

Indeed "some U.S. dentists ... have conceded to the competition and begun a 'reverse migration' opening offices in Mexico to take advantage of lower costs". More American insurers are providing coverage for travellers, as the out-of-pocket costs to them are much lower. "With healthcare costs in the United States continuing to rise, many employers in Southern California are turning to insurance plans that send their workers to Mexico for routine care, plans that are growing by nearly 3,000 people a year."

In addition to dental and plastic surgery, Mexican hospitals are popular for bariatric surgery for weight loss, considered an elective procedure that is not covered by some US insurers. A popular bariatric procedure, lap band surgery, which was approved by the FDA in the US in 2001, has been performed for longer by Mexican surgeons.

Panama

In Panama, health and medical tourism is growing rapidly. Factors drawing medical tourists include Panama's tourist appeal, position as a hub for international travel, and use of the American dollar as the official currency. Many of Panama's doctors are bilingual, board certified, and accustomed to working with the same medical equipment and technology used in the United States and Europe. On most procedures, Panama offers savings of more than 50% compared to the US and Europe. No Panamanian hospitals currently have international healthcare accreditation, whether through US, British, Australian or Canadian sources.

United States

Although much attention has been given to the growing trend of uninsured Americans travelling to foreign countries, a report from 2008 found that a plurality of an estimated 60,000 to 85,000 medical tourists were travelling to the United States for the purpose of receiving inpatient medical care. The availability of advanced medical technology and sophisticated training of physicians are cited as driving motivators for growth in foreigners travelling to the U.S. for medical care. Also, it has been noted that the decline in value of the U.S. dollar is offering additional incentive for foreign travel to the U.S. However, costs differences between the US and many locations in Asia far outweigh any currency fluctuations. Several major medical centres and teaching hospitals offer international patient centres that cater to patients from foreign countries who seek medical treatment in the U.S. Many of these organizations offer service coordinators to assist international patients with arrangements for medical care, accommodations, finances and transportation including air ambulance services. It should be noted that many locations in the US that offer medical care comparable in price to foreign medical facilities are not Joint Commission Accredited.

Uruguay

Uruguay recently entered the medical tourism market. A private medical tourism initiative, Uruhealth, has been created with support from the Ministries of Tourism and Public Health. The initiative involves the infrastructure, human resources and experience of two healthcare companies: MP Personalized Medicine (Montevideo) and SEMM-Mautone Hospital (Punta del Este).

Asia/Pacific

Many Asian Pacific countries are medical tourism destinations.

China

China is fast emerging as a desirable destination for individuals seeking medical care in a wide range of medical specialties, including cardiology, neurology, orthopedics and others. A number of private and government hospitals in major cities have established international departments. Many leading hospitals provide treatments integrating Traditional Chinese Medicine with Western medical technology and techniques. China is home to leading stem cell research and treatment hospitals that offer Westerners who want to take advantage of stem cell treatments that are still considered experimental or have yet to be approved in their home country.

Hong Kong

As of 2006, Hong Kong had 12 private hospitals and 39 public hospitals, providing 3,124 and 27,755 beds respectively. A wide range of health care services are offered. All 12 of Hong

Kong's private hospitals have been surveyed and accredited by the UK's Trent Accreditation Scheme since early 2001. This has been a major factor in the ascent of standards in Hong Kong's private hospitals.

The Trent scheme works closely with the hospitals it assesses to generate standards appropriate to the locality (with respect to culture, geography, public health, primary care interfaces etc.), and always uses combinations of UK-sourced and Hong Kong-sourced surveyors.

Some of Hong Kong's private hospitals have now gone on to obtain dual international accreditation, with both Trent and JCI (and have therefore attained a standard surpassing some of the best hospitals in Thailand and Singapore). Others are looking towards dual international accreditation with Trent and the Australian group. Hong Kong public hospitals have yet to commit to external accreditation.

India

India's medical tourism sector is expected to experience an annual growth rate of 30%, making it a Rs. 9,500-crore industry by 2015. Estimates of the value of medical tourism to India go as high as $2 billion a year by 2012. Advantages for medical tourists include reduced costs, the availability of latest medical technologies and a growing compliance on international quality standards, as well as the fact that foreigners are not likely to face a language barrier in India. The Indian government is taking steps to address infrastructure issues that hinder the country's growth in medical tourism.

Most estimates claim treatment costs in India start at around a tenth of the price of comparable treatment in America or Britain. The most popular treatments sought in India by medical tourists are alternative medicine, bone-marrow transplant, cardiac bypass surgery, eye surgery and orthopedic surgery. India is known in particular for heart surgery, hip resurfacing and other areas of advanced medicine.

Ministry of Tourism India (MoT) is planning to extend its Market Development Assistance (MDA) scheme to cover Joint Commission International (JCI) and National Accreditation Board of Hospitals (NABH) certified hospitals. A policy announcement of this effect is likely soon.

The south Indian city of Chennai is regarded as the healthcare capital of India.

Korea, Republic of

Listed on CNN.com as one of the "hot destinations" for medical tourism, Korea is quickly establishing itself in the field of medical tourism. However, *The Korea Times* reported in a series of articles that Korean hospitals have adopted a discriminatory pricing policy, charging foreigners two to three times more than the full-fee for locals.

The paper revealed that the price disparity in medical fees for foreign patients is extremely high, considering that the difference between the lowest and highest fees for the most-sought-after procedures exceeds more than 10 times on average. It claims the government is overlooking soaring medical fees on foreign patients, who are unprotected from malpractice, discriminatory charging, overpricing and patient privacy rights under the Korean Medical Law.

In 2008, Korea had 27,480 foreign-based patients and the Korean health ministry expects that number to increase to 140,000 by 2015. Due to legislation passed in May 2009, state-licensed clinics and hospitals are now allowed to directly seek out foreign patients through various promotional activities.

Korean hospitals and clinics provide a variety of medical services for medical tourists including comprehensive health screening, cancer treatment, organ transplantation, joint/rheumatism care, spinal treatment, ophthalmology, dental care, infertility treatment, otorhinolaryngology, and Korean traditional medicine. Currently, the most popular treatments for medical tourists are cosmetic procedures such as eyelid surgery, nose jobs, facelifts, and skin lightening.

Over 30 Korean hospitals and clinics are member providers under the Council for Korea Medicine Overseas Promotion (CKMOP). Among these facilities are the "Big Four" – Seoul National University Hospital, Samsung Medical Centre, Asan Medical Centre, and Yonsei Severance Hospital.

Malaysia

Malaysia is well on its way to develop itself as a medical tourism hub. The country has excellent hospitals, English is widely spoken, and many staff have been trained to a high level in the UK or in the US.

There is a highly active Association for Private Hospitals of Malaysia working to develop medical tourism. However, while Malaysia has a national accreditation healthcare scheme (MSQH) and many Malaysia's hospitals are currently firmly on the way to achieve international healthcare accreditation.

Malaysian hospitals International Specialist Eye Centre, Penang Adventist Hospital and many others such as Gleneagles Hospital Kuala Lumpur have or are going to be JCI accredited. The Ministry of Health has launched a medical tourism page with medical tourism portals such as Wellness Visit.

New Zealand

New Zealand is a relatively new destination to medical travel. It has all the hallmarks of a very successful destination especially for North American based patients. This includes being a first world, developed economy with a sophisticated and comprehensive medical system. It is first and foremost English speaking with a rich heritage of producing world class doctors and medical research.

Many of its private hospitals are internationally accredited, state of the art and offer an integrated package of care. The surgeons in New Zealand are trained both in New Zealand and abroad, usually spending years of their training in either North America or Western Europe.

While New Zealand is aligned medically and culturally to North America, the cost of the surgical care is significantly cheaper. On average it is considered that New Zealand's surgical costs are around 15 to 20% the cost of the same surgical procedure in the USA. One patient who had his prosthetic hip replaced in New Zealand said the total cost including travel, lodging and the surgery at a private hospital was $20,000, as opposed to the $80,000 - $140,000 he was told the operation would have cost at home.

Added to this the personalized level of medical care, the world renown natural beauty and tranquility, the fact that New Zealand is one of the safest places in the world and only 12 hours direct flight from the west coast of North America, then New Zealand as a medical travel destination looks set to develop.

Philippines

The Philippines has been growing as a destination for medical tourism. The US Medical Tourism Association magazine reported that this services sub-sector grew 8.0% in 2007. The number can be expected to grow as American health-care costs rise, or if pending legislation results in an increase in patient wait times for surgical procedures (as has been seen in other countries where care has been nationalized), due to the traditional political, economic and cultural connections between the United States and the Philippines.

The Philippines is one of a few countries that sends qualified nurses, physicians and dentists to the US, the thousands serving in American medical facilities being a testament to its quality of medical education. According to year 2000 WHO rankings of the world's health systems, the Philippines takes its position on no.60.

Singapore

Singapore has a dozen hospitals and health centres with JCI accreditation. In 1997 (published 2000), the World Health Organization ranked Singapore's health care system sixth best in the world and the highest ranked system in Asia.

"Singapore Medicine" is a multi-agency government-industry partnership committed to strengthening Singapore's position as a medical hub and promoting Singapore as a destination for advanced patient care. Patients come from neighboring countries, such as Indonesia and Malaysia, and patient numbers from Indochina, South Asia, the Middle East and Greater China are growing. Patients from developed countries such as the United States and the UK are also beginning to choose Singapore as their medical travel destination for relatively affordable health care services in a clean cosmopolitan city.

Taiwan

The Taiwanese government has declared its determination for the country to become a medical tourism centre. In 2007, the Department of Health launched a campaign to promote inbound medical tourism, focusing on integrating the resources of the government and academia to build Taiwan's brand as a medical tourism destination. Costs for procedures remain comparatively low. Taiwan is known for liver transplants, joint replacement surgery, bone marrow transplants, and reconstructive and plastic surgery.

Thailand

Medical tourism has been a growing segment of Thailand's tourism and health-care sectors. In 2005, one Bangkok hospital took in 150,000 treatment seekers from abroad. In 2006, medical tourism was projected to earn the country 36.4 billion baht.

Treatments for medical tourists in Thailand range from cosmetic, organ transplants, cardiac, and orthopaedic treatments to dental and cardiac surgeries. Treatments also include spa, physical and mental therapies. One patient who had coronary artery bypass surgery at Bumrungrad International hospital in Bangkok said the operation cost him US$12,000 (8,200 euros), as opposed to the $100,000 (68,000 euros) he estimated the operation would have cost him at home. Bumrungrad treated approximately 55,000 American patients in 2005 alone, a 30% increase from the previous year.

Hospitals in Thailand are a popular destination for other Asians. Bangkok Hospital, which caters to medical tourists, has a Japanese wing, and Phyathai Hospitals Group has interpreters for over 22 languages, besides the English-speaking medical staff. When Nepal Prime Minister Girija Prasad Koirala needed medical care in 2006, he went to Bangkok.

Many Thai physicians hold US or UK professional certification. Bumrungrad International hospital states that many of its doctors and staff are trained in the UK, Europe and the US. Bumrungrad International was accredited most recently in 2005 by the Joint Commission. Some of the country's major hospitals have also achieved certification by the International Organization for Standardization's ISO 9001:2000. However, ISO 2000 is not an accreditation scheme.

The World Health Organization's 2000 ranking put the Thai healthcare system at number 47, below the USA's ranking at 37 and the United Kingdom's ranking at 18. Serious political problems during late 2008, including mass demonstrations and the complete closure of major airports, have made travel to Thailand less appealing than in the past, and the US State Department has issued a travel alert for the country.

Europe

Countries in Europe that have active medical tourism sectors include Turkey, Cyprus, Germany, Hungary, Lithuania, Malta, Poland, Portugal, Czech Republic, Slovakia, Spain, and Ukraine.

Czech Republic

Czech Republic has built its medical tourism on spas and medical care equalling the world standards.

Germany

Germany is a destination for patients seeking advanced medical technology, high standards, safety, and quick treatment. All German citizens have health coverage, resulting in a high hospital density, with twice as many hospitals per capita as the United States. The high hospital density results in shorter waitlists for treatment. Costs for medical treatment compete well with other developed European countries and are commonly 50% of those in the USA.

Germany is an attractive destination for patients from the Middle East since travelling to the USA has become more difficult for them since the September 11 attacks. US citizens sometimes travel to Germany to seek treatments such as artificial cervical disc replacement that are not US Food and Drug Administration (FDA) approved.

Poland

Since 2004, when Poland joined the European Union, it has become another locale for people seeking cheaper medical treatments. The quality of care in Poland must comply with EU standards.

Turkey

Turkey has since many years attracted medical tourists from Europe and the Balkans, the United States, Eurasia and the Middle East.

The Turkish private healthcare system is striving to become a strategic global health service provider manufacturing centre. The site contains information on prices and hospital statistics, information about the healthcare, pharmaceutical and insurance environments as well as an international patient guide.

Turkey has the highest number of JCI accredited healthcare institutions in the world except for the US. The German Hospital in Istanbul operates the country's first ISO-certified IVF centre, while Memorial Hospital was the first private hospital to receive American JCI accreditation. Since then, over 34 hospitals and medical institutions have achieved Joint Commission International accreditation.

Tourism Development in Kerala

Kerala, a state situated on the tropical Malabar Coast of southwestern India, is one of the most popular tourist destinations in the country. Named as one of the *ten paradises of the world* by the National Geographic Traveler, Kerala is famous especially for its ecotourism initiatives.

Its unique culture and traditions, coupled with its varied demography, has made Kerala one of the most popular tourist destinations in the world. Growing at a rate of 13.31%, the tourism industry is a major contributor to the state's economy.

Until the early 1980s, Kerala was a hitherto unknown destination, with most tourism circuits concentrated around the north of the country. Aggressive marketing campaigns launched by the Kerala Tourism Development Corporation—the government agency that oversees tourism prospects of the state—laid the foundation for the growth of the tourism industry. In the decades that followed, Kerala Tourism was able to transform itself into one of the niche holiday destinations in India.

The tag line *Kerala- God's Own Country* was adopted in its tourism promotions and became synonymous with the state. Today, Kerala Tourism is a global superbrand and regarded as one of the destinations with the highest brand recall. In 2006, Kerala attracted 8.5 million tourists–an increase of 23.68% in foreign tourist arrivals compared to the previous year, thus making it one of the fastest growing tourism destination in the world.

Popular attractions in the state include the beaches at Kovalam, Cherai and Varkala; the hill stations of Munnar, Nelliampathi, Ponmudi and Wayanad; and national parks and wildlife sanctuaries at Periyar and Eravikulam National Park. The "backwaters" region—an extensive network of interlocking rivers, lakes, and canals that centre on Alleppey, Kumarakom, and Punnamada—also see heavy tourist traffic. Heritage sites, such as the Padmanabhapuram Palace, Hill Palace, Mattancherry Palace are also visited. Cities such as Kochi and Thiruvananthapuram are popular centres for shopping and traditional theatrical performances.

The state's tourism agenda promotes ecologically sustained tourism, which focuses on the local culture, wilderness adventures, volunteering and personal growth of the local population. Efforts are taken to minimise the adverse effects of traditional tourism on the natural environment, and enhance the cultural integrity of local people.

Historical Context

Since its incorporation as a state, Kerala's economy largely operated under welfare-based democratic socialist principles. This mode of development, though resulted in a high Human Development Index and standard of living among the people, lead to an economic stagnation in the 1980s (growth rate of 2.3% annually) This apparent paradox — high human development and low economic development — lead to a large number of educated unemployed seeking jobs overseas, especially in the Gulf countries. Due to the large number of expatriates, many travel operators and agencies set shop in the state to felicitate their travel needs. However, the trends soon reciprocated with the travel agencies noticing the undermined potential of the state as a tourist destination.

By 1986, tourism had gained an industry status. Kerala Tourism subsequently adopted the tagline *God's Own Country* in its advertisement campaigns. Aggressive promotion in print and electronic media were able to invite a sizable investment in the hospitality industry. By the early 2000s, tourism had grown into a fully fledged, multi-billion dollar industry in the state. The state was able to carve a niche place for itself in the world tourism industry, thus becoming one of the places with the 'highest brand recall'. In 2003, Kerala, a hitherto unknown tourism destination, became the fastest growing tourism destination in the world. Today, growing at a rate of 13.31%, Kerala is one of the most visited tourism destinations in India.

Major Attractions

Beaches

Flanked on the western coast by the Arabian Sea, Kerala has a long coastline of 580 km (360.39 miles); all of which is virtually dotted with sandy beaches.

Kovalam beach near Thiruvananthapuram was among the first beaches in Kerala to attract tourists. Rediscovered by back-packers and tan-seekers in the sixties and followed by hordes of hippies in the seventies, Kovalam is today the most visited tourist destination in the state.

Other popularly visited beaches in the state include those at Alappuzha Beach, Nattika beach[Thrissur], Vadanappilly beach[Thrissur], Cherai Beach, Kappad, Kovalam, Marari beach, Fort Kochi and Varkala. The Muzhappilangad Beach beach at Kannur is the only drive-in beach in India.

Backwaters

The backwaters in Kerala are a chain of brackish lagoons and lakes lying parallel to the Arabian Sea coast (known as the Malabar Coast). Kettuvallam (Kerala houseboats) in the backwaters are one of the prominent tourist attractions in Kerala. Alleppey, known as the "Venice of the East" has a large network of canals that meander through the town. The Vallam Kali (the Snake Boat Race) held every year in August is a major sporting attraction.

The backwater network includes five large lakes (including Ashtamudi Kayal and Vembanad Kayal) linked by 1500 km of canals, both manmade and natural, fed by 38 rivers, and extending virtually the entire length of Kerala state. The backwaters were formed by the action of waves and shore currents creating low barrier islands across the mouths of the many rivers flowing down from the Western Ghats range.

Hill Stations

Eastern Kerala consists of land encroached upon by the Western Ghats; the region thus includes high mountains, gorges, and deep-cut valleys. The wildest lands are covered with dense forests, while other regions lie under tea and coffee plantations (established mainly in the 19th and 20th centuries) or other forms of cultivation.

The Western Ghats rises on average to 1500 m elevation above sea level. Certain peaks may reach to 2500 m. Popular hill stations in the region include Devikulam, Munnar, Nelliyampathi, Peermade, Ponmudi, Vagamon, Wayanad and Kottanchery Hills.

Wildlife

Most of Kerala, whose native habitat consists of wet evergreen rainforests at lower elevations and highland deciduous and semi-evergreen forests in the east, is subject to a humid tropical climate. however, significant variations in terrain and elevation have resulted in a land whose biodiversity registers as among the world's most significant. Most of Kerala's significantly biodiverse tracts of wilderness lie in the evergreen forests of its easternmost districts.

Kerala also hosts two of the world's Ramsar Convention-listed wetlands: Lake Sasthamkotta and the Vembanad-Kol wetlands are noted as being wetlands of international importance. There are also numerous protected conservation areas, including 1455.4 km² of the vast Nilgiri Biosphere Reserve. In turn, the forests play host to such major fauna as Asian Elephant (*Elephas maximus*), Bengal Tiger (*Panthera tigris tigris*), Leopard (*Panthera pardus*), and Nilgiri Tahr (*Nilgiritragus hylocrius*), and Grizzled Giant Squirrel (*Ratufa macroura*).

More remote preserves, including Silent Valley National Park in the Kundali Hills, harbor endangered species such as Lion-tailed Macaque (*Macaca silenus*), Indian Sloth Bear (*Melursus (Ursus) ursinus ursinus*), and Gaur (the so-called "Indian Bison" — *Bos gaurus*). More common species include Indian Porcupine (*Hystrix indica*), Chital (*Axis axis*), Sambar (*Cervus unicolor*), Gray Langur, Flying Squirrel, Swamp Lynx (*Felis chaus kutas*), Boar (*Sus scrofa*), a variety of catarrhine Old World monkey species, Gray Wolf (*Canis lupus*), Common Palm Civet (*Paradoxurus hermaphroditus*).

Many reptiles, such as king cobra, viper, python, various turtles and crocodiles are to be found in Kerala — again, disproportionately in the east.

Kerala's avifauna include endemics like the Sri Lanka Frogmouth (*Batrachostomus moniliger*), Oriental Bay Owl, large frugivores like the Great Hornbill (*Buceros bicornis*) and Indian Grey Hornbill, as well as the more widespread birds such as Peafowl, Indian Cormorant, Jungle and Hill Myna, Oriental Darter,

Black-hooded Oriole, Greater Racket-tailed and Black Drongoes, bulbul (*Pycnonotidae*), species of Kingfisher and Woodpecker, Jungle Fowl, Alexandrine Parakeet, and assorted ducks and migratory birds. Additionally, freshwater fish such as *kadu* (stinging catfish — *Heteropneustes fossilis*) and brackishwater species such as *Choottachi* (orange chromide — *Etroplus maculatus*; valued as an aquarium specimen) also are native to Kerala's lakes and waterways.

Festivals

The major festival in Kerala is Onam. Kerala has a number of religious festivals. Thrissur Pooram and Chettikulangara Bharani are the major temple festivals in Kerala. The Thrissur Pooram is conducted at the Vadakumnathan temple, Thrissur. The Chettikulangara Bharani is another major attraction. The festival is conducted at the Chettikulangara temple near Mavelikkara. Parumala Perunnal, Manarkadu Perunnal are the major festivals of Christians. Muslims also have many important festivals.

Radiation Tourism

Karunagappally Taluk Karunagappalli#Places of Interest in Kollam District is the world's hottest spot of natural radiation. The radiation is caused by monazite sands which contain the radioactive element, thorium. The people in the area are exposed to radiation which is 10 times greater than the worldwide average. Tourist spots that offer the chance of the Radiation experience are very rare in the world.

Ayurveda

Medical tourism, promoted by traditional systems of medicine like Ayurveda and Siddha are widely popular in the state, and draws increasing numbers of tourists. A combination of many factors has led to the increase in popularity of medical tourism: high costs of healthcare in industrialised nations, ease and affordability of international travel, improving technology and standards of care.

However, rampant recent growth in this sector has made the government apprehensive. The government is now considering introduction of a grading system which would grade hospitals and clinics, thus helping tourists in selecting one for their treatments.

Culture

Kerala's culture is mainly Dravidian in origin, deriving from a greater Tamil-heritage region known as Tamilakam. Later, Kerala's culture was elaborated on through centuries of contact with overseas cultures. Native performing arts include *koodiyattom, kathakali* – from *katha* ("story") and *kali* ("play") – and its offshoot *Kerala natanam, koothu* (akin to stand-up comedy), *mohiniaattam* ("dance of the enchantress"), *thullal, padayani,* and *theyyam.* Other arts are more religion- and tribal-themed. These include *chavittu nadakom, oppana* (originally from Malabar), which combines dance, rhythmic hand clapping, and *ishal* vocalisations.

However, many of these artforms largely play to tourists or at youth festivals, and are not as popular among most ordinary Keralites. These people look to more contemporary art and performance styles, including those employing mimicry and parody. Additionally, a substantial Malayalam film industry effectively competes against both Bollywood and Hollywood.

Several ancient ritualised arts are Keralite in origin; these include *kalaripayattu* (*kalari* ("place", "threshing floor", or "battlefield") and *payattu* ("exercise" or "practice")). Among the world's oldest martial arts, oral tradition attributes *kalaripayattu's* emergence to Parasurama. Other ritual arts include *theyyam, poorakkali* and *Kuthiyottam.*

Kuthiyottam is a ritualistic symbolic representation of human bali (homicide). Folklore exponents see this art form, with enchanting well structured choreography and songs, as one among the rare Adi Dravida folklore traditions still preserved and practiced in Central Kerala in accordance to the true tradition and environment.

Typical to the Adi Dravida folk dances and songs, the movements and formations of dancers (clad in white thorthu and banyan) choreographed in Kuthiyottam are quick, peaks at a particular point and ends abruptly. The traditional songs also start in a stylish slow pace, then gain momentum and ends abruptly.

Kuthiyotta Kalaris', run by Kuthiyotta Asans (Teachers or leaders), train the group to perform the dances and songs. Normally, the training starts about one to two months before the season. Young boys between 8 to 14 years are taught Kuthiyottam, a ritual dance in the house amidst a big social gathering before the portrait of the deity.

Early in the morning on Bharani, after the feast and other rituals, the boys whose bodies are coiled with silver wires, one end of which is tied around his neck and an arecanut fixed on the tip of a knife held high over his head are taken in procession to the temple with the accompaniment of beating of drums, music, ornamental umbrellas, and other classical folk art forms, and richly caparisoned elephants.

Advertising Campaigns

Kerala Tourism is noted for its innovative and market-focused ad campaigns. These campaigns have won the tourism department numerous awards, including the *Das Golden Stadttor Award for Best Commercial, 2006, Pacific Asia Travel Association- Gold Award for Marketing, 2003* and the Government of India's *Best Promotion Literature, 2004, Best Publishing, 2004* and *Best Tourism Film, 2001.* Catchy slogans and innovative designs are considered a trademark of brand Kerala Tourism. Celebrity promotions are also used to attract more tourists to the state. The Kerala tourism website is widely visited, and has been the recipient of many awards. Recently, the tourism department has also engaged in advertising via mobiles, by setting up a WAP portal, and distributing wallpapers and ringtones related to Kerala through it.

Economic Development of Tourism

Time is a valuable commodity for today's travellers. Dual-income families find it difficult to schedule vacation time; family members often have jobs or activities that conflict; or an individual's job makes long vacations impractical. As a result, more families and individuals are taking long weekend or holiday vacations, or extending business trips into short getaway vacations. Packaging is a popular technique used for attracting these customers, because packages make travel easier and more convenient.

In the hospitality and tourism industry, "packaging" is the process of combining two or more related and complementary offerings into a single-price offering. A package may include a wide variety of services such as lodging, meals, entrance fees to attractions, entertainment, transportation costs (air, auto, train, cab or bus), guide services, or other similar activities.

Packaging can also create a variety of benefits for participating businesses. This publication will: Identify reasons for the increased popularity of packaging. Address issues a business should consider when developing a package. Describe the components of successful packages. Discuss the process of pricing a package.

Why Packages Are Popular

Travel packages have become increasingly popular over the years. They are attractive because they benefit both the customer and participating businesses; packaging provides convenience and value to the customer, and added revenue for participating businesses.

Items to Consider in Developing a Package

Before developing a tourism packaging program, the business should devise a marketing plan through practical marketing research. The business owner should ask him/herself the following questions: Are you willing to do market research to determine who your customers are and what they want? What are the potential attractions, businesses, or marketing service firms that could provide a part of the package? Meet with the managers of these businesses and public attractions to discuss their interests and ideas. What are potential marketing and promotional networks that will help spread the word about your product?

Convention and visitors bureaus, chambers of commerce, retail travel agents, clubs and organizations, state offices of tourism, and other attractions or travel businesses all have the potential to play an important role in merchandising your package. Will the physical appearance and service skills of your business match the target audience? Does your business have the ability to manage and service the customers you generate through your packaging program? Are you prepared for a risk? Because you will be including customer service activities that are not under your direct control, you will be required to develop formal, written agreements between the cooperating businesses.

Benefits to the Customer

Packaging can be an effective marketing tool to provide several customer benefits. These may include: Ability to budget for trips. Packages include most of the components a customer must pay for during a trip. The customer pays at one time and has a good idea of the trip's total cost. Increased convenience. Trips can be time consuming and difficult to arrange. Several telephone calls and letters may be required to arrange for tickets, accommodations, reservations, and other components of a trip. A package allows a customer to arrange many components of a trip with one call or letter and one payment, saving the customer time and aggravation.

Greater economy. Businesses that package can frequently purchase tickets, meals, and other package components at wholesale prices. The business can add in the cost of packaging and still provide a competitive price to the customer. Thus, the cost to the customer is usually more economical than purchasing the package components individually. Popular programs and activities. Visitors and travellers are often unfamiliar with many of the activities and attractions in an area: a package can help customers find them easily.

Specialized interests. Packaging provides a unique opportunity to design components of a package for specialized interests. These so-called "benefit bundles" can include a package component not readily available to individual customers. For example, a package weekend may feature a cooking demonstration by a well-known chef or a lecture by a well-known author. Benefits to Participating Businesses Packaging can be used by businesses to help improve profitability and build customer volume. Examples include:

Improved profitability. During peak or high-demand periods, use packaging to add value to an existing product. Purchasers may be required to stay a prescribed period or purchase a combination of goods and services. Packaging may also allow a business to price its product at a premium by adding special goods and services. Smooth business patterns. Use packaging during low demand periods to add attractive features to the business's service or product, thus generating additional business. Other businesses may also be willing, to discount their services during this time. Adding these services to the existing product mix may generate new business.

Joint marketing opportunities. Packaging can allow the business to reduce marketing costs or start a new program one could not normally afford by joining with one or more businesses to conduct a marketing or advertising program. This strategy can be especially effective if the businesses involved have similar customers. Improved target marketing. Packaging can be an effective tool to tailor tourism and travel products for specific target markets. Examples can be ski, sports, or theatre weekends. Good market research is needed so an appropriate mix of tourism and travel services will meet the needs and desires of a target group of customers.

Greater holiday weekend business. Packaging can be used to highlight special holiday weekends by developing services appropriate to the theme of the weekend. New Year's, Valentine's Day, or Mother's Day are just a few of the holidays that can be used to develop special programs for parties, couples, or family gifts. Unique recurring events. Businesses can create their own events that can occur throughout the year. Events could be tournaments such as chess or bridge or crime re-enactments that let guests do the detective work. Events of this type will require imagination and inventiveness to take advantage of the wide variety of activities that take place in the community. This technique is often called "programming."

Redirected traffic to lesser-known attractions. Directing visitors to often overlooked attractions can help in two ways: heavily visited attractions may be offered some relief, while newly discovered attractions may thrive and prosper. Businesses can use many different strategies in designing a package product. Success will depend on good market research, an understanding of existing customers, research, an understanding of existing customers, and a good knowledge of the community and its activities.

Pricing a Package

Lodging or transportation—the most expensive parts of a package product-are usually the first contact points for customers who purchase a packaged vacation or travel product. Lodging operations or travel agents are usually the key to organizing a packaging program, even though an area's attractions may bring visitors to a community. Although accommodations and transportation are the basic ingredients of a package, tickets to attractions, dining, and other services are other key parts of the product mix that make the package marketable. It is necessary for a business to understand its target market and conduct basic practical market research in order to develop a successful package. Experimenting with a set of packages can also help you identify which sets of activities are most attractive to your customers.

Issues to consider when pricing a package include: The package must be a good value and competitive in the market. Customers should not be able to purchase separate items in the package for less than the package price. A large user of package components should be able to receive discounts from businesses that provide them. Evaluate the role packaging can play in the business's marketing program. While packaging can be used to implement many different strategies, the basic intent is to generate additional business. Determine if the package is feasible by applying a break-even analysis to help determine how many packages a business must sell before earning a profit.

Break-Even Analysis

Break-even analysis is a tool used to determine total sales needed to recoup costs, hence the name "break-even." This analysis technique can also be used to evaluate alternative pricing levels.

Elements of a Successful Package

Putting together a successful package is not easy. However, by following the suggestions listed below, the chances of success will be greater. Include attractions or demand generators. Every package needs one or more core attractions. These could be tickets to a special event, specialized programming, or reduced prices. Provide value to the customer. Many travellers buy packages because they perceive they will receive greater value for the travel dollars they spend. For some, this translates into a package that costs less than the sum of the regular prices of individual elements. Almost everybody is interested in getting something for nothing or next to nothing. Be well planned and coordinated. A successful package must be well planned and coordinated. Each element should flow naturally from one to the next. Use a theme to hold the package together and create a positive experience for the tourist.

Offer consistent quality and compatibility among elements. Many customers buy packages because they expect consistency in quality. Combine only package components that are compatible and enhance the overall quality of the traveller's experience. Customer dissatisfaction with one part of the package will often spoil the entire experience. Provide a distinctive customer benefit. The best packages provide customers something they would not get if they purchased package elements separately. Sometimes this benefit is the offer of value, but in other cases, it is a component that is not readily available to individual customers. This might involve incorporating special lectures or appearances, unique dining experiences, or other activities. Cover all the details. The temptation might be to throw a package together, but the close attention to detail makes some packages more successful than others. Remember, it is often the little things a business does for guests that matter the most. Some things to consider include a policy on refunds and cancellations and complete information on all package elements included in the price, as well as items not included. Generate a profit. Clearly, packages offer a unique way to satisfy traveller needs and wants. Of course, the package should also be designed to generate a profit. The ideal time to offer packages is when demand is low and when the package will not displace customers who may generate higher revenues.

Tourism Contribution to Economic Conservation

The main positive economic impacts of tourism relate to foreign exchange earnings, contributions to government revenues, and generation of employment and business opportunities. These are discussed briefly here; further information on economic contributions from tourism can be found at the World Travel & Tourism Council's home page.

Foreign Exchange Earnings

Tourism expenditures and the export and import of related goods and services generate income to the host economy and can stimulate the investment necessary to finance growth in other economic sectors. Some countries seek to accelerate this growth by requiring visitors to bring in a certain amount of foreign currency for each day of their stay and do not allow them to take it out of the country again at the end of the trip. An important indicator of the role of international tourism is its generation of foreign exchange earnings. Tourism is one of the top five export categories for as many as 83% of countries and is a main source of foreign exchange earnings for at least 38% of countries.

Contribution to Government Revenues

Government revenues from the tourism sector can be categorized as direct and indirect contributions. Direct contributions are generated by taxes on incomes from tourism employment and tourism businesses, and by direct levies on tourists such as departure taxes. Indirect contributions are those originated from taxes and duties levied on goods and services supplied to tourists. The United States National Park Service estimates that the 273 million visits to American national parks in 1993 generated direct and indirect expenditures of US$ 10 billion and 200,000 jobs.

When visits to land managed by other agencies, and to state, local, and privately-managed parks, are added, parks were estimated to bring around US$ 22 billion annually to the US economy. These expenditures also generate significant tax revenues for the government. The World Travel and Tourism Council estimates that travel and tourism's direct, indirect, and personal tax contribution worldwide was over US$ 800 billion in 1998-a

Employment Generation

The rapid expansion of international tourism has led to significant employment creation. For example, the hotel accommodation sector alone provided around 11.3 million jobs worldwide in 1995. Tourism can generate jobs directly through hotels, restaurants, nightclubs, taxis, and souvenir sales, and indirectly through the supply of goods and services needed by tourism-related businesses. According to the WTO, tourism supports some 7% of the world's workers.

Stimulation of Infrastructure Investment

Tourism can induce the local government to make infrastructure improvements such as better water and sewage systems, roads, electricity, telephone and public transport networks, all of which can improve the quality of life for residents as well as facilitate tourism.

Contribution to Local Economies

Tourism can be a significant, even essential, part of the local economy. As the environment is a basic component of the tourism industry's assets, tourism revenues are often used to measure the economic value of protected areas. For example, Dorrigo National Park in New South Wales, Australia, has been estimated to contribute 7% of gross regional output and 8.4% of regional employment. The importance of tourism to local economies can also be illustrated by the impacts when it is disrupted: the catastrophic 1997 floods that closed Yosemite National Park in California cause locally severe economic losses to the areas around the park. In the most heavily impacted county, Mariposa County, 1997 personal income was reduced by an estimated US$1,159 per capita (US$18 million for the entire county)-a 6.6% decline. The county was also estimated to have lost US$1.67 million in county occupancy and sales tax revenues, and 956 jobs, a significant number in a county of fewer than 16,000 residents.

There are other local revenues that are not easily quantified, as not all tourist expenditures are formally registered in the macro-economic statistics. Money is earned from tourism through informal employment such as street vendors, informal guides, rickshaw drivers, etc. The positive side of informal or unreported employment is that the money is returned to the local economy, and has a great multiplier effect as it is spent over and over again. The World Travel and Tourism Council estimates that tourism generates an indirect contribution equal to 100% of direct tourism expenditures.

The Economic Impacts of Eco-tourism

There are two related, but distinct, economic concepts in Eco-tourism: economic impact and economic value. This issues paper focusses on economic impact, which refers to the change in sales, income, jobs, or other parameter generated by Eco-tourism. A common Eco-tourism goal is the generation of economic benefits, whether they be profits for companies, jobs for communities, or revenues for parks. Eco-tourism plays a particularly important role because it can create jobs in remote regions that historically have benefited less from economic development programs than have more populous areas. Even a small number of jobs may be significant in communities where populations are low and alternatives are few. This economic impact can increase political and financial support for conservation.

Protected areas, and nature conservation generally, provide many benefits to society, including preservation of biodiversity, maintenance of watersheds, and so on. Unfortunately, many of these benefits are intangible. However, the benefits associated with recreation and tourism in protected areas tend to be tangible. For example, divers at a marine park spend money on lodging, food, and other goods and services, thereby providing employment for local and non-local residents. These positive economic impacts can lead to increased support for the protected areas with which they are associated. This is one reason why Eco-tourism has been embraced as a means for enhancing conservation of natural resources. Several studies in Australia and elsewhere have assessed the economic impacts of Eco-tourism.

Predictably, the level of benefits varies widely as a result of differences in the quality of the attraction, access, and so on. In some cases, the number of jobs created will be low, but in rural areas even a few jobs can make a big difference. Still, Eco-tourism benefits should not be oversold, or there may be a backlash as reality fails to live up to expectations. The impacts of Eco-tourism, or any economic activity, can be grouped into three categories: direct, indirect, and induced. Direct impacts are those arising from the initial tourism spending, such as money spent at a restaurant. The restaurant buys goods and services (inputs) from other businesses, thereby generating indirect impacts. In addition, the restaurant employees spend part of their wages to buy various goods and services, thereby generating induced impacts. Of course, if the restaurant purchases the goods and services from outside the region of interest, then the money provides no indirect impact to the region — it leaks away. By identifying the leakages, or conversely the linkages within the economy, the indirect and induced impacts of tourism can be estimated.

In addition, this information can be used to identify what goods are needed but are not being produced in the region, how much demand there is for such goods, and what the likely benefits of local production would be. This enables policy makers to determine priorities for developing inputs for use by the tourism or other industries. How, then, are these direct, indirect, and induced impacts to be estimated? For small areas with non-diverse economies, there are relatively few indirect and induced impacts, and there are relatively little data available for modelling these impacts. Therefore, surveys of visitors, residents, and/or businesses often are used to identify tourism's direct impacts. For larger areas, such as states or countries, economists have developed various techniques for estimating indirect and induced impacts, including computable general equilibrium (CGE) and input-output (IO) analysis.

Negative Economic Impacts of Tourism

There are many hidden costs to tourism, which can have unfavourable economic effects on the host community. Often rich countries are better able to profit from tourism than poor ones. Whereas the least developed countries have the most urgent need for income, employment and general rise of the standard of living by means of tourism, they are least able to realize these benefits. Among the reasons for this are large-scale transfer of tourism revenues out of the host country and exclusion of local businesses and products.

Leakage

The direct income for an area is the amount of tourist expenditure that remains locally after taxes, profits, and wages are paid outside the area and after imports are purchased; these subtracted amounts are called leakage. In most all-inclusive package tours, about 80% of travellers' expenditures go to the airlines, hotels and other international companies (who often have their headquarters in the travellers' home countries), and not to local businesses or workers. In addition, significant amounts of income actually retained at destination level can leave again through leakage. A study of tourism 'leakage' in Thailand estimated that 70% of all money spent by tourists ended up leaving Thailand (via foreign-owned tour operators, airlines, hotels, imported drinks and food, etc.). Estimates for other Third World countries range from 80% in the Caribbean to 40% in India.

Bibliography

Baker, S. H.: *Character Building Clubs for Boys. The Scientific Management of Clubs for Boys*, London, YMCA Boys Department, 1919.

Brunt, Paul: *Market Research in Travel and Tourism*, Oxford, Butterworth Heinemann, 1997.

Cukier, J. : *Tourism Employment in Bali: Trends and Implications*, London: Thompson, 1996.

Donald E. : *Public Personnel Management: Contexts and Strategies*, Upper Saddle River, NJ: Prentice Hall, 1998.

Douglas C: *Practical Tourism Forecasting*, Oxford, Butterworth Heinemann, 1996.

Eckel, Peter J.: *College & University Foodservice Management Standards*, Westport, AVI Pub. Company, 1985.

Foster, Douglas: *Travel and Tourism Management*, London, Macmillan Educational, 1985.

Frechtling, Douglas C: *Practical Tourism Forecasting*, Oxford, Butterworth Heinemann, 1996.

Gamble, P. R: *The Educational challenge for Hospitality and Tourism Studies*, Tourism Management, 13, 1992.

Getz, D.P. : *Effects of Tourism on the Host Population, A Case Study of Tourism and Regional Development in the Badenoch-Strathspey District of the Scottish Highlands*, Edinburgh: University of Edinburgh, 1980.

Ghimire, Krishna: *The Native Tourist*: Mass Tourism within Developing Regions, London, Earthscan, 2001.

Hinkin, Timothy R.: *Cases in Hospitality Management: A Critical Incident Approach*, New York, Wiley, 1995.

Hoffman, Edward: *Project Management Success Stories: Lessons of Project Leaders*, New York, John Wiley & Son, 2000.

Ireland, Lewis: *Quality Management for Projects and Programs*, Upper Darby, PMI, 1991.

Judi Radice: *Restaurant & Food Graphics*, Glen Cove, PBC International, 1994.

Kharbanda, O. and E. Stallworthy: *Waste Management Towards a Sustainable Society*, Auburn House, New York, 1990.

Klein, S. : *Information & Communication Technologies in Tourism*, Springer-Verlag, Wien-New York, 2000.

Kotler, Philip: *Marketing for Hospitality and Tourism*: New Jersey, Prentice-Hall, 1998.

Larkham, P J: *Building a New Heritage: Tourism, Culture & Identity in the New Europe*, London, Routledge,1994.

Lewis, Robert C.: *Cases in Hospitality Marketing and Management*, New York, John Wiley, 1997.

Lock, Dennis: *Project Management*, New York, Wiley, 1996.

Marjorie, E.: *Careers in Travel, Tourism, and Hospitality*, Lincolnwood, VGM Career Horizons, 1997.

Morrell, J. : *Employment in Tourism*, London: British Tourist Authority, 1985.

Nancy, N.: *Choosing a Career in Hotels, Motels, and Resorts*, New York, Rosen Pub. Group, 1997.

Norman G.: *Hotel, Restaurant, and Travel Law: A Preventive Approach*, Albany, Delmar Publishers, 1993.

Prentice, R: *Conceptualising The Experiences of Heritage Tourists*, 1997.

Robert C.: *Cases in Hospitality Marketing and Management*, New York, John Wiley, 1997.

Rocco, M.: *An Introduction to Hospitality Today*, Orlando, Educational Institute, 1998.

Rogers, H Anthea and Slinn, Judy A: *Tourism: Management of Facilities*, London, Pitman: M & E, 1993.

Rosemary, E.: *Managing Employee Relations in the Hotel and Catering Industry*, London, Cassell, 1995.

Rosenzweig, J. E.: *Organisation and Management*, New York, McGraw Hill International, 1963.

Rue, Nancy N.: *Choosing a Career in Hotels, Motels, and Resorts,* New York, Rosen Pub. Group, 1997.

Schwaninger, M: *Trends in Leisure and Tourism for 2000 - 2010,* Prentice Hall, 1989.

Scottish Tourist Board: *Visitor Attractions: A Development Guide,* Edinburgh, Scottish Tourist Board, 1991.

Sharma Sunil : *Planning and Development of Tourism and Hospitality,* Rajat Pub, Delhi, 2007.

Slinn, Judy A: *Tourism: Management of Facilities,* London, Pitman: M & E, 1993.

Smith, G. : *International Tourism and Hospitality Careers through Education and Training,* CHRIE Annual Conference, Washington DC, 1996.

Swarbrooke, J.: *Marketing Tourism, Hospitality and Leisure in Europe,* London, International Thomson Business Press, 1996.

Thomas, F.: *Introduction to Management in the Hospitality Industry,* New York, Wiley, 1995.

Timothy, R.: *Cases in Hospitality Management: A Critical Incident Approach,* New York, Wiley, 1995.

Vallette, J.: *The International Trade in Wastes: A Greenpeace Inventory,* Washington, Greenpeace, 1989.

Walden, Richard: *Genetic Transformation in Plants,* England, Open University Press, 1988.

Index

M

O

P

R

T

W

❑❑❑